Please remember that this is a library book,
and that it belongs only temporarily to each
person who uses it. Be considerate. Do
not write in this, or any, library book.

WITHDRAWN

WITHDRAWN

CREATIVE PROGRAMMING FOR OLDER ADULTS

WITHDRAWN

CREATIVE PROGRAMMING FOR OLDER ADULTS

A Leadership Training Guide

FLORENCE E. VICKERY, A.C.S.W.

ASSOCIATION PRESS / NEW YORK

CREATIVE PROGRAMMING FOR OLDER ADULTS

Copyright © 1972 by Association Press
291 Broadway, New York, N.Y. 10007

All rights reserved. No part of this publication may be reprinted, reproduced, transmitted, stored in a retrieval system, or otherwise utilized, in any form or by any means, electronic or mechanical, including photocopying or recording, now existing or hereinafter invented, without the prior written permission of the publisher.

International Standard Book Number: 0-8096-1835-4
Library of Congress Catalog Card Number: 79-167884

PRINTED IN THE UNITED STATES OF AMERICA

362.63
V637c

Dedication

In grateful acknowledgment
to all the older men and women
of San Francisco, who as members of
the San Francisco Senior Center taught
me about the potentials and promises
of the later years; and in sincere
appreciation of their courage, enthusiasm,
and loyalty, which daily validated the
fact that the later years may bring
enrichment and fulfillment.

29426

Contents

III—Development and Administration of
Social Programs for Older Adults

Charts, Tables, and Forms

Preface

Understanding the social and emotional needs of older adults is essential in order to work effectively *for* and *with* them. The growing body of knowledge from research and demonstration projects on the physical, psychological and social aspects of the normal aging process cited in this book, translated into practice principles, will help leaders understand the dynamics of the behavior of those with whom they work.

This book deals essentially with the goals and programs of multiservice senior centers but the basic philosophy and principles for operating a senior center are applicable in other settings where older adults are served.

Creative Programming for Older Adults is a textbook for preparing students for positions in professions through which the needs of older adults are met. It is a manual for in-service training of agency staff, aides and technicians; and it serves as a guide for leadership training workshops for board, council and committee members, and other volunteers working with older adults.

Finally, the content will be helpful to young adults who seek more objective, yet warm, understanding of their own parents. It will be pertinent reading for older adults themselves as they search for increasing self-awareness and fulfillment as they grow into the later years.

FLORENCE E. VICKERY

Mill Valley, Calif.
October 1, 1971

Acknowledgments

I wish to express my deep appreciation to all those who have read all or part of the manuscript. Their helpful suggestions have led to clarification and conciseness. Special appreciation goes to Leslie Silverglad, who edited the manuscript, and to Florine Miller, who conceived the design for the charts and whose suggestions have enriched the content. I am also appreciative of the patience, skill, and helpfulness of my secretary, Florence Prince, in the laborious task of typing the material.

I — OLDER AMERICANS IN A TECHNOLOGICAL SOCIETY

1 / The Older Adult in a Climate of Change

"Nothing is permanent except change," observed Heraclitus during the fourth century B.C. As modern man moves into the twenty-first century, far reaching changes are apparent. Dissent and demonstration, riot and revolution, violence and vituperation challenge long established political and economic philosophies. Educational and social institutions, religious beliefs, and moral standards are questioned. Changes, which have been more extensive during the past thirty years than in all the preceding thirty decades, are appearing so rapidly in our technological culture that modern man often feels himself unable to cope with or control them.

Especially vulnerable to the emotional impact of these changes are twenty million Americans who are now older adults and in the retired segment of the population. In 1940, when they were at the peak of their productive years carrying the roles and responsibilities of mature adults, electronic technology was in its infancy and the computer had not been designed. Space exploration was only the subject matter of science fiction, and nuclear power, with its great potential for industrial development as well as destruction, was known only to the scientist in his research laboratory. The first public television broadcast had taken place in London four years before; antibiotics were in the experimental stage and did not become commercially available until 1950.

Modern electronic technology is radically changing ways in which man has traditionally functioned

The impact of the computer on contemporary life and its role in the future staggers the imagination. Today the physician can feed laboratory data and the results of his examination into a computer by means of his office teletypewriter and receive an almost instantaneous reply to aid him in diagnosing his patient's illness. The machine now supplements the instructor in many teaching and testing procedures. More students can be accommodated in classes and they can be taught in more precise and efficient ways. The news media carry advertisements announcing computerized procedures for choosing mates, and successful marriages are assured if the computer indicates that young people have certain desirable traits in common. In another decade there may be a cashless society with no worker handling his own salary checks or paying bills directly. Purchases of goods and services will involve electronic transfers of money and credit by the bank. Shopping patterns will tend to isolate individuals further in high-rise living cubicles. People will no longer need go to the market or the store and rub elbows with neighbors or those from across town. Instead, they will shop from their living rooms by means of closed television networks. A picture phone will enable the shoppers to inspect merchandise, select, and give orders without any face-to-face contacts with other human beings.

In the culture that technology is creating, man will necessarily become dependent on the speed and accuracy of the computer. The computer will sort and process the data of daily living; deliver goods and services; and may, in some instances, displace man in thinking, judging, reasoning, and calculating.

The computer cannot replace man's unique capacity to feel

Although the machine may, in the years ahead, take over more and more of the instrumental functions of man, it can never replace that which makes him uniquely human—his capacity for and his need to express his feelings and deep emotional reactions to his life experiences and to his fellowmen. The computer can never replace the doctor's compassion and reassurance to his patients or the teacher's inspiration and encouragement to his students. The friendly helpfulness of the shopkeeper to his customers and the tenderness and devotion of two young persons learning to know and love one another cannot be reduced to components for programming by a computer. Man's sense of self and his mental health will always be dependent upon encounters and meaningful relationships with other human beings.

The emergence of the love generation and the hippie culture among youth is basically a remonstrance against the values and mores of a society that—in the opinion of young people—depreciates the individual and denies him the freedom to be himself. As more and more aspects of his daily life become depersonalized, man will need to develop new ways for being aware of and sensitive to other persons and their feelings. Sensitivity training and encounter groups are popular today. In such groups employers and employees, husbands and wives, faculty members and administrators, church members and non church members, meet together during extended periods to express honestly and openly their true feelings about themselves and one another. Through such experiences individuals strive to become more understanding and accepting of one another's differences.

Confrontations among racial and poverty groups and established organizations and agencies, university administrators and students, activists and the police, youth and parents—all give evidence of the increasing inability of people to communicate, to understand, to feel with and for other people.

The widening generation gap increases the older adult's feelings of rejection and alienation

As society has moved during the early twentieth century from an agricultural to an industrial economy, the aged have become uniquely vulnerable to feelings of uselessness and rejection. The loss of jobs through compulsory retirement policies in business, education, government, and industry results in feelings of isolation for the older adult within the youth culture. It has always been recognized that the oncoming generation would view life in ways differing widely from those of their parents. Today the generation gap takes on unprecedented proportions.

In commenting on the seriousness of these generational differences, Margaret Mead, the eminent American anthropologist, points out that in the past adults have played the vital role of transmitting culture and mores to the next generation. Cultural changes evolved so slowly that members of the older generation were able to keep up with them as they occurred and communicate their values and meanings to the younger generation. Today social institutions, patterns of behavior, and ideologies and attitudes change so rapidly that adults are unable to assimilate, evaluate, and integrate them into value systems that will prove relevant to the problems of the next generation. Youth no longer believe that their elders are all-wise. They no longer look to them to give continuity to yesterday's values and today's demands. Young persons do not experience the security and stability that come from knowing that their elders have things under control and are able to make the best decisions to achieve a stable and peaceful society. Thus, Margaret Mead points out, the members of the younger generation today are in a unique position; never before have young people grown up in a world without adult interpretation of what is happening.[1]

Plato, in the fourth century B.C., wrote: "It gives me great pleasure to converse with the aged. They have been over the road that all of us must travel. They know where it is level and where it is rough and where it will lead." How different the situation is today! The world alters even as one walks in it. Anxieties and fears mount and many older people begin to feel themselves no longer adequate to cope with such far-reaching changes. They seek to protect themselves against the hurts and frustrations they experience by withdrawing more and more from all involvement with persons and situations that disturb them. When any age group becomes marginal to the society of which it is a part, and some of its members do not know or understand what is going on around them, feelings of disorientation, isolation, and an overwhelming sense of uselessness result. This development has become the plight of many older adults today.

The growing cleavage between generations becomes critically significant in view of the projected changes in the population growth during the next decade. According to the United States Bureau of the Census, the number of people over sixty-five years of age will increase in the next ten years by 4.1 million or 22 percent; the segment of the population between twenty and thirty-four years of age will increase by 18.3 million or 46 percent.[2] Unless there are opportunities for older persons to continue to learn and relearn the facts and forces that will be operating in society in the twenty-first century, a subculture of the aged, psychologically isolated from younger age groups, will develop.

There is a growing awareness and concern about the needs of older adults in our society

During the past twenty-five years, as the number of older persons in the population has increased and their needs have become more apparent, government at all levels, voluntary planning groups, and individuals have recognized their responsibility to take some action. This trend is noted in the creation of many new programs and agencies within the federal

[1] "Generation Gap," Adaptation of an address by Margaret Mead, *Science*, 11 April 1969, p. 135.
[2] U.S. Department of Commerce, Bureau of the Census, *Current Population Reports 1966*, P-25, No. 359.

Chart 1
Growth of U.S. Population 65 and Over

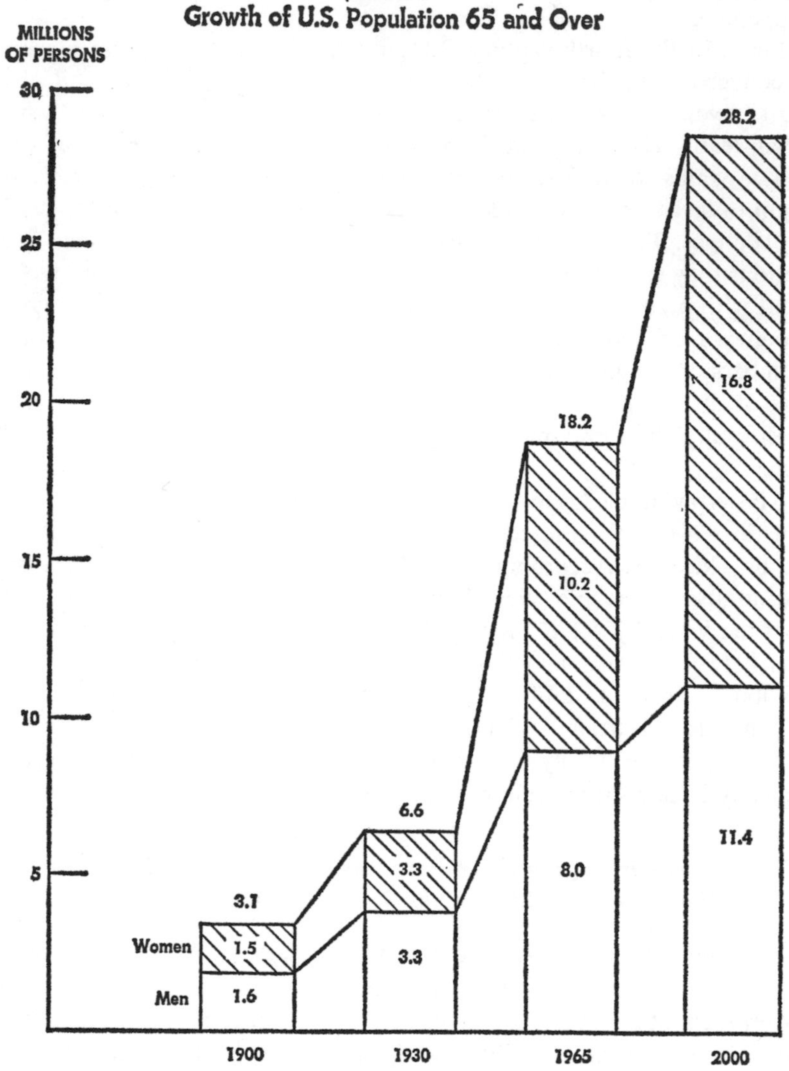

MILLIONS
OF PERSONS

Source: Bureau of the Census, Administration on Aging

government. These include (1) The Administration on Aging within the Department of Health, Education and Welfare, with the related state Commissions on Aging, (2) the Older Americans Act whereby federal funds are made available to local communities to initiate needed services to the aged, (3) Medicare and Medicaid legislation, (4) the Model Cities Act and Senior Citizens Housing legislation, (5) and Programs for Elderly Poor, a part of the Economic Opportunities Act. These significant developments mark some of the initial steps in what must become a greatly expanded program in the future. How rapidly this expansion can be made will depend on how successfully programs for the aged are able to compete with other pressing problems that face the country: poverty and ghetto living; educational and training opportunities for disadvantaged youth; redevelopment of deteriorating inner cities; cleaning up the natural environment; meeting commitments in foreign countries and underdeveloped nations; and launching this nation farther into the space program.

The needs of older people have too long been ranked low in importance. Ignoring their needs is no longer sound public policy in a nation whose population over sixty-five years of age will have increased from three million in 1900 to a projected twenty and eight-tenths million in the year 2000, half of whom will be more than seventy-two years old. (See Chart 1.)

Communities are recognizing the social and emotional needs of their older adults

The following chapters consider cultural changes that determine how an individual experiences aging and the sociological, psychological, and physical processes of aging that affect one's ability to remain a functioning, contributing member of society. Parts II and III will focus specifically on social programs that have been developed exclusively for older adults during the past twenty-five years in all large cities and many smaller communities in the United States. These programs are called by a variety of names and are sponsored by various community agencies, churches, libraries, labor unions, and municipal government departments. They use many different kinds of facilities and differ widely in the scope of their programs. The fundamental purpose of these programs, however, is the same: to provide settings and opportunities in which older adults can experience not only a continuing sense of personal enrichment and fulfillment but also a sense of being needed by society and having a place in it.

Future social programs must not be bound to the traditional molds of the past. Administrators and community leaders must look critically at present practices and patterns and move in bold and imaginative ways in the future. Current knowledge and continuing research on the growth and development potentials of the later years; an awareness of the rapidly changing cultural factors in America today; the experiences of practitioners—all must be utilized if programs are to provide the opportunities and motivation needed for continuous personal development and fulfillment. Only then can older adults experience meaningful involvement, rather than alienation, in contemporary American society.

BIBLIOGRAPHY

Brotman, Herman B. *Who Are The Aged: A Demographic View*. Washington, D.C.: Administration on Aging, 1968.

Burgess, Ernest W., ed. *Aging in Western Culture: A Survey of Social Gerontology*. Chicago: University of Chicage Press, 1959.

Drake, Joseph T. *The Aged in American Society*. New York: Ronald Press, 1958.

Federal Security Agency, Committee on Aging and Geriatrics. *Fact Book on Aging*. Washington, D.C.: Government Printing Office, 1952.

Ginzberg, Raphael. "The Negative Attitude Toward the Elderly." *Geriatrics* 7 (1952): 297-302.

Heyman, D., and Jeffers, Frances. "Study of the Relative Influence of Race and Socioeconomic Status Upon the Activities and Attitudes of a Southern Aged Population." *Journal of Gerontology* 19 (1964): 225-229.

International Association of Gerontology, Proceedings of the 3rd Congress, London, 1954. *Old Age in the Modern World*. London: Livingston, Ltd., 1955.

Martin, Lillian J., and De Gruchy, Clare. *Salvaging Old Age*. New York: Macmillan Company, 1930.

Reisman, David. "Some Clinical and Cultural Aspects of the Aging Process," *American Journal of Sociology*, 59 (January 1954): 379-383.

Riley, Matilda W., and Fouer, Anne. *Aging and Society*. New York: Russell Sage Foundation, 1968.

Rose, Arnold M. "The Subculture of the Aging: A Topic for Sociological Research." *Gerontologist* 11 (1962): 123-27.

Sheldon, Henry D. *The Older Population of the United States*. New York: John Wiley & Sons, 1958.

Simmons, L. W. *The Role of the Aged in Primitive Societies*. New Haven: Yale University Press, 1945.

Tibbetts, Clark. *Middle Aged and Older People in American Society*. U.S.

Department of Health, Education and Welfare, Administration on Aging, no. 227, 1965.

Tobin, Shelden S. "Basic Needs of All Older People: Planning Welfare Services for Older People." United States Department of Health, Education and Welfare, and Committee on Human Development. Chicago: University of Chicago Press, 1965.

United Nations, Department of Economic and Social Council. *The Aging of Populations and Its Economic and Social Implications* (Population Studies, no. 26), 1956.

2 / Social and Cultural Influences on the Aging Experience

HOW DIFFERENT LIFE LOOKS to those who today are over sixty-five! They have experienced two World Wars as well as the Korean and Vietnam conflicts. They have seen the shrinking of time and distance by mass communication, satellite broadcasting, and air travel. They have lived through a major economic depression followed by the development of one of the most affluent societies that man has ever achieved. Their lives have been extended by the elimination of the killer diseases of childhood and dramatic advances in medical knowledge. They have benefited from the automation of many of the processes of business and industry and have been awed by the potentials for the advancement as well as the destruction of mankind through the splitting of the atom. They have been amazed and inspired by flights into space and landings on the moon. All of these developments and more are bringing about far-reaching changes in the social institutions and cultural patterns of all societies.

Any study of older adults today must consider these revolutionary social changes and the efforts of individuals to cope with them. Successful aging for the individual will depend on his ability to adapt his thinking and behavior to these changes and maintain his sense of ego identity and integrity within the framework of his own times. This chapter will review some of the developmental changes in American culture since the turn of the century.

Employment and retirement practices have changed

Compulsory retirement at a specified chronological date, now an accepted practice in most corporations, industry, government, and education, was unheard of in the early decades of this century. The worker's labor was needed in a fast growing industrial economy. A job and the right to work were demanded for all. A man was primarily judged by how well he provided for the material needs of his family. As the population rapidly expanded and technology progressively automated industrial and business processes, more and more workers have become available for fewer jobs.

There have been many changes in the place of women, as well as of men, in the labor force since the last decades of the nineteenth century. At the turn of the century young girls began leaving their farm homes to work in the mills and factories or as domestics in the big cities. During World Wars I and II, as men went off to distant battle fronts, women took over their jobs in order to produce needed war materials and maintain the domestic economy. This development marked the beginning of the now generally accepted pattern of women, married and unmarried, working outside the home either by necessity or by choice. The early 1900s also found an increasing number of women enrolling in colleges and universities and entering professions other than teaching or nursing.

The passage of the Social Security Act in 1936, after the major financial depression of 1929–1935, gave recognition to the fact that the federal government had some responsibility to keep the job market open for younger workers and to encourage the retirement of older workers by providing a cushion—as additional regular income—to supplement individual savings and pension plans that unions were beginning to negotiate. Revisions in social security legislation during the years have extended coverage to additional workers and increased monthly benefits. The inflationary spiral and the devaluation of the dollar during the years, however, has meant that the buying power of retirement incomes has become less and less. Finding an adequate income to meet increasing living costs in an affluent society is one of the gravest problems older persons face. Some seek part-time jobs to supplement inadequate incomes, but for many others a sharp reduction of expenditures becomes necessary. Many older adults on limited retirement incomes must move into less expensive housing, purchase cheaper foods, limit medical and dental care, and curtail social activities and contacts. Such steps often decrease the individual's sense of self-worth and feelings of adequacy.

Inflation and high taxes reduce
the income of many older adults

In an advertisement appearing in 1948 in many national magazines a retiree remarks:

Fifteen years ago I bought an endowment insurance; now I have a comfortable income. . . . no business worries. . . . my security is guaranteed. . . . each month I get a check for $150 and will as long as I live. . . . my friends are envious: they didn't discover the endowment plan my insurance company offered. . . . today I am only 55. . . . I have everything I want, lifelong security, a chance to hunt and fish, to play, to live a full life, no financial worries bother me. . . . I can be sure my future years will be happy and comfortable for I have a guaranteed income of $150 a month for life.

(Parker Corporation newsletter)

Advertisements appearing in 1960 had only minor changes in the text but the needed monthly income increased to $300. In 1970 the ad read $500 a month. Financial experts predict that by the year 2000 further inflation will bring prices of food and services to a new level that represents a 100 percent increase over 1970 prices. Houses purchased during employment years become an increasing financial burden as maintenance costs and property taxes rise.

In 1962 the United States Bureau of Labor Statistics estimated the cost of a "modest but adequate" budget for an older retired couple to be $2,500 and for an older retired individual to be $1,800. In 1969 their estimates had risen to $2,902 for the couple and to $2,000 for an individual. For an intermediate level of living the estimate for a couple was $4,192 and for a high level it was $6,616.[1] In 1962 the median income for aged couples was $2,875 and for the unmarried individual, $1,130.[2] In 1969, with increases in social security benefits, 50 percent of the aged families had incomes under $3,928, and 50 percent of the elderly living alone or with nonrelatives had incomes under $1,480.

Although social security benefits were increased at the beginning of the 1970s, many older Americans must continue to live at and below poverty levels.[3] Poverty in the United States is more prevalent among elderly persons than among any other age group. In 1968 the elderly poor (sixty-five years of age and over) numbered 4.6 million or 18 percent of the total poor, and they constituted about 25 percent of all aged persons. Of the total 4.6 million aged poor, about 3.9 million persons (85 percent) were whites. The nonwhites comprised only 15 percent— a relatively small fraction—of the aged poor. However, the proportion of

[1] Mary H. Hawes, "Measuring Retired Couples' Living Costs," *Monthly Labor Review*. U.S. Department of Labor, 92:3 (November 1969).

[2] Lenore A. Epstein, "Income of the Aged in 1962: First Findings of the 1963 Survey of the Aged," *Social Security Bulletin* 27:3-24 (March 1964).

[3] Walter W. Kolodrubetz, "Employee-Benefit Plans in 1968," *Social Security Bulletin,* 33:35 (April 1970).

those among the elderly who are poor is much higher among nonwhites (47 percent) than among whites (23 percent).[4] It is unrealistic to urge older people with limited incomes to keep up social contacts and remain active in the life of the community. It is difficult, if not impossible, for them to afford bus fares, a telephone, or appropriate clothing—all essential for socialization with family and friends.

Plans are currently being proposed in certain communities for some tax relief on property owned by older people. State and federal governments are considering further relief on income taxes and escalation of social security benefits to be commensurate with the cost-of-living increases. All of these measures to improve the financial position of older adults offer some hope that people will not continue to be pushed into poverty in their old age.

There is wide variation in the wealth of older adults. Some own nothing at all and others are very wealthy. Over 17 percent of the holders of listed securities on the stock market are older adults. Furthermore, people over sixty-five years of age as a group have a forty-five billion dollar consumer purchasing power, and the affluent spend unprecedented amounts on travel both in this country and abroad, on cosmetics, alcohol, cigarettes, insurance, and housing.[5] Today older people are creating national movements in order to give voice and visibility to their needs and interests. The importance of this group as an economic force and a political power cannot be minimized as they form lobbies and vote for measures to improve their economic and social position.

Changing social patterns result in changing generational roles

For the woman whose primary responsibilities are centered on homemaking and the supervision of children, retirement has been a gradual process that extends over a long period of time. Today, with youth asserting their independence at an earlier age, women are younger when their homemaking responsibilities terminate. Children leave home after high school graduation to live independently in apartments with friends, enter military service, go to college, travel, and marry and establish homes and families of their own. The woman's role as a homemaker changes drastically and she must make adjustments to new roles and life-styles.

[4] Committee for Economic Development, *Improving the Public Welfare System*, (New York: Committee for Economic Development, April 1970).
[5] "The Forgotten Generation," *Forbes*, 15 January 1969, p. 22.

The woman's role as a grandmother has become less functional and more symbolic. The mass production of children's clothing from drip-dry, no-iron materials and their availability in suburban shopping centers and supermarkets at reasonable prices make it unnecessary and impractical for the grandmother to sew for her grandchildren. Clothing for special events, however, are often her gifts. Grandmothers are no longer needed to help with food preparation, for freezers and shelves are regularly filled with frozen and preprepared foods bought at the supermarket.

Families today, as a convenience and as an economy, often depend on grandparents to serve as baby-sitters for the younger generation in cases of illness or their absence from home, but more and more young mothers who are financially able prefer to hire baby-sitters rather than impose on grandmothers. Nursery schools and child-care centers, where youngsters can spend a portion of a day or longer if both parents are employed, have become a part of our cultural pattern. When their children became ill, today's older adults had a ready supply of home remedies on which they confidently depended; if the illness persisted the family doctor was called to the house to diagnose the child's condition and prescribe medication. Grandchildren today are taken regularly by parents to the office of a pediatrician for periodic physical examinations. Tests and shots to immunize against many childhood illnesses are part of the accepted health care of all children. A telephone call to the pediatrician replaces the one that a young mother, only a few years ago, would have made to her mother seeking advice and direction about her child's illness.

Emotional and intellectual distances
between generations have increased

Head-of-the-family has been the symbolic role that grandparents have always played in relation to the younger generations. The adult children and their children returned to the family home for special holiday and traditional celebrations. This practice provided continuity, cohesiveness, and stability for the family. This role becomes diluted and often non-existent in our mobile society when family members are living at distances too far from one another to make frequent reunions possible. Furthermore, great emotional distances develop between grandparents and grandchildren in a society where one in every 3.7 marriages ends in divorce and remarriages occur.[6] Grandchildren must be shared with multiple sets of grandparents, and relationship becomes more casual and

[6] "Marriages and Divorces in the U.S. 1968," *World Almanac Book of Facts* (New York: Newspaper Enterprise Association, Inc., 1970), p. 72.

less meaningful to children and grandparents alike. Family stability and continuity are changed as barriers among religious, nationality, and racial groups disappear and marriages across group lines become more acceptable. Many members of the older generation view such intergroup marriages with alarm and as a threat to their long-held views and their moral and ethical standards.

Current attitudes and practices related to the role of advanced education for all youth are creating greater ideological and emotional distances between the generations. To grandparents, student campus revolts and demands for some voice in making decisions affecting their lives and for courses that are relevant to making a life rather than a living are confusing and bewildering. Fifty years ago only the children of the middle- and upper-class families had opportunities for college educations. For the majority, formal education was over at the end of high school, and many young people from the lower socioeconomic groups left school at the end of the eighth grade in order to take jobs and help supplement their families' incomes. In 1940 over 80 percent of those sixty-five years of age and over had completed only the eighth grade or less. By 1985 this proportion will drop to a projected 39 percent.[7] In the past, the sons in a family who planned to enter one of the professions left home after high school graduation to attend college in another community—a pattern that was not generally considered appropriate for girls. The expectation was that a daughter would remain in her parents' home until she married and established a new home, with her husband, usually in the same community.

Today further education or training of some kind is the goal and expectation of most young people. With scholarships and government grants and loans available for able students, a college education can be a reality for all youth who desire it, whatever their socioeconomic status or racial background. Some grandparents feel inferior to their college educated young people and unable to understand or communicate with them on an intellectual basis. Since the grandparents' school days, tremendous new areas of knowledge about man and his universe have become known and these facts fill the textbooks and laboratories available to today's students. Learning the three Rs—reading, writing, and arithmetic—seemed an adequate program for their grandparents, but today even the methods of teaching these fundamentals have changed and seem incomprehensible to the bewildered members of the older generation.

Because of the marked decline in immigration after the early years of

[7] Matilda White Riley and Anne Fouer, *Aging and Society,* Vol. 1, *An Inventory of Research Findings,* (New York: Russell Sage Foundation, 1968) p. 114.

this century, the retired segment of the population of this country will never again contain such a large number of immigrants and second generation Americans. These older people today experience language and emotional difficulties in communicating with younger members of their families. Their acculturation has been slower than that of their children and grandchildren who have learned the language and adapted to American ways as they have worked and gone to school. Ethnic newspapers and social groups related to nationality churches have, in the past, filled the social needs of older family members who have not become involved with groups whose language and ways they could not understand. As members of the younger generation of immigrant families take on more and more of the American attitudes and ways, their elders are experiencing a deepening sense of being forgotten and left behind.

Housing and family living patterns have changed

In the central neighborhoods of American communities—if redevelopment projects have not completely destroyed them—there still can be found some of the old houses and yards that were typical family homes at the turn of the century. These dwellings could accommodate the three generations that generally made up the average family. Not only did the young parents and their children live there, but also, when "Mama" or "Papa" died, the remaining spouse moved in. Many times an unmarried aunt or uncle whose help was needed and welcomed was also part of the family.

As high-rise apartments with limited space and one-family homes in outlying neighborhoods and suburban areas replace traditional housing, the number of three-generational families living under one roof decreases. Space has become too limited to provide the freedom and privacy needed for the members of all three generations. Separate housing in geographical proximity to children and grandchildren is preferred by most older adults. Today nearly 80 percent of all older Americans live in the homes in which they raised their children. These homes are generally still located in the older neighborhoods in the central parts of cities. They have now become too large, too difficult and expensive to keep in repair, and too awkward for the infirmities of old age. If they move from them, older people are forced, because of limited incomes, to live in older apartments and second-rate hotels in the deteriorating cores of cities. Nostalgic ties with neighbors, merchants, and church friends and the unavailability of other more desirable housing at rents they can afford, keep many older people stranded in their too large and run-down homes.

New housing patterns for
older adults are emerging

More adequate housing for older people at rents they can afford has become a concern in all communities within the past decade. The supplemental rent program, made possible through federal funding, is making it possible for older people of low incomes to live independently in any neighborhood of the community, in housing units they could not otherwise afford. Many new projects are being built by local housing authorities and nonprofit sponsors with funds from the federal Department of Housing and Urban Development. It is estimated that at least 2.8 million more units of housing are needed to accommodate all older adults now living in substandard conditions— approximately ten times the number now built or planned. Some projects are exclusively for retired adults; others have within them larger units for families. Many high-rise apartment houses for older people are situated within a complex of similar buildings for younger families. Thus, the older person can live among younger people and avoid the noise and confusion of living close to active children.

Some of the most creative planning today provides a network of related units housing a maximum of thirty or forty residents built in various neighborhoods of a large community and close sponsoring churches. The church serves as the social center for each housing unit, and a multiservice center in the downtown area provides the recreational, health, and counseling services for the residents from all units.[8] From central kitchens in the multiservice center hot meals are prepared and sent each day to the sponsoring neighborhood churches where the residents in the satellite units gather for congregate meals. These low-cost housing projects—with units well designed and easy to care for, with many built-in protective and safety features, and with rents geared to minimum incomes—are highly desirable and sought after by more individuals than can be accommodated.

Housing construction for a growing older adult population has now captured the interest of private builders and promoters. In many parts of the country high-rise condominium apartments and entire new communities are being built. In addition to attractive living units, clubhouses, res-

[8] Satellite Senior Homes, Inc., of Oakland, California, is an example of such a project.

taurants, swimming pools, golf courses, and craft and hobby shops of all kinds are provided. Maid service, maintenance of garden and grounds, and limousines to take residents back and forth to town assure them of freedom from unwanted responsibilities. Such settings attract individuals who have sufficient incomes and are physically well, socially adequate, and activity oriented.

Viewpoints about congregate living for older adults vary. Many gerontologists are most critical of housing projects built exclusively for older adults, arguing that older people are happier, more independent, and more mentally alert if they continue to live in the midst of younger families where the action is. The contrary was found to be true, however, in a study by Irving Rosow of Case Western Reserve University.[9] The findings show that older people who live predominantly with members of their peer group who share broadly similar backgrounds and social class and life experiences are happier, have more friends, and remain more active in the community than their age mates who live alone in the midst of younger families. Living in physical proximity to other age groups whose interests and life-styles differ widely from theirs does not result in meaningful relationships being formed between the generations. On the contrary, the research shows that the opposite is true—psychological and social barriers *do* exist between the generations, and the old are not readily accepted outside of the immediate family either by young or middle-aged adults.

Phrases such as "ghettoizing the aged" and "isolating older people as second-class citizens" are used by those who oppose separate housing patterns for older adults. Individual older people are all different. Many will not, and should not, choose to live in projects designed exclusively for their age group. For others, segregated living with age mates provides the best potential for social contacts and meaningful friendships.

Developments in medical knowledge and care have been far-reaching

Probably the most dramatic development during the century has been in medical knowledge and care. This development is evidenced by the fact that people are living longer and there is an increasing percentage of older persons in the population. In 1900, life expectancy was 48.2 years. In 1964, life expectancy for women was 74.6 years and for men, 67.7 years. For nonwhite females it was 67.2 years and for non-white males,

[9] Irving Rosow, *Housing and Social Integration of the Aged* (Cleveland, Ohio: Case Western Reserve University, 1964).

61.1 years. On an average day 3,800 Americans become sixty-five years old and 3,000 over sixty-five die; the country has a net gain of approximately eight hundred elderly people daily.[10]

As technical equipment and mechanical devices have been improved, many successful new surgical procedures have been developed. Surgery for removal of deposits of cholesterol from clogging arteries, open heart surgery to repair malfunctioning valves, kidney dialysis to keep poisonings from entering the blood stream, and organ transplants are being accepted as safe and effective procedures by the staffs of many of the nation's larger hospitals. Hormone and vitamin therapy, the use of antidepressants and tranquilizers, drugs to thin the blood and halt the progress of senility—all give promise of control of, and may eventually eliminate, some physical and mental illnesses.

The family doctor who made house calls and treated his patient there for any and all ailments is being replaced by teams of highly trained specialists in different fields. Today the physician and surgeon are assisted by paramedic personnel of all kinds who, under their direction, carry out many routine tests and medical procedures. Hundreds of lives are saved as the early stages of physical conditions that would result in early death are detected by multiphasic screening processes. Many who suffer strokes and fractures are restored to high levels of physical functioning through physical medicine and rehabilitation programs. The modern physician, however, has limited time to devote to each one of his many patients. Older people often feel bewildered and confused when a doctor is unable to take the time to interpret his diagnosis patiently and repeatedly and to explain his directions for care. A trend to train doctors once again as family doctors to fill this recognized need in younger families and among older people is noted in medical schools.

The passage of Medicare legislation in 1965 has been one of the most significant developments in providing medical care for older Americans without imposing on them and their families the possibility of medical indigency. The cost of medical care has risen phenomenally within even the last ten years. In 1964 medical costs were 116 percent over their 1957–1959 averages; in 1968 the average cost of hospital care in this nation was $55 a day. In several leading medical centers it ran as high as $100 a day.[11] Even though the present generation of older adults set as a goal the saving of enough money to pay for a last illness and burial,

---

[10] U.S., Department of Health, Education and Welfare, National Center for Health Statistics, 1966 data.

[11] Stanley Rosenthal, "Medical Costs Are Getting Out of Hand," *Forbes,* 15 March 1968, p. 24.

few could possibly have saved enough to cover the cost today of hospital care for long-term chronic and catastrophic illnesses. With Medicare supplemented by additional health insurance under union contracts and voluntary prepayment plans, no older person is limited to public clinic doctors and hospitals for care. He may choose any physician and be treated in the hospital he prefers.

Medical attention was difficult to obtain—and inadequate by today's standards—for those who lived on farms scattered in rural areas in the early twentieth century. Few young men, as they left medical school, chose the rural community as the locale for their practice. There might be one doctor in a community that was the seat of county government, and he may have been miles away from people in the smaller surrounding communities. There were no freeways or high-speed automobiles and ambulances to speed the patient to what were then inadequate county hospitals. How different the picture is today. Already, in many parts of the nation, there is a melding of private and public facilities in the enlarging concept of adequate community health care for rich and poor alike. It is predicted that, in the near future, every American will be covered for medical and dental care either through union contracts, cooperatives, or government programs. Every community, however small, will be served by a major medical center staffed by an organized group of physicians and linked by helicopters to rural areas. These centers, serving all ages, will feature an intensive care hospital that is flanked by diagnostic and rehabilitation facilities and out-patient departments. They will be teaching centers and will sponsor institutes on alcoholism, mental illness, and health problems of the aging. Such centers will be very different from the present inadequate health care services in many communities.

Serious public health problems
affect older people

Some of the public health problems that threaten modern man were unheard of when the present generation of grandparents were young adults. Overpopulation, pollution, smog, and the disposal of urban garbage were not front page news. The abusive use of tobacco, alcohol, and drugs had not become such threatening social problems. Today the health of the aged, as well as that of the total population, is being seriously affected by the overcrowding in the slums of big cities and by the pollution of air and water caused by automobile exhausts and gases that pour from the smokestacks of huge industrial complexes. The fish in the streams and oceans and the cattle and the produce from the fields are all becoming increasingly unsafe from the indiscriminate use of detergents, insecticides, and chemical fertilizers. The cutting away of hills and other natural watersheds, the destruction of orchards and forests, and the utilization of the few remaining green and open areas in big cities to make way for freeways, gas stations, carwashes, and housing developments are severely threatening the physical environment and the well-being of all Americans. Many older people with decreased physical resistance are particularly affected.

Mass communication helps to keep older adults in touch with their world

The instruments and processes of mass communication are important and cohesive forces in any society. In 1938 television broadcasting had just been initiated and the dial telephone did not exist. That sound and sight would be transmitted between distant points of the globe by means of Telstar satellite relay or that individuals could be visible to one another on a videophone would have been considered fantastic. Today fifty-five million homes have television and prime time audiences exceed sixty million viewers. Studies show that over two-thirds of older people sixty-five and over spend an average of three hours each day watching television. More viewers select programs devoted to information rather than to entertainment.[12] As retired individuals, their days hold many leisure hours. For many older people the radio and television are a boon that provides companionship and a source of information about happenings at home and around the world, thus keeping them in touch with their society. For other aged people television increases isolation, serving as a crutch and substitute for human companionship. This situation is especially true for the older adult who has limited physical strength and who easily gives in to apathy and inertia. For many the programs intrude too intensely with overdocumentation of the violence and turbulence of present days. The aged become apprehensive and alarmed by the impact of accounts of current events by newspapers, radio, and television. Extreme anxiety, frustration, and insecurity may develop, especially for those who live alone with few human contacts and emotional supports.

[12] Glenn H. Beyer and Margaret E. Woods, *Living and Activity Patterns of the Aged,* Research Report, no. 6 (Ithaca, N.Y.: Cornell University Center for Housing and Environmental Studies, 1963).

*New days call for new ways
of coping with change*

This review of some of the changes in societal and cultural patterns points up the specific impact on older adults. When a society changes so rapidly and with such turbulence as it does today, many older people are left psychologically and emotionally behind, in eddies of unrelatedness and alienation. In all societies changing patterns create problems of adjustment for the men and women who live in them. New ways of coping have to be learned. New patterns must be designed today to create an environment of opportunity for all older Americans, the majority of whom are relatively healthy and largely self-directing.

Opportunities for older people to age with dignity and usefulness and to participate, as they are able, in the common life must be an integral part of community planning. Meaningful involvement in society, rather than alienation from it, must be the goal.

BIBLIOGRAPHY

Beyer, Glenn H., and Woods, Margaret. *Living and Activity Patterns of the Aged.* Research Report No. 6. Ithaca, N.Y.: Center for Housing and Environmental Studies, Cornell University, 1963.

Clark, Margaret, and Anderson, Barbara. *Culture and Aging.* Springfield, Ill.: Charles C. Thomas, 1967.

Commager, Henry S. *The American Mind: An Interpretation of American Thought and Character Since the 1880's.* New Haven: Yale University Press, 1950.

Jung, Karl. *Collected Works.* Edited by Herbert Reed et al. New York: Pantheon Books, 1953.

Kluckholn, Clyde, et al. *Personality in Nature, Society, and Culture.* New York: Alfred A. Knopf, 1953.

Kutner, Bernard, et al. *Five Hundred Over Sixty, A Community Survey on Aging.* New York: Russell Sage Foundation, 1956.

Niebauch, Paul L., and Pope, John B. *The Elderly in Older Urban Areas.* Philadelphia: University of Pennsylvania, Institute for Environmental Studies, 1965.

Old Age As a Social Issue. Special issue of *The Journal of Social Issues* 21 (1965).

Riley, Matilda White, and Fouer, Anne. *Aging and Society.* New York: Russell Sage Foundation, 1968.

Rosow, Irving. *Social Integration of the Aged.* New York: Free Press of Glencoe, 1967.

Shock, Nathan W. *Trends in Gerontology.* Stanford: Stanford University Press, 1957.

Taeuber, Conrad, and Taeuber, Irene. *The Changing Population of the United States*. New York: John Wiley & Sons, 1958.

Tibbitts, Clarke, ed. *Living Through the Older Years*. Ann Arbor: University of Michigan Press, 1949.

————, *Aging and Society: A Handbook of Social Gerontology*. Chicago: University of Chicago Press, 1959.

United Nations, Economic and Social Affairs Council. *The Aging of Populations and Its Economic and Social Implications*. Population Studies, no. 26, 1956.

U.S., Department of Commerce. Bureau of the Census. *Senior Citizens—18 Million*. Washington, D.C.: Government Printing Office, 1964.

3 / The Use of Time and Social Adjustment in the Retirement Years

Leisure, LIKE *age,* IS A WORD that has different meanings depending on the viewpoint of the person defining it. For the employed adult, it is the time remaining after the day's work is over, which he uses for tasks necessary to maintain himself and for rest and recreation in order to return refreshed to his job. When he retires, free time makes up the worker's total day and has different meanings and potentials. Some retirees complain about having too much "time on my hands," while others find that there are not enough hours in the day for the many new interests that challenge them. Some older adults use their free time as they did before retirement: in homemaking, visiting, reading, watching television, gardening, sewing, enjoying recreational and cultural activities, and participating in civic, church, adult education, and social groups. Other retirees need help to discover themselves and to use their new leisure to develop their potentials as total human beings.

The meaning of his new leisure and the retiree's ability or inability to use it in satisfying and fulfilling ways are largely determined by the place his former job held in his life. In our pragmatic American society great emphasis is placed on the acquisition of money and things. Work is the socially approved role for adults and most workers invest the greater portion of their time and effort in their jobs. From them they derive feelings of personal worth and self-esteem. What one does becomes the frame of reference by which one is recognized and approved by others. If a worker has developed no interests other than his job, retirement and the increase in uncommitted time it brings can produce tension, frustration, and a sense of personal worthlessness.

Individuals react to retirement
in different ways

Studies of the meaning of retirement to individual workers show that attitudes differ widely. Many individuals anticipate the time when pressures are less. They look forward and plan for it as they have for other important milestones in their lives. Other workers dread the prospect of being retired and reject for as long as they can all thought of it. Differences in attitudes about retirement are related to many concomitant factors. The kind of work done, whether retirement was mandatory or by choice, adequacy of retirement income, state of health, marital relations and preretirement planning—all directly affect a worker's readiness for retirement.

The adequacy of income is an important
factor in readiness for retirement

Although overall satisfaction with life remains high among older people who continue to work, many move into retirement with minimum emotional trauma if they are confident they will have enough income, not only to maintain accustomed patterns of living, but also to travel and do things they never had time to do when employed. National surveys show that no appreciable loss in life satisfactions or rise in depression rates occurs among retirees if they are assured of incomes that to them seem adequate. This finding is true for corporation executives as well as for industrial workers. The surveys show that nearly 70 percent of all men who retire by plan and are in good health are content with their lot as compared with fewer than 30 percent of those who retire involuntarily because of ill health or compulsory retirement policies.[1]

Some retirees must look for new jobs

When workers are required by compulsory retirement policies to leave their jobs, some find they must seek other employment in order to meet financial responsibilities. This need occurs especially when there is illness in the family or when there are aged parents to support. Because the overwhelming proportion of people retiring today receive total pension income—from both private and public sources—that is only 20 to 40 percent of their average earnings in the years prior to retirement, these

[1] Gordon Streig, "Morale of the Retired," *Social Problems,* 3:270-276 (April, 1956).

responsibilities add heavy demands on their already limited retirement income. Technological developments that constantly decrease the manpower needs in business and industry limit the number of second career jobs available for older workers. The cost of retraining an older worker to qualify him for a job requiring new skills is high and, from the viewpoint of the employers, impractical when the work span may be relatively short. A recent study conducted by the Committee on Aging of the National Institute of Industrial Gerontology questions the efficacy of prematurely forcing older people, at a specific age, out of jobs they have held all their lives and creating the necessity of retraining them for new jobs in order for them to remain gainfully employed. According to the study 84 percent of the people between sixty-five and seventy years of age had jobs in 1954. At the beginning of 1970, 75 percent of the male workers between sixty and sixty-five and 34 percent of those between sixty-five and seventy were still in the labor force. For women the figure was only 17 percent. Labor force participation for both sexes dropped off even more rapidly for those seventy years of age and older.

Early retirement, the study points out, has important implications for society as a whole because it increases the ratio between the economically nonproductive segment of the population—the very young and the old—and the employed, economically productive portion. As this ratio is enlarged, social security payments of the middle-aged workers are increased to meet the costs of social programs for children and the aged.[2] Many economists believe that a favorable income position for older persons can best be maintained by more flexible retirement policies that set no specific cutoff age for employment. Other economists, however, believe that in an affluent society older people can be assured adequate income not by reentering the labor force after compulsory retirement but by a curb in inflation and an increase in social security and other benefits to be commensurate with increases in living costs.

Some workers are not emotionally prepared for retirement

Some men and women seek continued employment even though their retirement income is adequate to maintain a high standard of living. Work has become for them an emotional necessity. They have allowed their jobs to become the dominant interest in their lives. They work overtime and on weekends and often refuse to take vacations. Their jobs have

[2] "The Older Worker," a study conducted by the Institute of Industrial Gerontology, National Council on Aging, 1969.

sometimes become a defense against their inability to make strong human relationships and develop creative and satisfying leisure time interests. They feel threatened by retirement and are anxious and unable to use their new freedom. They reflect the Judeo-Christian ethic that predominates in Western society that work is good and to be economically nonproductive is an unworthy adult role indicating laziness and irresponsibility. Such individuals feel valued and useful only if they are paid for what they do and have a sense of deep personal guilt when they are not working.

Poor health and early death are not caused by retirement

Until recently it has been a popular belief that the increase in the number of deaths, especially among men recently retired, was a direct result of the trauma of compulsory retirement and the depression that followed. No comparative studies of the health of workers during a period immediately preceding their retirement and after have proved that there are any clear causal relationships between retirement and early death; nor have studies indicated that working per se has any positive effect on health. Studies do show that when death occurs soon after retirement, declining health is the factor that necessitated that the worker terminate his job. The possibility that the health of the worker will improve after retirement is just as great as the possibility that it will decline.[3] The probability that an individual may experience poor health, however, which may become a factor gradually limiting an older adult's social functioning, increases with age. Data from the National Health Survey indicate that, from July 1961 to June 1963, 43 percent of middle-aged persons forty-five to sixty-five years of age and 37 percent of older respondents sixty-five and older were limited in or unable to carry on their major activity because of poor health.[4] In a study of 1,716 workers past the age of sixty-five, made at the University of Missouri in 1967, 79 percent were recently retired. One-half gave poor health as the reason for their retirement.[5] Compulsory retirement at a specified age makes it emotionally much easier for a worker to give up a job that he is no longer

[3] Wayne E. Thompson and Gordon F. Streib, "Situational Determinants: Health and Economic Deprivation in Retirement," *Journal of Social Issues,* 14:18-34 (1958).

[4] U.S. Public Health Service, National Health Survey, *Chronic Conditions and Activity Limitations: United States, July 1961–June 1963.* Washington, D.C.

[5] C. T. Pihlblad and Henry A. Rosencranz, "Poor Health Not the Result but the Cause of Retirement," *Aging,* 173-174:11, 12 (March–April 1969).

physically able to carry. There is no need to explain his action or reveal his encroaching illness.

Marital and family relations
affect adjustment to retirement

When family and friendship groups remain unbroken and are close and supportive, the individual's adjustment to his new status as a retiree is relatively easy. For women the adjustment to being at home is not as disruptive as it is for most men. Women who have worked have usually managed a home in addition to a job and can return to homemaking tasks with little loss of status or sense of having nothing to do. A man, however, may have serious adjustment problems in the absence of a regular daily schedule to structure his time; he may also miss the opportunities to participate in the male culture that his job gave him.

With retirement and the departure of children from the home, older couples have long periods of time to spend together. Studies of retired couples indicate a wide difference in the effect on marital relationships of the husband's retirement and his increased time at home. Sharing with a retired husband some of the responsibilities in the home, adjusting to his spending more time there, living on a reduced income, and spending more time with him and less with other women in social groups will be difficult for some older wives. This difficulty will be especially true if the couple has not developed, through the years, common interests and the enjoyment of each other's company. For others, increased time together adds depth and meaning to relationships and interests.

Many older adults find themselves vulnerable to increasing isolation in the later decades of life as marriage partners are lost through death or through separation and divorce. Some marriages, although unhappy, are maintained until the children are grown and out of the home and then terminated. The partners find themselves isolated and extremely lonely unless they seek new associates. Doing so is not easy when one is alone and old. There are countless ways to keep busy *doing* and *going,* but opportunities to develop relationships that provide meaningful substitutes for primary persons who have been lost are few.

Participation in preretirement planning programs
has positive effects on attitudes about retirement

Company sponsored preretirement planning courses are one of the fast growing employee relations services among business and industrial corporations today. Television programs and adult education classes on preparing for retirement are increasingly popular and helpful. Studies show that an acceptance of compulsory retirement at a specific age and positive attitudes toward it are directly related to the opportunity the worker has had to participate in preretirement counseling programs. A report issued in 1964 of a study of 1,200 retirees from Inland Steel Company found that notable changes had taken place in a ten-year period in the attitudes of those who had participated in preretirement planning. In 1954, 55 percent of the employees said no to the query, "Do you want to retire?" Ten years later only 31 percent said they did not want to leave their jobs. Of the employees who were positive about retirement, 81 percent had made specific plans for the use of their time after retirement.[6]

New life goals may be
needed in retirement

How any individual will react to retirement is dependent upon many personal factors. It has been estimated that if a person lives at least fourteen years after retirement, he will have as much free time as a retiree as he had during his working years.

Positive attitudes toward leisure and new goals for its use will help give an older adult assurance that his life continues to be significant and meaningful. The measure of a man's worth during his working years has been his ability to produce goods and services. In retirement, his sense of worth will be based not on what he produces for the market, but on his success in achieving his own highest potential as a mature human being and on what he does that is socially useful and desirable. Achieving a sense of self-worth will require for many a reassessment of life values, a new emphasis on things that are useful to society, and a unifying of interests around new goals. An individual who does not adapt his values and goals to his new situation may become overwhelmed by the apparent meaninglessness of his existence.

There are many kinds of time
and options for its use

Alexander Reid Martin, former chairman of the National Committee on Leisure and Its Use of the American Psychiatric Association, dis-

6 Philip Ash, "Pre-retirement Counseling," *The Gerontologist,* 6:97-99 (June 1966).

tinguishes between two kinds of time the uses to which they can be put.[7] Dr. Martin describes time as being *occupied* or *unoccupied*. *Occupied time* is made up of those day-by-day routines essential for self-maintenance, such as eating and sleeping, shopping and preparing food, cleaning the house, and caring for the garden. The hours remaining in the course of the day are designated as *unoccupied time*. These hours may be used as *free time* or for *leisure*. *Free time,* according to Dr. Martin, is objective in nature. It can be measured and controlled and specifically planned for. The choices that an individual makes for its use will depend on his personality, health, social class, and ethnic and racial backgrounds. His interests, skills, and educational background will also influence how he will choose to use his free time. He may use some time in political and social action and in volunteer service for his community. Many older adults, as well as individuals in other age groups, use all or most of their free time in activities that are totally for their own enjoyment, diversion, and pleasure.

Some men and women, as they retire, depend heavily on commercial recreation, sports events, television, and entertainments in which they can be spectators. For most older adults, however, the most meaningful activities will be those that call for sustained interest and effort and through which relationships with congenial age mates can be developed. Golf courses, parks, recreation centers, adult education programs, churches, and senior centers are all important community resources for those older adults who need routines to structure their days and the companionship of peers for the enjoyment of their free time.

Free time, according to Dr. Martin, also has a subjective quality. This quality, which he calls *leisure,* is not measured by minutes and hours but is rather a state of mind. It is a readiness for the opening of the self—which has been trained in our culture to attend only to stimuli outside of the self—to an awareness of its own inner meanings and purposes. Within leisure an individual has the opportunity to achieve an awakened awareness, to rediscover himself, to think about what he is and what he ought to be, to contemplate, reflect, and marvel on events and things around him and on the universe itself. The growing interest in gurus and Eastern philosophies and such techniques for turning inward as Yoga and Zen Buddhist meditation is evidence of man's search to find deeper meaning in the events of his day-by-day existence. The inability of modern man to achieve this consciousness through the use of his own mental and spiritual powers and the increas-

---

[7] Alexander Reid Martin, *Leisure Time—A Creative Force.* (Washington, D.C.: National Council on the Aging, 1963).

ing use of mind-expanding drugs by many to experience this heightened awareness is one of today's tragic realities.

Demonstrating uses of leisure that add meaning to life could be a significant social role for older adults

The retirement years, when one is no longer preoccupied with the anxieties and pressures of job and family responsibilities, could provide opportunities to develop meaningful content for leisure. It is questionable whether many older adults of this generation will be able, or even interested, to use their leisure in these ways. Most people resist bringing problems into their consciousness. They are more comfortable in using their leisure for distracting amusements that enable themselves to run away emotionally from facing their innermost selves and the transitory nature of their lives.

Most adults in Western culture need training and opportunity to develop their powers of sensitivity, contemplation, and awareness before they will be able to experience the richness that such a use of some of their leisure time can add to life. The programs of senior centers offer many options for the use of time for personal enjoyment and diversion, for enrichment and the development of skills, for citizenship and community volunteer responsibilities. There are, however, few opportunities in such programs to gain insights into one's inner self and feelings, as well as an understanding and appreciation of other people. With the recent space exploration and interstellar discoveries, man also faces the need to reflect on the expanding wonders of the universe and the meaning of life within it. Leisure may enable older adults to face with inquiring minds and spirits the major issues of their own, and of all, human existence: life and death, God and man, truth and justice, freedom and responsibility, change and enduring reality. Such a use of a portion of time will bring greater heights and depths to the days of older adults and broader dimensions to their remaining years of life.

New values will be important in our automated society

As the polarization of the generations continues, there is an imperative need to define the unique roles and contributions of the elderly in our rapidly changing society. It is becoming increasingly evident that in the years ahead we will need to rethink some of the values and goals of an automated society. Work and the material possessions and pleasures that it makes possible can no longer be the only measure of a man's worth! Equally important and of significant value to society will be the quality of a man's life and his relation to his fellowmen wherever they live on this planet. The tenor of our times and the events in our world make it essential to begin to actualize human values in society. Older adults can make a significant contribution by demonstrating in their own lives how time can be used to enhance the dignity of man, the growth of his spirit, and, in turn, the quality of his society.

BIBLIOGRAPHY

Ash, Philip. "Pre-retirement Counseling." *The Gerontologist* 6 (1966): 97-99.

De Grazia, Sebastian. *Of Time, Work, Leisure.* New York: The 20th Century Fund, 1961.

Donahue, Wilma, et al. *Free Time: Challenge to Later Maturity.* Ann Arbor: University of Michigan Press, 1957.

Frank, L. K. "Education for Later Maturity." In *Education for Aging,* edited by Wilma Donahue. New York: Whiteside Press, 1955.

Freedman, Eugene A., and Havighurst, Robert J. *The Meaning of Work and Retirement.* Chicago: University of Chicago Press, 1954.

Gordon, Margaret. "Work and Patterns of Retirement." In *Aging and Leisure,* edited by R. W. Kleemeier. New York: Oxford University Press, 1961.

Havighurst, Robert J. "Life Beyond Family and Work." In *Aging in Western Societies,* edited by Burgess, Ernest W. Chicago: University of Chicago Press, 1960.

Kleemeier, Robert W. *Aging and Leisure: A Research Prospective into the Meaningful Use of Leisure and Time.* New York: Oxford University Press, 1961.

————, "Leisure and Disengagement in Retirement." *The Gerontologist* 3 (1964): 180-84.

Krep, J. *Employment, Income and Retirement Problems of the Aged.* Durham, N. C.: Duke University Press, 1963.

Martin, Alexander Reid. *Leisure Time: A Creative Force.* New York: National Council on the Aging, 1963.

————, "Urgent Need for a Philosophy of Leisure in our Aging Population." *Journal of American Genetics Society* 9 (1962): 215-24.

May, Rollo. "The Nature of Creativity." In *Creativity and Its Cultivation,* edited by Harold Anderson. New York: Harper and Brothers, 1950.

Morse, Nancy C., and Weiss, Robert. "The Function and Meaning of Work and the Job." *American Sociological Review* 20 (1955): 191-198.

Outdoor Recreation Resources Review Commission. *National Recreation Survey*. Study Report, no. 19. Washington, D.C.: Government Printing Office, 1962.

Pieper, J. *Leisure, The Basis of Culture*. New York: Pantheon Books; Mentor—Omega Books, 1963.

Thompson, Wayne E. "Pre-Retirement Anticipation and Adjustment in Retirement." *Journal of Social Issues* 14 (1958): 35-45.

Wilensky, H. L. *Work and Leisure*. Glencoe, Ill.: The Free Press, 1963.

Youmans, E. Grant. "Objective and Subjective Economic Disengagement Among Older Rural and Urban Men." *Journal of Gerontology* 21 (1966): 439-441.

II — EFFECTS OF THE AGING PROCESS ON SOCIAL FUNCTIONING

4 / Who Is Old and What Is Aging?

IN DESCRIBING THE PHYSICAL AGING PROCESS and its social, psychological, and emotional aspects, it is important to know the precise meaning of some of the terms that are used, such as old, aging, senescence, maturity, and senior citizens.

Old age is a relative concept

In America's youth culture it is a very difficult psychological task for many individuals to recognize the passing of time and their own aging within it. Consciously and unconsciously and for as long as possible, they try to retain a youthful self-image. "I don't feel a day older than I did twenty years ago. Why all this interest in old people? I'm not different from anybody else," says the sixty-five-year-old.

Old age for any individual is a relative matter and depends on many personal and environmental factors. Anyone over thirty is old to a member of the younger generation. "Someone who is ten years older than I am is old," says the middle-aged individual. "A man of sixty is a mere kid," according to the octogenarian. "I don't want to be around a lot of old people," says the seventy-five-year-old woman looking at a group of sixty-year-olds. Society's acceptance of an individual's ability to perform a certain kind of job sometimes serves as an index of age. A professional person in contemporary America is not considered too old to practice through his seventies and into his eighties, but clerical workers find it difficult to find new jobs after they are forty-five. In some primitive societies the beginning of old age is marked by an event rather than chronological time. Traditionally the Apache Indian becomes old at the birth of his first grandchild and is made an elder in the Tribal Council. For the physiologist the menopause for women and failing health and reduced physical vigor for men may mark the beginning of old age.

50

The sixty-fifth year as the statutory beginning of old age was first established for actuarial computation for pensions in the early nineteenth century when Otto von Bismarck was chancellor of Germany. Then life expectancy was only fifty years. Much has happened since then to improve physical health and extend the life span, and the sixty-fifth year is no longer a realistic index of old age. Chronological definitions are convenient but they are not precise enough because they tell us only how much calendar time has passed since an individual was born. The answer to the question of "How old is old?" will depend upon who is asking the question and what kind of facts he is gathering. The biologist, physiologist, anthropologist, sociologist, psychologist, and economist are all interested in specific aspects of the aging process. They gather different facts and therefore formulate different definitions.

Aging is a physical process
common to all animal life

In the eighteenth century George Louis Buffon, a French naturalist, became interested in the varying life spans that he observed in the animal kingdom. He theorized that within each species some regulatory factor operates that predetermines its life expectancy. He calculated the life span to be approximately five or six times the period that it took for the species to mature physically. A rat is mature at 10 months and lives for about 4 years. Dogs mature at 2 years and become old at 14. Man's physical body is completely developed at 25 or 30 years and his life expectancy, according to Buffon's theory, could be 125 or even 180 years. This possibility is difficult for modern man to conceive although isolated instances of individuals' living to be 110 years have been reported in this and other countries. In such instances, however, the reliability of birth records is questioned. The chances that a person will live to be 100 years old today are only 1 in every 500. In the twenty-first century, no doubt, the age span will be further extended. The far-reaching implications of this possibility are reflected in proposals of British medical societies for a social policy on euthanasia for individuals who become so old and so ill that they lose all capacity for mental and physical functioning.

According to recent biological research, the patterns of individual growth and maturation are linked to genetic factors and the length of an individual's life can be fairly accurately predicted by knowing how long his progenitors lived. Biologists describe the life process as a continuum beginning with conception and ending with death. The aging process within this continuum can be accelerated by illness, accident, poor nutrition, radiation, and psychological stress, but it can never be reversed. It can, however, be slowed down. With regular multiphasic screening examinations and improved diagnostic techniques, the life span of an individual may be extended by the early detection and treatment of conditions that might otherwise become chronic.

The locale of the aging process is within the millions of cells that make up the organs and tissues of the body. During the life process they have continued to mature and divide; the new cells have replaced the dying ones and have thus continuously renewed the body. At some point in this ongoing process metabolic changes occur and reverse the cell's capacity for self-repair and reproduction. When changes occur in the structure of cells and the rate of dying cells overtakes the rate of the new ones being formed, senescence, or old age, has set in. Biologists believe these changes are due to a chemical agent that is inherent in the genes, but none of their research is conclusive as to what triggers the change and upsets the homeostasis, or balance, that the body had achieved between cells dying and new ones being formed. The research gives evidence that this process takes place at different rates in different individuals and even within different organ systems in the same body. One person may have a senile mind and a strong, healthy cardiovascular system. Another may be able to see without glasses into his eightieth year, but his skin may be completely wrinkled. In another a stroke may affect the locomotion and speech functions, but all vital organs may continue to function normally. Loss of hearing and vision is experienced by many individuals long before any other physical changes occur. Aging, then, is a universal physical process that is highly variable in individual experience.

Although there is no clinical definition as to when it takes place, the fifth decade is suspected as being the borderline of involution when senescence begins. Because much of the early research focused on the pathology rather than on the normalcy of the process, aging has often been equated with disease. Although the aging process does reduce the body's defense against infections, these time-related physical changes and pathological conditions, while often concurrent, are not synonymous. Old age as regression and decline is a biological rather than a personality concept.

*Although physical aging is an inevitable
human process, emotional maturity grows
out of individual life experiences*

While much of the early research in social gerontology has been directed toward an understanding of the biological aspects of aging, it is only within the last decade that serious studies have been undertaken to understand the psychological and emotional adjustments involved in achieving emotional maturity. The behavioral scientists, although dependent on biological facts, approach the problem on a broader and a more comprehensive base. They are concerned not only with the *soma* (the body) in which these changes occur but also with the psychological, social, and cultural factors as they interact within the *psyche* (the personality) of the individual. The following diagram shows some of these interacting factors within the *inner* (psychological) and the *outer* (social) environments of any one individual. The pattern of interaction will be different for every one because each individual is a living organism embodying varied stages of physical development and life experiences. The environment too is alive, complex, and dynamic, and from it a person must distill meanings and values. How well the older person is able to function in ways that meet his continuing needs for self-actualization and society's expectations of him will be a measure of his maturity and mental health. (See Chart 2.)

*Emotional maturity at each life stage
is dependent on the successful adjustments
achieved during earlier periods*

According to behavioral scientists, achieving emotional maturity is a developmental process beginning in infancy and lasting until the very end of one's life. Each life stage brings specific developmental tasks that must be achieved. Becoming mature depends on the degree to which the individual meets the stresses and achieves a sense of ego identity and integrity in each preceding stage. An understanding of what these psychological adjustments are at each period gives a perspective on developmental tasks in later years.

Infancy. Infancy is the period from birth to about six years of age. It is characterized by the individual's efforts to have his instinctual needs of hunger, thirst, warmth, and physical comfort met. If the mother is able to meet these needs in a satisfying degree, the child develops a feeling of trust and security. In time, he also learns to trust

Chart 2
A Construct of the Psychophysical and
Sociocultural Factors that Determine
How Individuals Experience Aging

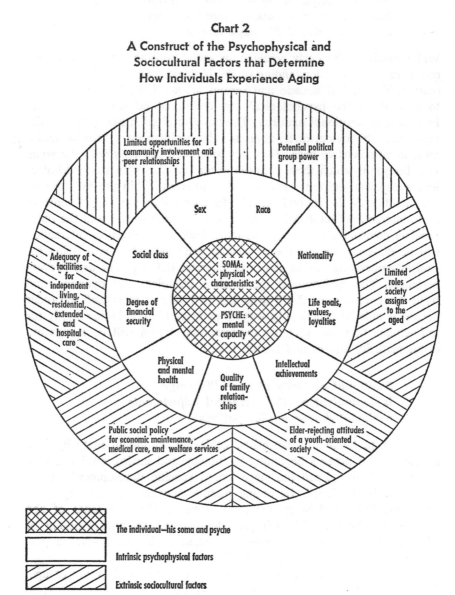

Limited opportunities for community involvement and peer relationships

Potential political group power

Sex

Race

Adequacy of facilities for independent living, residential, extended and hospital care

Social class

Nationality

Limited roles society assigns to the aged

SOMA: physical characteristics

Degree of financial security

Life goals, values, loyalties

PSYCHE: mental capacity

Physical and mental health

Intellectual achievements

Quality of family relationships

Public social policy for economic maintenance, medical care, and welfare services

Elder-rejecting attitudes of a youth-oriented society

The individual—his soma and psyche

Intrinsic psychophysical factors

Extrinsic sociocultural factors

and feel dependent upon other authority figures who care for and comfort him and give him approval. In learning experientially those things for which he receives approval and those things for which he receives disapproval from those adults he trusts, a child learns the acceptable patterns of behavior of the adult world.

Childhood. Childhood extends from age six to the beginning of adolescence. During these years a person achieves an awareness of his ego identity, an acceptance of his sex role, and an identification with the parent of the same sex. For the earlier part of this period at least, his peer relations are of a homosexual nature and he is strongly dependent on his parents and older siblings. School is a first and significant step in his lifelong task of achieving independence—the teacher, as well as his parents and other adults, encourages him to make independent decisions and become self-reliant. In meeting the expectations of these authority figures and in earning their approval, the child grows from dependency to independence. Basic emotional inadequacies that he experiences and suppresses into his unconscious will have a tendency to work their way into his adult actions as infantile behavior.

Adolescence. Adolescence falls roughly from the twelfth through the eighteenth years. During this transition from childhood to adulthood the ego vacillates between seeking to remain dependent and secure under parental control and striving to become independent; from looking to parents for direction to learning to internalize authority and become responsible for decisions and actions. The adolescent increasingly rejects the authority of his parents and identifies with his peers and accepts their values and patterns of behavior. His on-again off-again desire to maintain his childhood dependency and his attempts to demonstrate his independence as he learns to be a responsible adult are the source of many intergenerational conflicts. In adolescence, peer relations are heterosexual. Dating and learning to get along with members of the opposite sex are a primary developmental task, and life values and life goals are formulated.

Young adult years. This short period from eighteen through twenty-one years may be designated as one of preparation for the responsibilities of adult life. Extended professional education and military service are lengthening this period for many youth. Emotional independence from parents has normally been achieved, but continuing financial dependence on parents is common when young adults marry and have their first child during their college years. These years mark the beginning of full adult responsibility for many young people for whom further education is not a life goal. They have left their parents' home, taken jobs, married, and established their own homes and families.

Adult or *peak years.* These years range roughly from ages twenty-one through forty-five and represent the person's time of maximum responsibility. Men become well established in jobs and professions, and most of their time and energy are expended in meeting the demands of being adequate husbands and fathers and providing for the material needs of their families. If they are in the middle or upper classes, they may have undertaken roles of leadership in church, service clubs or the general community. The dominant role of the mother during this period is to be a "good" wife, to create a happy, comfortable home for her family, and to help her growing and grown children to become mature, responsible adults. If she works outside her home she has to learn to handle the pressures of her job along with the needs and demands of her growing family.

In the latter part of this period children leave home to attend college or to establish homes of their own. Parents find themselves again a family of two and are more dependent on one another for companionship and emotional support than they have been since the first years of their marriage. Continuing to grow together through shared interests, continuing to satisfy each other as marital partners, and making adjustments to basic physiological changes that begin in these years are essential developmental tasks. New responsibilities and concerns must now be carried—keeping in touch with siblings and members of the extended family and being responsible, perhaps, for providing increasing emotional and financial support for aging parents.

This period marked the end of life at the beginning of this century, when life expectancy was only 49.2 years. With life expectancy now being extended to a projected average of 78 years in 1975, three additional life periods, each with its own developmental tasks, have been identified by behavioral scientists. These will be described in more detail in subsequent chapters, but are described briefly below.

Middle age. Often described as the youth-of-old-age period, it includes the forty-fifth to the sixty-fifth years. Most of the responsibilities and tasks that began in the previous life stage are carried forward into this stage. Emotional and financial preparation for retirement take place and, for most older adults, job responsibilities are terminated. Progressive physical changes begin, but the detriments come slowly and a high degree of independent physical and social functioning is maintained by most people.

Later maturity. This period extends from sixty-five to eighty years of age, often sees the loss of one's spouse and the frequent loss of other significant persons. Physical detriments and dependency strivings increase. Bernice Neugarten, in her recent research into this period of old age, finds that the individual begins to view his physical environment as complex and dangerous. He feels that he can no longer be effective in changing it and accepts more readily the necessity to conform to the demands of his outer world. Preoccupation with the inner life becomes greater as he moves away from involvement in the outer world.[1]

Old age. The years after eighty are designated as the closure years and terminate with death. Although there are many brilliant examples of individuals who maintain a high level of mental and social functioning throughout these years, the physical, psychological, economic, and social resources of most individuals have become limited, and it is difficult for them to maintain themselves as independently functioning members of society. Physical and mental detriments mount and the aged person becomes more accepting of increasing and total dependency. The ego looks to the past for meanings, turns inward on itself, and often becomes preoccupied with physical needs.[2]

The behavioral scientist's functional definition of aging, which relates to the ability or inability of the individual to cope with the psychological and emotional stresses of physical and interpersonal change, is helpful in understanding the attitudes and behavior of individual older adults. To the behavioral scientist it is the degree of a person's emotional maturity and his ability to adjust to the changes that old age brings rather than the extent of the physical changes themselves that determines when he is old. This functional definition clarifies the question of why some individuals of more advanced chronological years, even though facing physical limitations, are more youthful in their attitudes, face their problems more positively, and manage their lives more independently than many others of lesser years.

Senior citizen is a term popularly used to designate older adults

Many prejudicial and stereotyped concepts and phrases characterize much of our thinking about older adults and their problems. To be called old or elderly constitutes an emotional threat to the self-image

[1] Bernice L. Neugarten and associates, *Personality in Middle and Late Life* (New York: Atherton Press, 1964), p. 194.

[2] Clark Tibbets, Middle Age and Older People in American Society, no. 227 (Washington, D.C.: U.S. Department of Health, Education and Welfare, Administration on Aging, 1965).

of most adults. More relative terms, such as aging, older American, or older adult, are more acceptable. The designation *senior citizen* has come into wide use and popularity in most community and governmental programs. Although a euphemism that attempts to connote status and respect—as did the word *elder* in primitive society—senior citizen is not a designation that is popular or acceptable to all older adults. To be separated from the rest of society by a special definition is psychologically inappropriate for any group. Everyone wants to belong. Some verbal frame of reference, however, is necessary to help focus interest and planning for needed services and programs for older adults. Until a more appropriate one is formulated senior citizen will continue to be the designation most widely used.

There is no universal definition of age

The continuing research of both the physical and behavioral scientists indicates that the complicated changes in the aging process cannot be reduced to any unitary principle in terms of biochemical substance, a physical state, or a psychological process. The question of when one is old can only be appraised on an individual basis when all of the physical, psychological, and social variables are known. Even then the investigators who are not themselves older adults cannot really answer the question, for they know nothing of how it feels to be old. They may know how it feels to be a child, an adolescent, or a young adult—for they have experienced these stages—but what it feels like to be old can only be described from within—by one who is himself involved in the experience.

BIBLIOGRAPHY

Birren, James E., ed. *Aging and the Individual: A Handbook of the Biological, Psychological and Social Aspects of Aging.* Chicago: University of Chicago Press, 1959.

Comfort, Alex. *The Biology of Senescence.* New York: Holt, Rinehart & Winston, 1956.

Curtis, Howard J. *Biological Mechanisms of Aging.* Springfield, Ill.: Charles C. Thomas, 1966.

Erikson, Erik H., "Growth and Crises of the 'Healthy Personality.'" in *Personality in Nature, Society and Culture,* edited by C. Kluckhohn, H. G. Murray, and D. M. Schneider, pp. 185-225. New York: Alfred A. Knopf, 1953.

Havighurst, Robert J. "The Sociologic Meaning of Aging." *Geriatrics* 13 (1958): 43-50.

Kastenbaum, Robert "The Foreshortened Life Perspective." *Geriatrics* 24 (1969): 126-133.

Milne, Louis J., and Milner, Margery. *The Ages of Life*. New York: Harcourt, Brace and World, 1968.

Neugarten, Bernice L., et al. *Personality in Middle and Late Life*. New York: Atherton Press, 1964.

Rough, Thomas A. "Emotional Needs and the Later Years." *Journal of the American Geriatrics Society* 13 (1965): 380-384.

Shock, Nathan W., ed. "Biological Aspects of Aging" in *Aging Around the World,* Proceedings of the Fifth Congress of the International Association of Gerontology (San Francisco, California). New York and London: Columbia University Press, 1962.

Strehler, B. L. *Time, Cells, and Aging*. New York: Academic Press, 1962.

Tanenbaum, David E. "Loneliness in the Aged." *Mental Hygiene* 51 (1967): 91-99. January, 1967.

Tuckman, Jacob, and Lorge, Irving. "When Aging Begins and Stereotypes About Aging" *Journal of Gerontology,* 8 (1953): 487-492.

5 / Physical Aging as It Affects Social Functioning[1]

THE NORMAL PHYSICAL AGING PROCESS is the result of age-linked changes in the body and their effect on the functioning of its vital systems. In addition to age-linked or intrinsic changes there are other physical changes that are the result of illness, poor nutrition, accident, radiation, and emotional stress that the individual has experienced during earlier life periods. All of these changes make the human body, in the later years, increasingly vulnerable to the onset of chronic illness. In youth, an individual usually returns quickly to his former level of well-being after an acute illness. During old age, an increasing loss of physical vigor results from each illness.

As the body ages the limits within which it can function normally become progressively restricted, and its susceptibility to disease increases. It is not the single change in the aging body that is of primary importance, but the accumulation of a series of changes. The aging process involves both *primary aging* associated with a decline of functional abilities and *secondary aging* resulting from disease and trauma. A comprehensive review of all of the physical changes and chronic illnesses that may take place is outside the scope of this book. This chapter will deal only with those conditions that curtail or seriously limit the mobility and social functioning of the older adult.

The aging process takes place in the cells

The individual cell, the basic component of all tissues and organs, is the locale of the primary aging process and age-linked changes. In each

[1] Public Health Service Publication No. 1459, Vol. II (April 1970) has been the source of the statistical material used in this chapter. Recent research reports on physical aging that are cited have been reviewed in *Geriatric Focus,* a monthly publication of the Knoll Pharmaceutical Company, Orange, New Jersey.

cell—cells are so tiny that it takes millions to form a half-inch cube of body tissue, highly complicated chemical processes occur. These internal cellular processes are controlled indirectly by the molecular structure of deoxyribonucleic acid (DNA), the genetic material that determines the biological properties of all living tissue. Three kinds of genetic effects have been suggested as possible contributors to the aging process.

1. A missing or incorrect genetic sequence in the DNA may result in genes that cause low resistance to disease.

2. The presence of genes that have had a beneficial effect in early life may slowly produce harmful changes as by-products of their normal function.

3. There may be a diminishing of those genes that are involved in the longevity of the cell.

More than twenty theories about the precise nature of these changes and what triggers them are now being tested in scientific laboratories around the world. Continuing research may soon make present theories obsolete.

The body is made up of many interrelated vital systems

Many intricately related organs and organ systems comprise the human organism. Each organ in turn is made up of various tissues and these are composed of cells. In simple organisms, the individual cell is capable of performing all necessary life functions, but as the organism becomes more complex, specialization of the various components (cells, tissues, and organs) requires complex interrelationships for proper maintenance of the entire organism. The following sections will review some of these intricately meshed and interrelated systems within the human body.

The skeletal and muscular systems give the body its shape and help it to stand upright

The skeletal system, which is made up of 206 bones, cartilage, and ligaments, gives the body its shape. This framework reaches its maximum size and strength in about twenty-five years and then begins to shrink as the cells in the body are reduced in number and as the cells themselves begin to atrophy and reduce in size. The muscular system gives support to the skeletal structure and is responsible for the movements of the body. Each part of the skeletal-muscular system performs perfect teamwork, with some muscles contracting to pull bones forward and others to pull them back. The tissues of this system are the most infection-free of the entire body and those of the bones have an extraordinary built-in capacity for self repair. Muscles do not have this ability. No new muscle cells appear in the body after the last month of fetal life. Growth in the muscles throughout life is by the enlargement of the original cells, and a damaged muscle can repair itself only through the formation of fibrous (scar) tissue.

Joints, bones, and cartilage. As the body ages, bones lose their density and become more brittle, and joints become less mobile. As the cartilage between the segments of the spinal column degenerates, the vertebrae come closer together and the body shrinks in height. Ligaments lose their elasticity, the spinal column becomes less flexible, and a hunched-over appearance results. As joints stiffen and moving about becomes increasingly painful, many older persons fall into sedentary habits in an effort to protect themselves from discomfort. They take elevators rather than use stairs, ride the bus rather than walk short distances, and in countless other ways protect the aching joints and muscles rather than continue to use them and keep them flexible. Protecting aching joints results in less demand being made on the circulatory system. As a result, the diameters of the blood vessels shrink and a poorer supply of blood to the whole body results.

Bones become weak when not used. Bones are made up of a network of osteons with canal systems for carrying the blood supply. The center core of the bone is comprised of fatty marrow also with a rich blood supply. The bone is about one-third mineral material and two-thirds a protein matrix in which the mineral is deposited by the blood. The largest amounts of calcium are deposited in those bones where the greatest stress comes and where the greatest weight is carried. These, of course, are the hip bones, which are so often fractured when an older person falls. Getting a person who has a broken hip onto his feet as quickly as possible is part of the rehabilitation program, for bones grow strong only under stress and longitudinal compression. Falls are more common in old age and are due to a variety of reasons: the decline in postural skills, gait changes, such as the tendency to drag the feet, changes in weight, attacks of dizziness, and difficulties of seeing in the dark. If the body remains prone for too long the blood collects in the legs and the blood pressure drops. There is a decrease then of blood to the brain and heart, and the individual experiences a tendency to faint. Persons over sixty-four years of age were victims in 73 percent of all accidental deaths from falls in 1967. Approximately three thousand fatal falls per year occur in various institutions for the aged.

The feet. The importance of the feet in keeping the individual ambulatory and active can hardly be emphasized enough. The normal foot is made up of twenty-six bones: seven tarsal, five metatarsal, two phalanges in the great toe, and three phalanges each in the other toes. These bones are arranged in four arches, which handle the body's weight and balance as one stands and walks, and are bound together by 112 ligaments that are moved by twenty muscles. As the tissues of the muscles and ligaments lose elasticity, the functioning of all these interrelated parts often becomes painful. The padding of fat between the bones and the bottom of the foot often becomes thinner, thus reducing the cushion between the foot and the ground. Corns and callouses form where there is pressure and, in turn, press more on the nerve endings in the foot, making walking very painful. Properly fitting shoes distribute the pressure evenly. While perhaps less attractive than those worn in earlier years, they do give comfort and enable the older person to remain mobile. The functioning of the foot in some degree of comfort and efficiency is of paramount importance to the individual's health and continuing involvement in activities. Discomfort of the feet becomes a too-ready excuse for some individuals to withdraw from activity and involvement. Information on foot care is important in any educational program for older people, and many organizations make the services of a podiatrist available for their members.

Poor functioning of the skeletal-muscular systems causes older adults to become accident prone

Educational programs to alert older adults to their vulnerability to accidents are important. The potential of accidents among older people who have ambulatory problems and whose reactions have also slowed down has increased markedly in our large urban cities: 47.6 percent of all deaths from injuries incurred while crossing at an intersection and 30.4 percent of those from jaywalking involved persons over sixty-five years of age. The National Safety Council takes the position that we need special crossings for the elderly—with ramps rather than high curbs on which they may trip or fall—and longer spacing of traffic signals at strategic intersections. A single green light often does not give an older person adequate time to cross city streets, especially if he uses crutches or walks with a cane.

Canes, crutches, and wheelchairs serve as aids when ambulation has become severely impaired by fractured bones, arthritis, peripheral vascular disorders, and partial paralysis resulting from small strokes and broken-down feet. Such aids necessarily limit movement when it is important to use a bus, climb stairs, or pass through doors and down halls of many community buildings. The transportation of the physically impaired and nonambulatory older person is a problem that calls for cooperation from officials of transportation systems who design the malls and crosswalks in redeveloped central cities as well as of the architects of public buildings and stores.

The oral cavity. Changes in the bones that make up the oral cavity cause dentures to fit poorly and result in discomfort in eating. Many older persons become dental cripples and accept toothlessness and the necessity to eat soft foods as inevitable. Good teeth and correctly fitted dentures are essential to good morale. They not only enable the individual to eat the foods that he really enjoys as well as needs, but they directly affect his appearance and his ready acceptance in a social group. A lack of understanding of the importance of good nutrition throughout life and the role that good teeth and properly fitted dentures play in insuring it keeps many aging men and women from spending their limited income on dental bills. Investigations have shown that with increasing age, visits to the dentist decrease while those to medical doctors increase. Too many older persons suffer dental discomfort from shrinking gums and changes in the oral cavity and wait until it is too late for preventive or rehabilitative measures. In embarrassment, these older adults retreat from socializing with other people.

The cartilage. Pads of cartilage cover the ends of the bones that form joints. When the pads slowly become less resilient and are worn down as a result of the wear and tear of normal life, stiffness occurs around the joints. When this condition becomes crippling, it is known as osteoarthritis. It occurs most frequently in the joints of the lower spine, hips, knees, and other areas that bear the body's weight, and is especially bad in the grossly obese person. As the cartilage ages it becomes rough and gradually wears away, allowing bone to move against bone. Bony outgrowths may form at the edge of the joint, and these may gradually interfere with the joint's normal movement. Any strain on the joint can make the condition worse although anything that improves the circulation—like massage, heat, and especially exercise—can improve it.

The bursae. Closely related to the cartilage are the bursae, which contain a lubricating fluid that reduces the friction as tissue moves over other tissue. Bursae lie in the connective tissue between the skin and bony structures, such as those in the elbow or shoulder. When they become inflamed as a result of degenerative changes, movement of the joints is limited and a painful condition known as bursitis results.

The muscles. As muscles age they lose their strength and become flabby from disuse, a condition that is known as loss of muscle tone. Those muscles that move the bones of the body work with less force and precision, and the older person, therefore, moves slowly and with poor coordination. As muscles in such organs as the bowels and bladder lose their tone, they become sluggish and sometimes lose function. Bladder infection, incontinence, and constipation result. Fear of possible loss of control over functions of elimination causes increased anxiety and embarrassment.

The skin. As sweat glands decrease their activity and the fatty layers underneath the skin are lost, wrinkles appear in the skin. Wrinkles are sometimes caused by the sun's active rays, which break down the elastic fibers in the skin. Skin changes and the loss of hair or its pigmentation are such obvious signs of aging that they become for some individuals a threat to their self-image. The large sums of money spent on cosmetics by aging women are evidence of their desire to maintain a youthful appearance.

Age-linked changes in the circulatory system affect all vital organs

The circulatory system is made up of the heart and the labyrinth of veins and arteries that carry blood to all parts of the body. The heart functions as a pump, and, as the body ages, it must pump harder to compensate for the decreasing elasticity of the walls and the smaller passages that result from the build-up of fatty deposits within them. Tests indicate that in one minute the average twenty-year-old heart pumps about four quarts of blood for each square meter of body surface, but the ninety-year-old heart pumps an average of slightly less than two quarts. This finding explains why older people have less total physical energy than the young. Obstructions in and the narrowing of the passages of the blood vessels is known as arteriosclerosis. When this condition occurs, less blood is able to pass through to be delivered to the various vital organs unless other blood vessels are able to compensate for the blockage.

Hypertension. When changes occur in the walls of the large arteries, other parts of the circulatory system are affected. High blood pressure, or hypertension, may result from tensions or unhappiness in the individual's personal life, but it is more often a warning of some physical condition or combination of conditions in the circulatory system. More women than men are affected. Early attention is aways important. Physicians now have available a growing number of drugs to treat high blood pressure. These, as well as diet control and any indicated change in living habits and attitudes to relieve tensions and anxieties, are often adequate to alleviate this condition.

Coronary heart disease. The heart has to feed itself as well as all the rest of the body. It does so through the coronary arteries by pumping blood back into its own muscles. Any weakness in the valves or any blockage or narrowing that cuts off the food supply to these arteries is more serious in the heart than in any other part of the body. It results in a coronary occlusion or heart attack.

Strokes. When blood vessels of the brain are blocked or a rupture occurs within the thinning walls of the small veins of the brain, slight strokes that bring on some temporary paralysis and changes in personality occur. When the rupture takes place over a large area of the brain, the individual is said to have suffered a cerebro-vascular accident. The damage caused depends upon what part of the brain is affected. If the damage is in the cerebellum, incoordination results and there is a paralysis of those specific areas of the body controlled by the cerebellum. If the accident occurs in that portion that controls speech, the individual loses all power to speak or speaks only haltingly. This disease is called aphasia. The body itself sets about repairing the affected portions by feeding blood to them through different circuits of veins. After assessing the damage that the stroke has caused, the skills of the physical therapist and the speech therapist supplement the natural rehabilitative processes within the body. This is a long and discouraging process for many people, and those responsible for care must use great patience in motivating the patient to make an effort to reuse the affected parts. Through a persistent use of all rehabilitative therapies many patients are restored to a high degree of social functioning.

Between the ages of forty-five and seventy-four, the third major cause of death for Americans is the stroke, and its incidence nearly doubles in these three decades. By age seventy-five, strokes become the second highest cause of death.

The endocrine system is a regulatory system

The endocrine system is made up of all internal gland secretions, from the pituitary, pancreas, thyroid, parathyroid, adrenal, and sex glands.

These glands secrete hormones and serve as regulatory mechanisms. They exert enormous control over such vital functions as metabolism, the clotting of blood, the level of blood sugar, body temperature, and the production of antibodies to fight infections. A breakdown in the protective mechanisms of the enzymes secreted by these glands is thought to be one of the major factors that trigger high blood pressure, arthritis, and arteriosclerosis.

The respiratory system is closely related to the circulatory system

Oxygen, which is crucial to life, is taken into the body from the outside environment by the minute air tubes in the lungs called bronchioles and is distributed in turn to the body by the blood. At the same time carbon dioxide, a waste product in the blood, passes through these bronchioles and is exhaled. The cleansed blood with its oxygen returns from the lung to the heart and is pumped to all parts of the body. In the later years the lung capacity remains very much the same but the lung's ability to transfer oxygen to the blood stream seems to decline. The decline results when bronchial tubes lose elasticity and the ability of the lungs to expel air is decreased. The average twenty-year-old person's lungs can transfer four liters of oxygen each minute to the blood stream, while at age seventy-five only a liter and one half per minute enters the blood from the lungs. The older person must breathe faster to transfer a given amount of oxygen to the blood in a given time, and as a result, he has less energy than the younger one.

When the bronchial tubes become clogged with scar tissues from inflammation caused by colds and bronchial attacks suffered throughout life, the condition is known as emphysema. The normal person breathes fifteen to twenty times a minute; a person with emphysema may breathe four times as fast and still not bring enough oxygen into the blood. His whole body is thus seriously affected.

The incidence of lung diseases, such as bronchitis and emphysema, is especially high among cigarette smokers and in large urban centers. It is now recognized that pollution of the air by exhaust from automobiles and industrial plants is accelerating the rate of death from lung disease. Thirty years ago emphysema caused only about one hundred deaths in the United States annually. In 1964 there were fifty thousand deaths. A large percentage of these was among people sixty-five years of age and older. Some of the increase may be the result of more accurate medical diagnosis of lung conditions. Nevertheless, it is sobering to remember that many deaths today are caused, not by disease, but by man himself. The excessive use of cigarettes, the pollution of air and the careless use of the automobile can all be controlled.

Tuberculosis and bronchopneumonia are also a serious problem for the older adult. More than half of the patients in tuberculosis hospitals are over fifty years of age, and bronchopneumonia often becomes the terminal condition in many older persons suffering from other physical illnesses. The collapse of any vital organ produces an accumulation of fluids in the lungs that interferes with normal breathing, and the patient dies.

The nervous system is the coordinating mechanism of all body processes

One of the most fascinatingly efficient systems of the body is the nervous system. It is made up of the brain, which weighs approximately three pounds, the spinal cord, and a complex network of nerves that are threaded throughout the entire body, reaching from head to toe. This system is constructed of some ten to twelve billion nondividing irreplaceable cells whose ultracomplex processes control all the body's activities —every thought, emotion, and action that is taken. It functions every second to control every vital bodily process. The brain controls messages as they travel through a system of eighty-six major nerves connecting it at the base of the skull and running down the spinal cord from which they fan out to thousands of smaller nerves all around the body. In some individuals as they age and in ways that are not yet fully understood, the substance of the brain wastes away. The loss of nerve tissue results in intellectual deficit, a condition that is known as senile brain syndrome. When the brain becomes poorly nourished because of changes in the circulatory system, conditions such as senile brain syndrome, strokes, and cerebrovascular accidents result. Because the cells in the brain can never be replaced, any impairment greatly affects social functioning. Chronic and acute brain syndrome are discussed in the chapter on mental illness.

The receptors of the central nervous system—the eye, ear, taste buds, and nerve endings in the skin and in the nose—bring to the brain all stimuli from the outside environment and enable the individual to relate to his environment. When these receptors are impaired the individual becomes drastically affected; research has shown that if all sensory input is cut off from a human being of any age, he begins to hallucinate and becomes severely mentally disturbed. Psychological health depends on a continuing perception of time and space. In general, the senses become less sharp with advancing age. To the extent that they are associated with changes in the nervous system, the aging process itself rather than any organic condition accounts for much of the decline of the senses.

The sensory perceptors keep the individual in touch with his outside environment

The eye and sight. The human eye is a mechanism of many intricate interrelated parts. It is through the muscles that control the shape of the eyeball and the dilation of the pupil that images are brought to the retina and, in turn, by the optic nerve to the brain. One is thus enabled to see both in dim and bright light, to see near and far objects, and to distinguish colors and judge distances. The lenses of the eye become less elastic as the fibers produced by cells accumulate in the lens, and the retina and optic nerve become less sensitive. As the muscles controlling the pupil of the eye become less flexible, the eye is unable to accommodate as rapidly to different degrees of light. A younger person can go into a darkened room or theatre and move quickly to a seat; the eyes of an older person take longer to adjust to the darkness and he must wait until they do if he is not to stumble and grope. Older people are uncomfortable in dimly lit restaurants because poor vision restricts movements and makes a person more liable to accidents. Illuminating engineers estimate that, on an average, twice as much light is required at age sixty as at age twenty. For this reason, night lights in bathrooms and stronger bulbs in reading lamps and craft areas must be used to enable the aging person to function. Age-related changes that begin in the eye by the fortieth year can be accommodated by means of glasses, which most people of all ages wear without feelings of personal discomfort or embarrassment.

Glaucoma and cataracts. Some serious changes that occur in the eye may result in blindness if they are not controlled or properly treated. Such conditions result from hardening of the arteries, high blood pressure, kidney disease, and diabetes. Glaucoma occurs when the channels through which the aqueous material of the eye is drained become obstructed, and increased intraocular pressure causes the optic nerve to atrophy. By a simple and routine test that measures the tension in the eyeball, the beginning of this condition can be detected by an ophthalmologist. Medication controls glaucoma in many patients, but for others surgery is essential to preserve vision. If glaucoma is neglected blindness results. Screening programs for glaucoma are part of the health services in many organizations serving older people.

Cataracts occur when the crystalline lens of the eye becomes opaque because of scarring. If cataracts progress slowly, many people can adjust to their limited vision and live out their lives without surgery. However, corneal transplants or surgical removal of the lens and wearing a specially ground or contact lens can take care of this condition. Glaucoma, cataracts, and some other less common conditions, according to the National Health Service survey, annually cause blindness in at least one million people, 47 percent of whom are sixty years of age or over. Blindness for older persons increases existing age-engendered feelings of uselessness, helplessness and isolation. All possible efforts should be made to keep the individual involved in activity and in relationships with others or withdrawal and depression will follow. The radio, talking books, large type books, and materials written in Braille are all useful tools in helping the older person relate to what is going on around him and to remain in meaningful communication with others.

The ear and sound. Hearing loss (presbycusis) occurs when there is damage to nerve cells in the inner ear or to nerve fiber. At least one out of every eight older persons in this country has a significant loss of hearing that affects his interpersonal communication. There are two major kinds of hearing losses. The first involves the auditory nerves when they become damaged and when sound can no longer be carried over to reach the brain. Such a condition cannot be helped by a hearing device because the nerve itself is dead. The second occurs when the bones of the ear become frozen; in other words, a blockage occurs and sound cannot be transmitted. Bone deafness can be corrected by a hearing device, which should be selected only after testing by an audiologist, or by surgery through a special microscope.

One can lose his hearing for fairly specific high audio frequencies. In such cases, the person can hear, but the loss of high frequency sounds results in his inability to discriminate between consonant sounds. Voices thus sound muddled, and it takes the older person a longer time than is normal to figure out what is being said. Many people refuse to recognize that they have hearing losses, even though such losses are indicated by tests, and they may resent suggestions that they need hearing aids. The loss of hearing is soon reflected in the individual's emotional adjustment. Because he cannot hear what is being said, an older person may accuse others of mumbling or of deliberately speaking in low tones to cut him out of the conversation. He often becomes suspicious or imagines that others are talking about him. The individual with a hearing loss can remain more independent than the blind person but he often becomes more cranky and demanding. People working with the elderly must be especially sensitive to symptoms of hearing problems that are often evidenced in behavior. The elderly man or woman who gives odd answers to questions, who fails to pay attention to others except when talking face to face, or who seems withdrawn from social contacts may be suffering from loss of hearing. An increase in background noises in a room where deaf older people are meeting has proved helpful in keeping them in touch with their environment.

Touch, taste, and smell. Knowledge about the senses of taste, touch, and smell is limited, but it appears that in the average person these senses begin to decline at approximately sixty years of age. A consciousness of taste comes to the brain through the nerve endings in the mucous lining of the nose and in the taste buds located on the papilla of the tongue. A reduction of 36 percent of their number in the later decades results in taste changes and a decreased interest in many foods. As the mucous lining of the nose and the skin is thinned out there are fewer nerve fibers to continue to activate all of these senses to the same degree as in youth. This explains why some say elderly people no longer enjoy the foods that were formerly such favorites with them.

The digestive system carries nourishment for the body's maintenance

The digestive system is made up of the stomach—a ten-inch-long organ that holds two quarts of food—and the small and large intestines, which fold and coil and could stretch for thirty feet. Within this system the chemical conversion of food takes place. Here carbohydrates and fats are turned into simple energy, and proteins becomes amino acids, the basic building materials of the body. Research has established that the amount of saturated fatty acids (cholesterol) taken into the body is related to arteriosclerosis and coronary heart disease. The unsaturated fatty acids appear to help keep other fats in solution and prevent their deposit in the vessel walls.

Nutrition. Good nutrition, like proper exercise, can contribute much to physical well-being and to the enjoyment of life through the later years. There are many reasons why older persons develop poor patterns of eating and a disinterest in food. They often lack knowledge of the basic nutritional content of foods and the essential daily intake of each food group. Too frequently, low incomes restrict the quality and quantity of foods that can be purchased, and many older people have inconvenient cooking facilities and inadequate refrigeration. Shopping can become confusing and exhausting in the modern supermarket with its bewildering variety, its many new packages, and its long aisles. Poor teeth and a dulled sense of taste and smell often diminish interest in food. Living and eating alone limit the enjoyment of food for many elderly persons. Companionship and the sharing of meals play a vital role in the maintenance of esential levels of nutrition. A study of 130 subjects at the Age Center of New England in Boston revealed that the ten persons with the best nutrient intake were among those rated as "most gregarious," whereas the ten rated as lowest in nutrition adequacy were among the most isolated.

Lack of activity and an increase in emotional anxiety decrease the appetite of many older persons. Others, who want to escape and to relieve tensions, eat too much. Food choices and practices represent a lifelong pattern that is influenced by social, economic, cultural, and religious factors. Attitudes about diet grow out of experiences of years of living. Older people tend to eat what they ate when they were younger, which can be a problem if their diets were poor during youth. Any suggestion that change might be beneficial as one grows older is often rebuffed with a defensive reply, "Well, I've managed pretty well up to this point; I see no reason why I need to change how I cook and what I eat now that I have become old." Research has been done on the nutritional needs of the aging human body, but such individuals are unable to benefit from the new knowledge gained.

The metabolic processes involved in physical aging seem to indicate little difference between young people and healthy older people in the basic food requirements and how foods are assimilated by the body. Poor nutrition among older people, then, is not so much a functional problem but rather one of omitting essential items in the diet. The importance of nutrition in the aging body is apparent when it is realized that the food that is eaten must provide the building materials by which muscles, organs, bones, teeth, blood, and all body fluids are maintained. The complex metabolic processes of the body that produce the enzymes and hormones that regulate and control bodily functions and keep the body in a state of homeostasis are dependent upon the nutrients supplied in the daily food intake. In some older persons presenile conditions do not necessarily reflect deterioration in the physiological processes of the body, but may rather be caused by inadequate nutrition.

Changing life patterns in age do demand less expenditure of physical energy, and fewer calories are needed; requirements for other nutrients, however, are not essentially different from those in early maturity. Nutritional experts have estimated that a total of 1,600 calories is needed daily for people seventy to ninety years of age. Too often bread and cereal products provide a disproportionate part of the total caloric intake and block the use of other essential foods, such as meat, eggs, milk products, fruits, and vegetables. The need for weight-producing calories that abound in fats and carbohydrates grows less in the older body while the need for proteins and minerals—those substances that repair and maintain cells—increases. So many older people who live alone, however, fall into the easy pattern of an unplanned diet of sweet rolls, cookies, toast, and coffee rather than using fresh fruits and milk and taking the time and effort necessary to prepare meat and fresh vegetables. Erratic nibbling many times during the day often replaces previous patterns of regular meals. Obesity and a decline in energy and strength needed to carry additional body weight result. Some studies indicate that obesity now is much more of a problem among older people than undernutrition.

Table 1, prepared by Pearl Swanson, professor emeritus of nutrition at Iowa State University, lists the caloric contributions from the key food groups for a 1400 to 1600 calorie diet appropriate for individuals seventy years of age and over:

TABLE 1. Diet needs for individuals 70 years and older

FOOD GROUP	Appropriate amount to be eaten per day	Calories per day
Fluid milk, including milk used on cereals,	½ cup, whole	85
fruits, and puddings	1½ cup, skim	131
Meat, fish, and poultry	3 oz.	225
Protein extenders		
Eggs (4 times a week)		
Legumes (once a week)	1 serving	90
Cheese (twice a week)		
Fruits and vegetables		
Vitamin-rich		
Dark green and deep yellow	½ cup	50
Citrus	½ cup	55
Potatoes	½ potato	50
Other fruits and vegetables	½ cup	80
Cereals		
Breads	2½ slices	165–225
Cooked	⅓ cup	50–100
Fats (table, cooking, cream, bacon, salad)	2⅓ tbsp	230–280
Sweets and desserts, other than fruit	1 serving	150–200
Soups and miscellaneous		20
Calories from "four essential food groups"		981–1,091
Calories from fats		230–280
Calories from other foods		150–200
Calories from miscellaneous foods		20
Total calories		1,381–1,591

In a study of 695 men and women sixty-five years of age and older, Dr. Swanson found that only one in twenty was eating a nutritionally adequate diet. Eight percent did not eat enough protein; 59 percent lacked Vitamins A and C; and 79 percent did not eat foods that produced adequate calcium. When the respondents in the study were asked to evaluate their diets, 34 percent considered them very good; another 65 percent rated their daily diets good; and only 2 percent thought that their diets were poor.[2]

Out of their basic ignorance about nutrition, older people often develop a dependence on so-called health foods and health fads. In much of their advertising, health food promoters focus on older people who have normal fears of failing health and bodily changes. Their sales approach is that some vital element or vitamin is missing from the regular foods that one purchases and must be added to the diet to insure health. Although doctors may recommend vitamins at specific times when the body needs to be built up, a person who is eating nutritional meals does not need them continuously. In relying on fads and on unnecessary vitamins, many older people deprive themselves of the help and advice of a doctor. As a result, delay in getting needed medical care can prove to be serious and even fatal. The National Food and Drug Administration is concerned about the number of older persons who are duped by the proponents of so-called health foods and by the large amounts of money spent on health care frauds and swindles.

Information on the importance of nutrition in maintaining health and educational programs to aid older adults in planning diets are essential. Many senior centers, housing projects, and other community groups for older people are including hot cooked noontime meals as part of their programs. Demonstrations are conducted on planning and preparing well-balanced meals for one person. The use of nutritionists as teachers and consultants can add much to the program in senior centers and make significant contributions to the improvement of the nutritional health of members. Nutritious meals attractively served and eaten in the company of other people are an important therapeutic factor in the rehabilitation of older persons in nursing homes and hospitals.

[2] Pearl Swanson, "Adequacy in Old Age," *Journal of Home Economics* 56: 651–58, 728-34; table, 730 (1964).

The function of the reproductive system ceases in old age but sexual interest and activity continue

In the study of human gerontology there is a dearth of data about the sexual behavior of older adults and how much poor adjustment in old age is related to sexual frustration. It was formerly assumed that men had sexual drives into old age but that women no longer experienced them after menopause. Recent studies of changes in hormone secretion and balance, especially those hormones concerned with sexual functions, show that these changes seem to be less critical in the whole aging process than had been believed. Although older people experience a decline in sexual activity and in the strength of the sexual drive, persons in reasonable good health, with partners who are physically healthy, continue to be sexually active into the seventh and eighth decades and beyond. At Duke University a ten-year study was made of ninety-five participants—all men and women who were over sixty when the study began. According to the report there was a tendency toward a gradual waning of sexual interest and activity from the fortieth year on. Sixty-five members of the group, who were between sixty and seventy-one years of age, reported that they still engaged in sexual intercourse with some frequency. Among those seventy-eight years old or over, 10 percent to 20 percent reported sexual activity. By the late eighties the frequency approached zero. Nevertheless, individual exceptions occurred. Among male subjects surviving into the eighties and nineties, continued sexual activity was no great rarity; about one-fifth of these men reported having sexual intercourse once a month or less.

Menopause, which occurs when viable ova are no longer likely to be produced, usually begins in women between the ages of forty and fifty. Because there is no longer a fear of pregnancy, many women experience heightened sexual satisfaction after menopause. Psychogenic factors, as well as the unbalanced endocrine system, determine the sex drive of postmenopausal women. Those who have happy marriages and enjoy sex continue to do so after menopause.

There seems to be no clinical evidence that comparable changes in the hormonal balance take place in men. Most men remain fertile well into old age. The steady decline in sexual performance after age sixty can be more directly attributed to a variety of fears rather than physical changes—fear of an inability to perform adequately, fear of rejection, fear of overexertion after an illness. Impotence may also be caused by alcohol, poor diet, and by certain drugs used to treat urologic disease, arteriosclerosis, diabetes, and arthritis. If neither acute nor chronic physical incapacity intervenes, doctors agree that aging males usually are able to continue some form of active sexual expression into the seventh, eighth, and even ninth decades.

In a 1960 national health survey, 95.5 percent of the men and only 5 percent of the women over eighty-five years of age were living with their spouses. Because life expectancy is longer for women and there are 145 females for every 100 males, women will continue to outnumber men and still have need of normal sex relations. More men remarry when widowed than women, and they usually choose younger spouses. Many men and women of this age group live together without marrying in order not to lose social security benefits.

Deviant sexual behavior is often caused
by changes in the central nervous system

Deviant sexual behavior especially on the part of older men can often be attributed to chronic brain syndrome and other arteriosclerotic changes in the central nervous system. A psychological study of fifteen elderly male sex offenders by Dr. Frederick Whisken of Harvard Medical School showed that nine of these men suffered in some degree from brain deterioration. Their sex offenses were most frequently exhibitionism and the caressing and fondling of children without physical hurt or injury, rather than violent aggressive acts, such as rape or rape-murder. Older women are much less frequently involved in sex offenses than men. It is considered natural for older females to hug and caress children, but the older male who does so becomes a "dirty old man." Dr. Whisken points out that these sex acts are related in part to the male's struggle to maintain his self-image as a sexually adequate person. Many older individuals become emotionally isolated in life because of a loss of sight or hearing. Touching a loved person reduces feelings of isolation and desolation. When such individuals are suffering any mental impairment, former controls and defenses are affected and sex offenses are sometimes committed. Society and the individual can best be protected by assuring that the environment provides opportunities for older adults to meet their emotional and social needs in acceptable ways.

Chronic illnesses accelerate physical aging

In the preceding paragraphs the focus has been on those time-linked changes that take place in the physical body. Many of these changes eventually develop into conditions that become chronic, irreversible, and progressive diseases. As persons live longer they become more subject to such chronic conditions as heart disease, high blood pressure, arteriosclerosis, angina pectoris, cancer, arthritis, diabetes, Parkinson's disease, and kidney disease. If these can be conquered, on the average a seventy-five-year-old man can expect to live 8.2 years longer, and a woman 9.7 years longer.[3]

Four out of every five individuals over sixty-five years of age have one or more chronic illnesses. Elderly people spend almost three times as much for drugs and drug sundries for the control of their illnesses as teen-agers. A 1968 study of the high cost of drugs to older adults indicates that 20 percent of the elderly people surveyed had no drug expenses. Costs annually were less than $50 for 41.5 percent of these elderly people; between $50 and $99 for 19 percent; between $100 and $249 for 15.5 percent; and $250 or more for 4 percent.

The severity as well as the frequency of chronic illnesses increases with the years. Many chronic illnesses begin with mild disabilities and progress slowly to the point where the elderly patients become helpless. It is estimated that chronic illness and resulting disabilities limit the mobility of about 60 percent of all persons over the age of seventy-five, and 40 percent of all of those between sixty-five and seventy-five.[4] Many chronic diseases are treatable although not curable. Early identification, diagnosis, and treatment may prevent many persons from becoming totally disabled. There is therefore a need for regular and complete multiphasic screening procedures, which are an important part of any comprehensive preventive medical care program for older people. Medical details of specific illnesses are beyond the scope of this book, but it is important that leaders working with older adults understand the emotional components of illness and their social implications.

Emotional acceptance of possible chronic illness and an adjustment to it is a developmental task of the later years

The acceptance of possible physical illness and its limitations and the adjustment to living happily and meaningfully with less than optimal health are developmental tasks of the later years. As many individuals

[3] Herman Brotman, *Who Are the Aged: A Demographic View* (Washington, D.C.: U.S. Department of Health, Education and Welfare, Administration on Aging, 1968).

[4] Study made by Public Health Service of the U.S. Department of Health, Education and Welfare, Task Force on Prescription Drugs, 1968.

age they seem to prepare themselves psychologically for coping with the crises that waning health and diminishing strength will bring. Most people behave as they are expected to behave by others. Because society has built up an expectation of illness around age, many individuals slip comfortably into playing a sick role. Illness for some serves as an excuse for shortcomings and as a defense against inactivity and withdrawal. They may exploit their illness to gain the attention and sympathy of the family and even to "punish" those who they feel have been neglectful. For others, illness becomes a refuge from unpleasant demands and an excuse for continuing dependency on and attention from a doctor. Such older persons can afford to be well only if in so doing they do not forfeit the interest and concern of their doctors. The physician who is aware of the emotional need of his patient to remain ill in order to assure his continuing attention will take part in the planning for care when the critical stages of the illness have passed. Arranging for care in a nursing home, or for representatives from Home Health Aides, Visiting Nurses, Meals-on-Wheels, and Friendly Visitors will make it possible for the patient to transfer his dependency feelings from the doctor to others who can help him again achieve a sense of health and well-being.

Long-term hospitalization
has some negative effects

Many doctors today believe that many patients overuse the hospital. Real damage is done to the patient if he spends too much time within the routine of the hospital, where he must give up physical activity and independence of spirit and lose contact with the outside world. From being a person who communicates with others on an equal basis, he becomes one who is talked "to," with the minutest details of his life, including eating, elimination, and even his position in bed, being subject to the order and control of others. All of these factors soon contribute to the breakdown of a patient's willingness to struggle to maintain control over his condition and environment. The older person especially is apt to relax into an unconscious acceptance of the protective care of the hospital. Often the doctor who makes the hospital stay as short as possible in his attempt to keep the older person from becoming too dependent as a sick person is accused of denying to the patient the benefit of hospital care. There must be more imaginative planning around the sick role and the quality of care and social opportunities within nursing home settings. Although they may become incapacitated to some degree, many older persons can maintain a degree of self-management and enjoy appropriate social activities with other people.

The effects of extended hospitalization soon tend to destroy in the patient all attempts at self-determination and actually cause him to become emotionally, if not physically, more ill than he was when he entered the hospital. The chronically ill older person, after the initial hospital stay, must be helped to accept the fact that he has been only temporarily excused from his social obligations and that his family and society will expect him to remain as active as his physical condition permits. Emphasis must be placed on what he can do, rather than on what he can no longer do. This emphasis will be basic to learning to live with a chronic persisting illness. The encouragement of family members, friends, and the minister, rabbi, or priest will be beneficial to the patient's emotional and social rehabilitation. Get-well cards and regular telephone calls from friends help to prevent the crystallization of such a sick role and establish the expectation of return to active participation in a social group. The socialization needs of older people persist even though they may become nonambulatory and hospitalized for long periods of time. These needs as well as those imposed by physical conditions must be of continuing concern to the doctor, family members and all others responsible for the individual's care.

Physical exercise is important in the later years

The importance of physical exercise in maintaining the body at its optimal level of physical and mental health is receiving increasing attention today. No hard-and-fast rules can be set about how much and what kinds of exercise are appropriate because no two persons have exactly the same physical needs or psychological preferences. In extreme old age, when physical strength and mental ability steadily decline, exercise beyond that involved in the acts of daily living may no longer be possible, but through most of the older years appropriate physical exercise contributes to positive physical and mental well-being. There is no evidence that vigorous exercise can in any way injure a healthy individual in the older age bracket if his body has been kept in good physical condition throughout his life. Contrary to popular misconceptions, heart attacks are not caused by too much exertion; rather, in many cases, prolonged inactivity is a major contributor to the development of heart disease. The heart is basically a muscle and must be exercised like any other muscle in order to operate efficiently. As the normal heart and circulatory system are required to move blood to the active regions of the body, the more efficient they become. The heart muscle is strengthened so that it can pump more blood with fewer beats, and blood vessels are strengthened and enlarged. Blood pressure often falls to better levels in individuals with high blood pressure who follow a regular exercise program that has been approved by their physicians. Better circulation also improves the distribution of oxygen to the brain and greatly increases mental alertness. This theory is related to the current widespread interest in jogging.

The benefits of regular exercise are not all physical. Moderate, continuous programs of exercise offer extra rewards of helping to maintain good posture, control weight, and generally improve the physical appearance. Paul Dudley White, internationally famous heart specialist, recommends that an individual follow some planned program of daily exercise involving as many muscles as possible in order to maintain good health through the later years. He himself is an enthusiastic bicyclist but points out that vigorous walking, too, is one of the best all-over forms of physical exercise. Dr. White notes the following benefits of exercise:

1. It establishes and maintains general muscular tone throughout the body. Good muscular tone of the aorta and other great arteries in the circulatory system helps to maintain an even flow of blood to and from the heart and other parts of the body.

2. It provides an antidote for nervous tension, strain, and anxiety. A pleasant sense of fatigue induces relaxation and sleep.

3. It helps to control obesity, which becomes a serious problem as the individual ages. Overweight can best be controlled by cutting down on the caloric intake, but exercise increases the metabolic rate and thus more calories are burned up.

4. It increases the breathing capacity of the lungs. The exchange of the air, with high levels of carbon dioxide and low levels of oxygen, gradually improves the state of the tissues themselves.

A study has recently been completed at the University of Southern California, under the direction of Herbert A. deVries, to determine how much exercise is beneficial for an individual and when exercise becomes excessive exertion. A group of 112 older Caucasian males aged fifty-two to eighty-seven (mean age 69.5) volunteered for participation in a vigorous exercise training regimen. Under supervision they did calisthenics, jogging, stretching exercises, and aquatics for approximately one hour three times each week. All participants were pretested and 66 were retested at six weeks, 26 at 18 weeks, and 8 at 42 weeks. The parameters included (1) blood pressure, (2) percent of body fat, (3) maximal consumption of oxygen, (4) the oxygen pulse at a heart rate of 145. The most significant findings were related to an increase in oxygen consumption. At a heart rate of 145, the oxygen pulse and minute ventilation increased by 29.4 percent and 35.2 percent respectively. Vital capacity improved by 19.6 percent. Significant improvement was also found in the percent of body fat, physical work capacity, and both systolic and diastolic blood pressure. Dr. deVries concludes that, in view of the improvements in function demonstrated, the exercise regimen developed was both safe and effective for a normal population of older men in the presence of medical and physiological monitoring. Through his research Dr. deVries hopes to lay a foundation for designing individual prescriptions to meet the differing physical and psychological needs of aging men and women.[5]

Too few older individuals are fully aware of the importance of physical exercise in their daily lives. Some understanding of the various functions of the vital systems of the body and how they are affected by exercise would help to motivate older adults to plan their own exercise regimen. Classes in geriatric calisthenics and relaxation are becoming popular programs in senior centers and community recreation departments. Their doctors' encouragement to participate will help motivate many older persons to become involved. Although a rocking chair concept of old age will have disappeared by the beginning of the twenty-first century, too many individuals in the twentieth century still spend too much of their time "just sitting."

Physical death is the last stage in the human life cycle

When the various organ systems of the body that have been described are all operating at their normal level of efficiency, the individual may be said to be in a state of high physical health. When age-related changes in any of these systems begin to be evident, they result in a progressive loss in the individual's ability to be active and socially involved. When disease and accidents are also present, the resulting limitations in social functioning are even more significant to the mental and emotional well-being of the older person. Progressive changes and deteriorating conditions in the senescent organism lead inevitably to death, the last and final stage in the human life cycle.

There are, for most individuals in our society, a conscious or uncon-

[5] Herbert A. deVries, *Physiological Effects of an Exercise Training Regimen upon Men Aged 52-88,* (Washington, D.C.: U.S. Department of Health, Education and Welfare, Administration on Aging, 1969).

scious dread of the physical and mental impairments of old age and a fear of dying. Although very mature persons may accept death as the natural end of life, the vast majority attempt to submerge their feelings and to deny and repress any thought of their own mortality. An acceptance of the finiteness of life and preparation for eventual death are the final major psychological tasks of all human beings. Individuals all react differently to the facts of aging and death.

The preplanning that many older persons do for their own funerals does not necessarily represent a morbid preoccupation with death. These are people who have managed their lives well in earlier periods and want, while they are able, to make such arrangements. Thus they can be assured of some posthumous notice that they have lived and left a mark. There is evidence that attitudes about dying are an accentuation of lifelong ego defense maneuvers. Reactions are related to personality factors, such as hysteria, dependency, and impulsivity. Those older persons who have had more physical and psychological disturbances throughout life show higher death concerns than those with fewer such complaints.

Death is still a subject that is very much taboo in our society. Many of the accepted norms of behavior in regard to funeral practices become blocks for the creative and purposeful review of its meanings. Some investigators have found that the subject of death is dealt with, in healthy older people, in very open and direct ways. Having lived long they have experienced the loss of so many significant persons that they have already faced its reality many times. Belle B. Beard reports that centenarians whom she interviewed seemed to be willing to speak freely about death and had no morbid fears or any special reticence in discussing it. It is younger persons who care for the aged who hold fears and inhibitions. The seriousness of the loss of loved persons by an older person, however, cannot be underestimated. Even the loss of a pet can sometimes precipitate depression.

Death is a universal experience that all living things share. Man, however, is the only creature who is able to look at himself objectively as he exists in time and space and to evaluate his achievements and his own nonexistence. Philosophers question whether man would ever look at himself deeply and ask about the meaning of life if death did not limit life. Self-awareness without a religious faith or philosophy can lead to overpowering fear and anxiety. Man needs to place his own finiteness within the context of the immortality of the species and believe that life has meaning. In considering the meaning of death many people place too much emphasis on negative feelings of hostility, guilt, fear, anxiety, and depression, and too little on positive feelings of faith, confidence, trust, love, and joy.

The literature reports very few systematic studies of elderly people's attitudes toward death. Some of the research now completed comes to contradictory conclusions. One of the difficulties is that different methods are used; in addition, people have a strong tendency to deny death, and it is difficult to design a study that is able to cut through their emotional defenses. Some researchers have had success in using Thematic Apperception Tests. These are projective tests in which the subject is presented with a series of moderately ambiguous picture cards and is asked to make up a story about each picture. The unconscious, not readily reported aspects of the personality can thus be more easily expressed than by answers to direct questions.

Using a check-list of thirty-five descriptive attitudes about death and the Cottrell scale for the measurement of religiosity, Wendell M. Swenson of the University of Minnesota queried 210 men and women, all over sixty years of age, about their attitudes toward death. He found that there is a significant relationship between religiosity and positive attitudes toward death. Persons with religious convictions accept death in more positive ways than do those with fewer beliefs and convictions. Religious faith seems to play a significant role in the attitudes of aged persons, and those who are not active participants in religious activities tend to manifest fearful attitudes. Dr. Swenson also found that a fear of death is found more often in those living alone than in those living with relatives or in homes for the aged. The fear of being ill and alone is more threatening than the thought of death itself. Less educated persons tend to be more evasive in regard to their attitudes toward death than better educated persons.[6]

Richard A. Kalish, a psychologist at the University of California at Los Angeles, describes four different levels at which death occurs:

1. *Physical Death.* The physical life begins at conception and continues until the organs cease to function. With advances in medical science, physical death is delayed for extended periods by the use of various artificial means. The extent to which such means should be used in situations where there is no hope of recovery is becoming an important moral question.

2. *Psychological Death.* Psychological life begins when the individual becomes aware of his own existence. Psychological death often precedes the physical death of those individuals who become hopelessly

[6] Wendell M. Swenson, "Attitudes Toward Death in an Aged Population," *Journal of Gerontology,* 16:49-52 (January 1961).

senile or comatose or who are kept heavily drugged. The time difference between these two levels of death leads many thoughtful people to question why the doctor does not allow physical death to occur when psychological death has already taken place. Dr. Kalish points out, however, that it is difficult to know when psychological death is reversible. Even individuals with severe brain damage evidence increased mental awareness when they are in social groups, where there is some communication.

3. *Social Death*. The third level is social death, which may be self-perceived as well as other-perceived. Too many old people accept social death for themselves long before their physical or psychological deaths occur. When urged to involve themselves in social relationships or to extend their interests beyond their own egocentric needs, they reply that they are too old and shouldn't be expected to be interested. It is the socially dead individuals who are the concern of those community services that try to make opportunities available for the social, intellectual, and spiritual needs of the elderly.

4. *Anthropological Death*. Anthropological life refers to the status of the individual in his community. Aged individuals as a group may truly be faced with this kind of death in a society in which they have no meaningful social roles and in which they face increased alienation as society becomes increasingly absorbed in a youth culture.[7]

Death of the personality is avoided for the person who lives a full life at every stage and always experiences a continual beginning. Death for this individual becomes the last great experience in life—its fruition.

BIBLIOGRAPHY

Birren, J. E., ed. *Handbook of Aging and the Individual: Psychological and Biological Aspects*. Chicago: University of Chicago Press, 1960.
————, *Human Aging: A Biological and Behavioral Study*. Public Health Service Pub. No. 986. Washington, D.C.: Government Printing Office, 1963.
Busse, Ewald D. "Some Emotional Complications of Chronic Disease." *The Gerontologist* 2 (1947): 153-56.
Duke University Center for the Study of Aging and Human Development. *Sexual Behavior in Senescence*. Durham, N.C.: Duke University, 1964.
Genn, Lillian G. "Boom in Retirement Marriage." *Modern Maturity* 13 (1970): 12-14.

[7] Richard A. Kalish, *Life and Death: Dividing the Indivisible*, vol. 2, *Sociology, Science and Medicine* (Oxford, England: Pergamon Press, 1968), pp. 249-59.

Geriatric Focus. Orange, N.J.: Knoll Pharmaceutical Company.

Howell, Sandra C., and Loeb, Martin B. "Nutrition and Aging: A Monograph for Practitioners." *The Gerontologist,* Part II, 9 (1969).

Jeffers, Frances C. "How the Old Face Death." In *Behavior and Adaption in Late Life,* edited by Ewald D. Busse and Eric Pfeiffer. Boston: Little Brown and Co., 1970.

Journal of the American Geriatric Society. Symposium on "The Emotional Basis of Illness." 17 (1969): 846-909.

Kalish, Richard. *Life and Death: Dividing the Indivisible,* Vol. 2, *Sociology, Science and Medicine.* Oxford, England: Pergamon Press, pp. 249-59.

King, C. G., and Britt, C. *Food Hints for Mature People.* Public Affairs Pamphlet, no. 336. New York, 1962.

Masters, William H., and Johnson, Virginia E. *Human Sexual Inadequacy.* New York: Little, Brown & Co. 1969.

Moss, Bertram. *Caring for the Aged.* New York: Doubleday & Co., 1966.

Robert, Dean W. "The Over-all Picture of Long-Term Illness." *Journal of Chronic Diseases* 1 (February 1955): 149-159.

Rubin, Herman H., and Newman, Benjamin W. *Active Sex After Sixty.* New York: Arco, 1969.

Savitsky, Elias, "Psychological Factors in Nutrition of the Aged." *Social Casework* 34 (1953): 435-40.

Shock, Nathan W., ed. *Aging: Some Social and Biological Aspects.* Publication No. 65. Washington, D.C.: American Association for The Advancement of Science, 1960, pp. 241-60.

Steiglitz, E. J. *The Second Forty Years.* Philadelphia: J. B. Lippincott Company, 1946.

Stokes, W. R. "Sexual Function in the Aging Male." *Geriatrics* 6 (1951): 304-308.

Swanson, Pearl. "Adequacy in Old Age. Part I, Role of Nutrition; Part II, Nutrition Education Programs for the Aging." *Journal of Home Economics* 56 (1964): 651-58, 728-34.

Thompson, Prescott W. "Understanding the Aged." *Journal of the American Geriatrics Society* 13 (1965).

Tibbetts, C., ed. *Handbook of Social Gerontology.* Chicago: University of Chicago Press, 1960.

U.S. Department of Agriculture. *Food Guide for Older Folks.* Bulletin no. 17, 1954.

U.S. Department of Health, Education and Welfare, Administration on Aging. *Fitness Challenge in the Later Years (An Exercise Program for Older Americans),* 1966.

U.S. Department of Health, Education and Welfare. *Task Force on Prescription Drugs Final Report,* February 1969.

Upham, Frances. *A Dynamic Approach to Illness.* New York: Family Service Association of America, 1949.

Wagner, M. C. "Evaluation of Dial-a-Dietician Service." *Journal of American Dietetic Association* 47 (1965): 381-390.
Worcester, Alfred. *Care of the Aging, the Dying and the Dead.* Springfield, Ill.: Charles C. Thomas, 1940.

6 / Mental Illness as It Affects Social Functioning

DECLINE IN THE MENTAL FUNCTIONING of an older adult parallels the decline in his physical functioning, but this decline usually occurs more slowly. It may not become conspicuous until deterioration in the central nervous system produces marked deficits in memory, orientation, comprehension, and judgment.

Extended life expectancy increases the possibility that more individuals will experience mental illness

Extended old age increases the possibility that an individual may experience a mental illness. It is estimated that at least one out of every three older adults develops some sort of mental disorder ranging in severity from mild eccentricity to violent paranoid behavior. Although patients who are over sixty-five make up more than 27 percent of all first admissions to mental hospitals, many other elderly people with comparable degrees of impairment are not hospitalized. Marked changes in behavior and personality that affect the ability of the individual to function responsibly in the community are caused either by actual disease in the brain and central nervous system or by severe psychiatric disturbances. There is a close relationship between these conditions, and physical illnesses often foster psychogenic illnesses. Even though community-based social programs may not include those older people with serious degrees of chronic brain syndrome, senile psychosis, and cerebral arteriosclerosis, group leaders need to understand the causes of such conditions and the resulting behavior.

87

*Acute and chronic brain syndrome are
physically-based mental illnesses*

Senile brain disease, a condition that seems more common in women than in men, results from a gradual wasting away of the substance of the brain. Certain spaces between parts of the brain enlarge and can be seen on X ray studies. The causes of this condition are not fully understood. Because the cells of the brain can never be replaced, the psychic and psychomotor functions become increasingly afflicted, intellectual activity gradually diminishes, and the patient is eventually reduced to a vegetative existence. For patients with senile brain syndrome custodial care in a simplified and protective environment is needed. The prognosis for recovery is poor.

Senility is also a factor in chronic brain syndrome, a chronic condition that is found in many aged individuals. When the amount of blood that reaches the brain is cut off or curtailed because of a hardening of the arteries and a narrowing of the artery walls, cerebral arteriosclerosis develops; damaged by the interruption of the blood supply for more than a few minutes, brain cells never regenerate. The symptoms of this condition vary according to which part of the brain is being denied the essential oxygen and nutrients. The brain-damaged patient shows loss of memory for recent events, impaired judgment, and a disturbance in his affective reactions that results in shallowness and altered moods. He becomes disoriented as to time, place, person, and situation, and the content of his thought often becomes paranoid. There are changes in judgment and the patient may become unable to evaluate factors and make decisions. When his defenses are no longer adequate to cover up these losses and he can no longer handle routine events, he may react in a variety of ways. Many individuals with chronic brain syndrome become depressed, fearful, and angry with people who bring out their helplessness. They become agitated, restless, and often get up at night and wander around. Lost, they are unable to tell who or where they are.

How the individual with chronic brain syndrome will react is determined by lifelong personality patterns. The well-educated person can function better than the deprived person even if his brain damage is greater; he has learned certain social graces and manners that he uses to cover up his inability to handle reality factors. The socially deprived individual becomes more violent in his reactions, and the better educated person shows more paranoid behavior. Some of the physical aspects of the chronic brain syndrome are treatable, but, by and large, it is a nonreversible condition and patients must be cared for in specialized settings. When the critical physical conditions are treated with appropriate drugs—supplemented by vitamin B-12 and adequate diets—a patient often shows improvement. Comfortable physical surroundings, a rigid, dependable daily routine, and the supportive relationships of those through whom his anxiety, fears, and angers can be drained off are essential for his care. He will become confused and frightened if sharp orders are given, but will respond in a cooperative way when the caring person is consistent and warm in his relationship with him.

Acute brain syndrome is often confused with chronic brain syndrome because some of the reactions are the same. Acute brain syndrome, however, is a reversible condition, and the patient may be restored to normal functioning if underlying physical conditions are treated. Chronic brain syndrome, which is accompanied by a loss of memory, delirium, poor comprehension, and severe disorientation, can be caused by malnutrition, excessive alcoholism, high fever from infections, excessive barbiturates, and even from acute anxiety reactions. The acute form of brain syndrome appears suddenly and most patients either die or recover completely within a few weeks. Because the acute condition is so similar in its outer manifestations to chronic brain syndrome, many patients may be rushed to a psychiatric institution rather than given immediate medical attention for the condition that has caused the acute reaction.

Mental illnesses are also caused by severe psychiatric disturbances

Not all mental illness is caused by physical changes in the brain and nervous system. Some result from severe psychiatric disturbances or psychogenic conditions that have become established in the personality in earlier life stages. The stress that accompanies the loss of a spouse, severe illness, or even the loss of a job reactivates these, and the individual may become seriously disoriented and retreat into acute depression and withdrawal. Such mentally ill older adults may be helped to deal with these stresses and be more comfortable when one of the new drugs that influence the moods and emotions is prescribed. Short-term psychiatric treatment will be helpful to some patients and others may even require short-term hospitalization. Group therapy sessions for older people often do not prove helpful because the inherent competition and personality conflicts with other group members are too threatening for the neurotically lonely older person to overcome. Unless seriously disturbed, many older adults with psychogenic illness can be helped to maintain themselves in the community and function in very normal ways even though there may be some residue of psychiatric dysfunctioning.

With the growing recognition that there is a direct relationship between social isolation and emotional deterioration, a senior center that provides a therapeutic environment and meaningful activities can become an important community resource to serve psychogenically ill older people. The services of a skilled psychiatrist to consult with the staff will be essential, however, so the staff can be understanding and deal with such members in supportive and creative ways.

Depression. Recurrent depression is perhaps the most common nonorganic mental illness. Mood changes and actual periods of depression occur in earlier stages of life, also, but investigators have found that elderly people experience a greater number of depressive episodes. Such individuals feel that their families have rejected them, that no one understands them, that they are all alone and abandoned, and that they have no reason to continue to live. They often express the wish that a painless death would intervene and even entertain thoughts of suicide. Depression is often an expression of anger at something or someone or a feeling of hostility turned inward. The older person who cannot overtly express these feelings may become psychotically depressed and withdrawn.

The physical complaints of the depressed person are of generalized distress—indigestion, aching all over, dizziness, nausea, and poor appetite. The depressed person complains of an inability to sleep, cries easily, and becomes easily fatigued. In addition, the neglect of regular habits of personal cleanliness is also a common symptom. Doctors often prescribe antidepressant drugs to relieve these conditions. They also are becoming increasingly aware that some involvement in creative and recreational activity after retirement is one of the best defenses against depression for their older patients. Through activities that require intellectual and physical effort, the older person experiences a sense of doing something worthwhile, which in turn gives him a sense of self-worth and fulfillment.

Loneliness. Loneliness is a basic human problem experienced by people of all ages. It is expressed pathologically in alcoholism, drug addiction, hypochondriasis, and compulsive eating. Elderly people often find themselves in social isolation and need to experience the warmth and affection of other individuals or groups to combat feelings of loneliness. Many individuals are "loners" all their lives, but feel free to acknowledge their loneliness only during old age; isolation is more socially acceptable for the elderly than it is for young people, who are more able to make social contacts. During their old age such isolate individuals do not have the capacity to make or enjoy close and warm relationships. They may be unaccustomed to small talk and lack the necessary social graces to feel comfortable around other people. It is difficult to interest these individuals in groups or in activities that involve interaction with others, and their well-established character patterns cannot easily be changed. Such older adults, with all their symptoms and complaints, will need to be warmly accepted by all group members if they are to benefit from a group experience.

Hypochondriasis. Hypochondriasis is a mental illness consisting of an anxious preoccupation with the body or a portion of the body that the individual believes is either diseased or not functioning properly. Such somatic complaints may have no organic basis. Some extreme preoccupation with bodily complaints may seem to indicate psychotic illness, but most seem to indicate only a neurosis or phycho-physiologic reaction. By preoccupying themselves with their own bodies, hypochondriacs use their complaints to withdraw from a threatening outer environment. They use their aches and pains—which are very real to them—as a means of punishing themselves or atoning for guilt feelings toward others. Subconsciously they feel that as long as they suffer they are protected from more serious punishment.

Doctors rarely confront the older person with the fact that there is insufficient organic evidence to support his physical complaints. To be stripped of these defenses would greatly increase his anxiety. The best therapy, they find, is to help the older person recognize the emotional problems that are making him anxious and give him the necessary support so that he can confront them. Only then will the patient find it unnecessary to retreat to complaints about bodily ailments.

Suicide. One of the tragic evidences of the increase of mental illness among older people is the dramatic rise in the suicide rate. The aged comprise approximately 9 percent of the total population; they commit 25 percent of the reported suicides. The rate is twice as high for individuals after sixty-five as for the population between the ages of forty-five and forty-nine. The highest rate of all occurs among white males after age seventy-five; most of the men in this group who commit suicide are widowers of the lower socioeconomic class who live in crowded parts of the big cities.[1] The highest rate for white females is between the ages of forty-five and fifty-five.

[1] U.S., Department of Health, Education and Welfare, *Mortality from Selective Causes by Age, Race and Sex,* 1960.

The individual who enjoys good health and happy social contacts is apt to regard life as rich and meaningful and accept its finitude. In contrast, the sick and the poor become lonely and discouraged and seek to escape life by dying suddenly and unexpectedly. An attempted suicide is in reality a cry for help, a kind of attention-getting device. Suicide prevention bureaus, with workers always available by telephone, are being established in many metropolitan areas today to be ready listening ears to people of all ages who are in trouble, hoping to deter them from taking their own lives. If the older person can get the help of a skilled interviewer and is quickly introduced to a group of his peers, his loneliness and depression may be alleviated. A threat of suicide or an expressed need to talk about death must never be ignored but patiently heard out. The anxiety that prompts this need to talk can sometimes be drained off by a warm person with a psychiatrical orientation who is well grounded in the conscious and unconscious anxieties that are being evidenced.

Alcoholism. Alcoholism is becoming an increasing problem among the elderly as well as for other age groups in this country. According to Dr. Alexander Simon, Medical Director of the Langley Porter Neuropsychiatric Institute in San Francisco, the death rate due to alcohol disorders has risen, since 1950, over 52 percent for white males between the ages of sixty and sixty-nine and 114 percent for white females at that age. For the group over seventy, the increase has been more than 27 percent for males and 39 percent for females. Alcoholism is a factor in many cases of acute and chronic brain syndrome and is usually an indication of lifelong emotional and personality disturbances. Some older people, however, begin to consume excessive amounts of alcohol late in life because of the new stresses and losses that these years bring. Today over 5 percent of all Americans sixty-five years of age and over may be classified as chronic alcoholics.

Alcoholism is the leading cause for police arrest of elderly individuals. A study made by Dr. Simon and his colleagues of 993 arrests of persons over sixty years of age in San Francisco revealed that more than 80 percent of the arrests were for drunkenness—a much higher proportion than for any other age group. Jailers report a great increase in arrests of elderly people for drunkenness during the Thanksgiving and Christmas season and cite numerous instances of older prisoners asking the judge for a jail sentence extending through the holidays. They attribute these requests to the fact that many elderly alcoholics are cut off from their families during holidays and suffer acute feelings of loneliness and rejection.

The intoxication of older individuals seldom involves acts of assaultive behavior and the arrest becomes a nonpunitive procedure equivalent to "psychiatric first aid." Most communities do not yet have wards in their general hospitals or in their alcoholic rehabilitation centers where older alcoholics can receive treatment that is more appropriate than commitment to a city jail. It is difficult to effect a complete cure in an aged person, but some emotional suffering can be alleviated if the environment is manipulated to eliminate some of the factors that have contributed to the condition. Many alcoholics are helped by participating in regularly scheduled meaningful activities with age-mates.[2]

For some individuals the satisfactions gained from such programs may not be great enough to substitute for their deprivations; others, however, may be helped by such opportunities to become stable for certain periods of time and to maintain more adequate social functioning in the community. Elderly alcoholics, Dr. Simon believes, deserve much more attention than they are now receiving from the community. A broadened public awareness of the severe adjustment problems that many older people face would point to the importance of establishing programs specifically designed for their treatment and social rehabilitation.

Maintenance of mental health must be the conscious goal of all programs for older adults

It is not known how many chronically brain damaged and depressed older adults whose adjustments are good enough so that their conditions remain unrecognized except to those closest to them live independently in their communities. Many are members of senior centers. Conservative estimates are that 50 percent of the older adult population show some degree of emotional handicap caused by brain impairment. About 40 percent of these show mild to noticeable changes in normal functioning and at least 10 percent show severe mental impairment. Approximately 80 percent of all older people, including the 50 percent without brain damage, are probably chronically mildly depressed and seek to form dependency relationships. The ability of senior centers to continue to serve their members who become severely mentally impaired will depend on the skill of the staff and the availability of funds to provide the supplemental programs that are needed. Consideration must be given to the effect that increasing services to such older adults will have on the climate of health that is needed for the larger number of well-functioning members.

[2] Alexander Simon, "Characteristics of Aged Alcoholics," *Geriatric Focus*, 7 (April 1, 1968): 7.

Communities must begin to provide opportunities for aging individuals to continue their lifelong quest for mental health. Mental health in old age is related to the ability of the individual to bring harmony to his desires, abilities, feelings, strengths, and weaknesses in order to meet the demands life makes on him. It enables him—if he is not overcome by poverty and physical illness—to face the last of life with courage, dignity, and calm. The great majority of American men and women who are over sixty-five remain mentally competent and can maintain themselves in their communities and experience an acceptable degree of life satisfaction.

BIBLIOGRAPHY

Albrecht, R. "Social Roles in the Prevention of Senility." *Journal of Gerontology* 6 (1951): 380-386.

Batchelor, I.R.C. *Clues to Suicide.* New York: McGraw-Hill, 1957.

Bortz, Edward L. "Stress and Aging." *Geriatrics* 10 (1955): 93-99.

Cameron, N. "Neurosis of Later Maturity." In *Mental Disorders in Later Life,* edited by O. J. Kaplan, pp. 201-243. Palo Alto: Stanford University Press, 1956.

Gitelson, Maxwell. "The Emotional Problems of Elderly People." *Geriatrics* 3 (1948): 135-150.

Goldfarb, Alvin I. "Psychiatric Problems of Old Age." *New York State Journal of Medicine* 55 (1955): 494-500.

———— "Depression, Brain Damage, and Chronic Illness of the Aged." *Journal of Chronic Diseases,* March 1959.

Hoch, Paul H., and Zubin, Joseph, eds. *Psychopathology of Aging.* New York: Grune and Stratton, 1961.

Hollingshead, A.B., and Redlich, F.P. *Social Class and Mental Illness: A Community Study.* New York: John Wiley & Sons, 1958.

Kaplan, Oscar J., ed. *Mental Disorders in Later Life.* Stanford, Calif: Stanford University Press, 1956.

Kiorboe, E. "Suicide and Attempted Suicide Among Old People." *Journal of Gerontology* 6 (1951): 233-236.

Lowenthal, Marjorie Fiske. "Social Isolation and Mental Illness in Old Age." *American Sociology Review* 29 (1964): 54-70.

———— *Lives in Distress: The Paths of the Elderly to the Psychiatric Ward.* New York: Basic Books, 1964.

Metropolitan Life Insurance Co., "Suicide Among Older People." *Statistical Bulletin, Metropolitan Life Insurance Company* 31 (1950): 9-11.

National Center for Health Statistics. "Characteristics of Residents in Institutions for the Aged and Chronically Ill." Public Health Service Publication No. 1000, Series 12, No. 2. Washington, D.C.: Government Printing Office, 1965.

Resnik, H. L. P. and Cantor, Joel. "Suicide and Aging." *Journal of American Geriatrics Society* 18 (1970): 152-158.

United Nations. World Health Organization. *Mental Health Problems of Aging and the Aged: Sixth Report of the Expert Committee on Mental Health*. WHO Technical Report Series, no. 171, 1965.

7 / Psychosocial Factors in the Aging Process

IN ORDER TO ADAPT to the constant and dynamic changes in his physical and social environment, each individual during his life develops certain characteristic ways of behaving. His individual style becomes his personality. The personality patterns of some older people enable them to maintain a high level of social functioning in spite of the losses and stresses that the later years bring. Others who experience similar physical changes and personal crises become depressed and despondent, withdrawn and disengaged. Explanations for these individual differences among older adults are the focus of many research studies by behavioral scientists. Many of their theories and assumptions must still be validated by longitudinal studies, but current findings are provocative and significant for the practitioner who gives direct services to older people. They provide insight into the varied behavior that he will observe in the individuals with whom he works.

Ego needs remain the same throughout life

The primary needs of the human organism for physiological satisfactions remain the same throughout life. Ego or personality needs—to be loved, to feel needed, to belong, to be thought of as worthful, and to feel one's self fulfilled—also remain unchanged. These needs are met through relationships with other human beings. With retirement from jobs, curtailed parental roles, the loss of a spouse, and decreased physical energy to invest in community activities, opportunities to have these ego needs met become progressively limited for the older adult.

Social roles change

Human relationships are structured through social roles. Roles are the specific functions one performs as a member of a family, a worker on a job, a member of an association, and a citizen of a community. Through his social roles an individual lives out his life goals and the community's expectations for him. Without the status and recognition that roles provide, many individuals are not able to sustain their sense of self-worth. Ten specific social roles of middle adult years have been identified by Robert J. Havighurst and his associates in their Kansas City Study of Adult Life. These include the roles of parent, spouse, worker, homemaker, user of leisure time, church member, club member, citizen, friend, and child of an aging parent.[1] If a person performs well in all or most of these roles, he is said to be a successful human being.

As he grows older many of these roles are lost or change, and there are fewer opportunities to find substitutes to replace them. A man's role as a worker has given him status, not only as head of a family and as a contributor to society, but his job also has provided him an identity and the companionship of fellow workers. Meaningful associations decrease as older adults relinquish to younger members roles of authority and leadership in church, lodge, service club, and community committees. As such status positions are lost, an individual often internalizes society's seeming rejection and begins to think of himself as a worthless individual. Some of the changes in roles that both men and women experience between middle and older adult years are pictured in Chart 3.

Changing spouse and parental roles demand difficult adjustments

When social roles change, an older adult experiences uncertainties around the demands of new roles. These uncertainties are especially true of parental roles as children leave the family to marry and establish families of their own. To the mature, well-adjusted couple this time of decreasing responsibility comes as a welcome period of less pressure and more time for pleasant relaxation. The new leisure brings opportunities to enjoy again the exclusive attention of each other and mutual interests and activities that the years devoted to child rearing have not

[1] Robert J. Havighurst, "Research Memoranda on Social Adjustment in Adulthood and Later Maturity," in *Psychological Aspects of Aging,* John E. Anderson, ed. (Washington, D.C.: American Psychological Association, 1956), pp. 293-302.

Chart 3

Diagrammatic Representation Showing the Continuities and Discontinuities

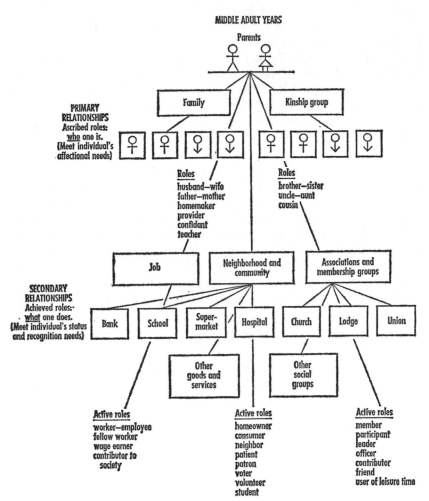

MIDDLE ADULT YEARS

Parents

PRIMARY RELATIONSHIPS
Ascribed roles:
who one is.
(Meet individual's affectional needs)

Family

Kinship group

Roles
husband—wife
father—mother
homemaker
provider
confidant
teacher

Roles
brother—sister
uncle—aunt
cousin

SECONDARY RELATIONSHIPS
Achieved roles:
what one does.
(Meet individual's status and recognition needs)

Job

Neighborhood and community

Associations and membership groups

Bank   School   Super-market   Hospital   Church   Lodge   Union

Other goods and services

Other social groups

Active roles
worker—employee
fellow worker
wage earner
contributor to
   society

Active roles
homeowner
consumer
neighbor
patient
patron
voter
volunteer
student

Active roles
member
participant
leader
officer
contributor
friend
user of leisure time

of Social Roles and Relationships in Middle and Older Adult Years

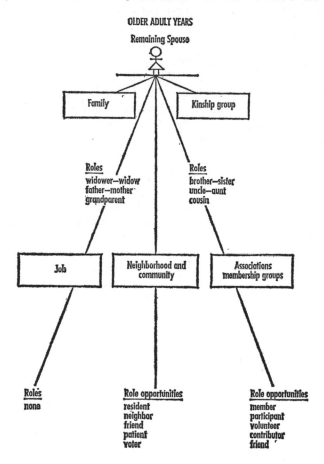

OLDER ADULT YEARS

Remaining Spouse

Family

Kinship group

Roles
widower—widow
father—mother
grandparent

Roles
brother—sister
uncle—aunt
cousin

Job

Neighborhood and community

Associations membership groups

Roles
none

Role opportunities
resident
neighbor
friend
patient
voter

Role opportunities
member
participant
volunteer
contributor
friend

made possible. To the less mature couple these years may be filled with new and disturbing anxieties, further complicated by the fact that many retired couples carry responsibility for one or more of their own parents or family members now eighty or ninety years old. Nurture and support of these older ones place additional strains on emotional and financial resources.

Most mature adults—especially those in the middle and upper economic classes—prefer to remain for as long as possible in their own homes and communities as independent, self-directing persons if they are physically and financially able. Little is known of the differences that exist in the expectations and living arrangements of older adults of nonwhite families. In a study of intergenerational relationships it was found that 75 percent of all older Americans maintain homes independent of their children; 25 percent of these live alone or with nonrelatives. Approximately 53 percent reported that at least one of their children lived close by—from ten minutes' to a day's traveling away—making possible daily or weekly visits. Only 8 percent of the widowed parents felt that their married children should invite them to share their homes.[2]

The death of a mate brings a traumatic loss and threat to the ego of the remaining spouse. Studies show that between the ages of sixty-five and seventy-four years 50 percent of all women and 18 percent of all men lose their spouses. In 1964, the wife was the surviving spouse in 70 percent of all marriages broken by death. The death of a marriage partner is more expected in the later years and is, on the whole, less emotionally disruptive to the remaining mate than if it had occurred earlier in life. If one of the couple is more emotionally dependent than the other and the stronger one dies first, the remaining mate often experiences deep depression and withdrawal. Studies have shown an increased mortality rate among such recently bereaved individuals. If the weaker one dies first, however, the remaining spouse goes through the normal grief period more rapidly and is able in time to make strong, new relationships and orient his ego-strengths around new life goals and satisfactions. Those individuals who experience a sense of guilt at the death of their mate because of real or imagined neglect or misunderstanding often experience extended and disruptive periods of grief and bereavement. With the loss of a spouse, the finiteness of life and the inevitability of death become a persistent reality to the widowed person.

[2] Ethel Shanas, *The Health of Older People: A Social Survey* (Cambridge: Harvard University Press, 1962), p. 98.

When marriage partners are lost, the remaining one—especially some women—reaches out in dependent ways to the children. The widowed parent may give up his own home to live with a married son or daughter before either carefully considers what would be involved. If the relationships between parents and children throughout life have been warm and mutually supportive, then problems that arise can be met with confidence and understanding. Such arrangements, however, often carry within them potentials for great unhappiness and disappointment if emotional distances and hostilities have existed. Often the aged parent feels himself the center and the cause of the inevitable tensions and misunderstandings that arise in all normal family living. Feelings of guilt and rejection develop and conflict follows.

If the house is large enough to provide the older person with the privacy of a room of his own, and he is made to feel a part of the family by carrying specific responsibilities, then this decision to live with children may be a happy one. The older person, whether living with his children or living independently, will earn his acceptance from members of the younger generation not automatically because he is the parent but because he continues to be an interesting and a likeable person. Too little, to date, has been attempted through adult education classes and family relations courses to help interpret the needs and behavior of the older parent to his middle-aged children and to help parents understand the life-style of their adult children. Given such understanding, there are few parents or children who are not willing to accept and adjust to one another's needs.

Traditional attitudes demanded respect and care for an aging parent whether he earned it or not, and society accepted the sacrifices of the younger generation to meet the demands of an ego-centered dominating parent. Today, a different attitude prevails. Parents are expected to give to their children and their children are expected to reciprocate, not so much by giving back to their parents but by giving to their own children. This idea is beautifully stated in an old Hebrew legend.

> There once was an eagle that set out to cross a windy sea with his fledgling. The sea was so wide and the wind so strong that the father bird was forced to carry his young one in his claws. When he was halfway across, the wind turned to a gale and he said, "My child, look how I am struggling and risking my life in your behalf. When you are grown will you do as much for me and provide for me in my old age?" "My dear father," the eaglet replied, "it is true that you are struggling mightily and risking your life in my behalf and I shall be wrong not to repay you when you are grown old, but at this critical time I cannot bind myself.

This, though, I can promise—when I am grown and have children of my own I shall do as much for them as you have done for me." [3]

Grandparent roles are
added during the later years

The parental roles of mother-homemaker and father-provider are replaced for many older adults by those of grandparent and great-grandparent. Studies of these roles show that 70 percent of all older adults over sixty-five years have living grandchildren and 40 percent have great-grandchildren.[4] Many older men and women report that they find more satisfaction and enjoyment in these new roles than in their parental years when the financial and emotional responsibilities of growing families weighed heavily upon them. There are, of course, great variations in individual experiences in the emotional and functional nature of the grandparental role. If adult children and their families live relatively near and family ties have been close, the role of grandparent will be more functional and satisfying. The grandmother's relationship to the grandchildren, which includes a wide range of helpful and meaningful activities, can be especially meaningful. There are also social class and ethnic differences in grandparental roles. In low-income families there is a strong tradition of mutual emotional and financial aid between the generations. In many middle-class families financial aid to children is on a much larger scale and may include the down payment on a home or special schooling and opportunities for the grandchildren.

The grandparent-grandchild relationship that is mutually warm and understanding provides meaningful emotional support for the members of each generation. The federally financed Foster Grandparents program, a project of the Administration on Aging of the federal Department of Health, Education, and Welfare, gives recognition to this fact. Through this program older adults become substitute grandparents for hospitalized neglected and deprived children. They visit regularly, play with and entertain the child, and provide the continuity of a warm, caring relationship that is mutually satisfying.

A recent study of the psychological and social dimensions of these grandparental roles in Western society has been made by Bernice Neugarten of the Department of Human Development of the University of Chicago. The sample studied included seventy middle-class grandmothers and grandfathers residing in Chicago living apart from, but close to,

[3] Source unknown.
[4] Robert J. Havighurst and Ruth Albrecht, *Older People* (New York: Longman, Green & Co. 1953), p. 276.

their grandchildren. Five different styles of grandparental roles were identified.

1. *The Formal Relationship.* Grandparents maintain a continuing interest in their grandchildren but do not become too emotionally involved or try to take over the responsibilities of the parents. They serve as baby-sitters occasionally and provide the extra treats and surprises their grandchildren enjoy.

2. *Mutual Enjoyment.* Grandparents and grandchildren alike share mutual feelings of close relationship and satisfaction. The grandparents view their grandchildren principally as the source of their greatest pride and enjoyment. They participate in all family celebrations with their children and grandchildren and visit them regularly if they live in different communities.

3. *Parent Surrogate.* In cases of crisis in the young family, such as death or divorce or when young parents are both working outside the home, grandmothers sometimes take over the management of the home and the disciplining of the children. Their physical presence is emotionally and financially essential to the young family.

4. *Reservoir of Family Wisdom.* In many upper-class and some ethnic families the grandfather plays an authoritarian role in relation to younger generation family members. He is seen as a reservoir of special wisdom and skills. Lines of authority are distinct and young parents maintain, sometimes with resentment, their subordinate position to the "head of the family."

5. *The Distant Figure.* Almost 50 percent of all grandparents in the sample studied had only infrequent and casual contact with their grandchildren. These contacts were mostly limited to birthday and special holiday celebrations. Such grandparents are benevolent figures to the children but their contacts with them are short and fleeting. The large percentage of older adults who experience this limited role indicates how devoid of emotional support and meaning the grandparent relationship is for many older adults.

The data collected in the study indicated that 59 percent of the grandparents experiencing the formal relationship role were sixty-five years of age or older. Mutual enjoyment and distant figure roles were more frequent among grandparents in the younger group. These differences may reflect the fact that the role of grandparent changes as one grows older.[5]

[5] Bernice Neugarten, *The Changing American Grandparents* (Chicago: University of Chicago Press), 1962.

Old age brings its own unique role

There is a certain degree of role uncertainty at each stage of the life cycle to which individuals must adapt in order to carry out the developmental tasks of the period. Developmental psychologists postulate that successful adaptation to problems of earlier life periods increases the likelihood that the older adult will be able to cope with the tensions that result from the physical, economic, and social stresses of aging. Erik H. Erikson, a proponent of this theory, describes the eight stages of ego development from infancy to old age and the developmental tasks of each stage. The attainment of either integration or despair in old age will be dependent on the success or failure of the ego in accomplishing the psychosocial tasks of each preceding life stage.[6]

Disengagement and involvement in continuing activity are adaptive patterns of the ego to maintain a high level of life satisfactions

As life roles are lost and health deteriorates, a decrease in activity is noted in the lives of many older adults. Both the activity theory and the disengagement theory are used to account for this decreasing involvement and the resulting low life satisfactions that many older adults experience.

Proponents of the activity theory hold that life satisfactions in old age are dependent upon opportunities to find substitutes for the meaningful social roles and relationships of the middle adult years that have become progressively lost. These new relationships and roles will be less personal and broader in scope than the primary ones of earlier life stages, but they will provide some of the needed recognition and affectional responses to give individuals a sense of belonging and a sense of usefulness. Such organizations as multiservice senior centers, the Senior Citizens Service Corps, Volunteers in Service to America, and the International Executive Corps attempt to provide older adults with these new relationships and roles.

Proponents of the disengagement theory take the position that during the later years an inevitable withdrawal process takes place between society and the older person. As physical energy becomes limited and mobility sometimes restricted, the individual comes to terms with the necessity to relinquish meaningful roles and relationships. According to

[6] Erik H. Erikson, "Growth and Crises in the Healthy Personality," in *Personality in Nature, Society and Culture,* Clyde Kluckhohn, ed. (New York: Alfred A. Knopf, 1953), pp. 185-225.

this theory, those individuals who are able to adapt to a pattern of relationships and activities that is commensurate with changing physical
and psychological strengths make the best adjustments. If the individual remains in control and his withdrawal is voluntary, morale remains
high as he reengages his remaining energy in less demanding interests
and relationships.[7] Low morale results when the withdrawal is involuntary and results from widowhood, retirement, illness, and other
losses of old age. Although these two theories of successful aging provide helpful insights, they do not in themselves account for the great
diversity of social behavior that one finds among individual older persons. The question of why some individuals retain high morale by
staying busily involved in activities while others maintain an equally
high morale after giving up lifelong activities, interests, and relationships is still unanswered. Such factors as good health, adequacy of income, and marital status are, of course, related.

Certain psychic changes appear to be part of the normal aging process

Carl Jung, a Swiss psychologist who worked with patients of all ages,
observed that an individual during the first half of life is dominated
mainly by the task of adapting to the pressures and expectations of the
outside world. In the second half he is confronted with the need to discover his own inner world and the meaning of his life in particular and
of all life in general. Recent studies under the direction of Bernice Neugarten and her associates at the University of Chicago also find that
there are certain observable interpsychic changes that occur in the later
years. There seems to be greater preoccupation with the inner life and
an evaluation of the self in terms of success or failure in achieving life
goals and resolving earlier life conflicts. The individual seems to show
an increasing dedication to his central core of values and his own life-
style and habit patterns. Older adults, the research shows, verbalize
their opinions in more dogmatic terms than younger people and seem
to experience a lessening sensitivity to the reactions of others. As they
become less able to integrate all of the stimuli coming from the outside
world, their behavior tends to become more rigid, consistent, and pre-
dictable. The individual now views his life span from the years remaining rather than from the number of years he has already lived.

There is also some evidence of a reversal in the emotional compo-

---

[7] Elaine Cumming and William E. Henry, *Growing Old: The Process of Disengagement* (New York: Basic Books, 1961).

nents of the male and female roles in some couples. Many women become more aggressive and develop a greater sense of security and freedom in expressing themselves. On the other hand, men seem to assume a secondary role, often becoming more docile and emotionally dependent upon their wives. If the wife has resented her husband's dominance in the early years she may now use his increasing dependency to make him feel unsure of his adequacy and insecure in their relationship.[8]

Other identifiable personality patterns influence the life satisfactions of individuals in the later years

Behavioral scientists have identified at least four different lifelong adjustment styles that become more apparent in individual behavior in the older adult years. The terms used to describe these types in various studies differ but the content of the behavior is essentially the same.

1. *The Mature-Integrated Person.* This term describes individuals who function well and are able to integrate their aggressive as well as passive dependent drives and exert a strong sense of mastery and control. They do not want to be waited on by other people but have a strong sense of self-worth and often assume new responsibilities to replace those that are lost. They are not especially aggressive but relaxed and outgoing. When individuals of this type join social groups of age mates, they use the programs well and take on leadership roles and responsibilities.

2. *The Armored-Active Person.* Such persons seem to fight against growing old and deny their age by keeping compulsively busy and striving in competitive ways to outdo others in what seems a desperate defense against age. They tend to be authoritative, set great value on independence, and maintain a rigid control on their feelings and impulses. Such persons have high defenses against anxiety and protect themselves by overactivity and involvement.

3. *The Rocking Chair Personality.* This term describes passive, dependent persons whose characteristic attitude is, "I worked hard all my life; now I just want to relax and rest and let someone else take over." Men become increasingly dependent on their wives; women, whose interests and activities have almost exclusively been centered around their roles as wives and mothers, live a comfortable, contented, low-

---

[8] Bernice L. Neugarten and associates, *Personality in Middle and Late Life* (New York: Atherton Press, 1964).

gear pattern of life. If they join a group, which they rarely do, they take no initiative to carry any responsibility for the good of the group as a whole. They participate only in passive, unstructured activities and hold low expectations for themselves and others.

4. *The Unintegrated Person.* These are generally unhappy individuals with an exorbitant need to be loved, and who seem totally unable to help themselves find happiness. They pity themselves and always seem to have a chip on their shoulders. They are suspicious and hostile and constantly feel that other people are against them. Sometimes their actions are irrational and even bizarre but, by and large, they are able to function on a casual basis and get along if emotional relationships are at a superficial level. They are able to maintain themselves acceptably in the community but at a low activity and life satisfaction level.[9]

In any group of older adults these four personality types may be easily identified among the members. In the Kansas City Study of Adult Life, the proportions of the four life-styles—in a group of fairly active and healthy individuals seventy to eighty years old—were 32 percent mature-integrated, 27 percent armored-active, 22 percent rockingchair, and 19 percent unintegrated. All personality types except the unintegrated seem able to maintain adequate levels of life satisfaction if their social environment is accepting and supportive.[10]

The ego adapts to aging by the use of certain coping mechanisms

In order to cope with the many uncomfortable changes that life brings, an individual develops certain unconscious, though healthy, psychic reactions known as defense mechanisms. Some of the more common ones used by older adults.

1. *Denial.* In this familiar defense a person treats situations in the outer environment that make him feel uncomfortable as though they did not exist. This reaction in older people is often mistaken for courage rather than as the ego's need to turn away from things that are too painful to face. When their own aging is too uncomfortable, many individuals refuse to identify with groups of their peers. Some marriages that take place in the later years are evidences of the individual's need to deny his aging and prove to himself and others that he is still attractive to the opposite sex. Frequently denial is used in an effort to cope with

[9] Suzanne Richard, *Aging and Personality* (New York: John Wiley & Sons, 1962).

[10] Havighurst and Albrecht, *Older People,* p. 286.

an awareness of failing health. Many individuals refuse to recognize signs of physical weakness and illness and state that their health is good even though physical examinations may show recent heart damage or other chronic conditions.

2. *Exclusion of Unwanted Stimuli* is a mechanism closely related to denial but of quite different dynamics. In this defense, the individual experiences lowered psychic energy and an inability to deal with all stimuli coming to his consciousness from the outside. To protect his waning capacities he begins to exclude some, hearing what he wants to hear and seeing what he wants to see. Thus, he invests his waning energy only in that which is emotionally comfortable to him.

3. *Rationalization* is another commonly used coping mechanism. To avoid the discomfort of acknowledging the truth, the ego formulates more acceptable explanations. A parent who longs for more attention from an adult child may say, "My son would like to come to see me more often but, after all, he is such an important and busy man." A widow who feels inadequate to manage financial matters will say, "I wouldn't be so helpless but my husband never shared such concerns with me." As some people become forgetful they are often heard to remark, "No wonder I forgot that appointment! I have so many things on my mind." One who finds it necessary to compete with others will say, "I could be an interesting person, too, if only I had had the advantages that he had."

4. In *Projection* the ego ascribes to another person what are in reality his own traits and his unconscious wishes. Jealous mothers-in-law will say, "What more could you expect from such a thoughtless, demanding, self-centered person as my son's wife!" One who feels hostile to another club member will remark, "She always gets the best seat in the bus because she knows how to play up to the tour leader." Untruths told by one person in an effort to discredit another are ways of unconsciously wishing something else were so.

5. *Sublimation.* Many times the environment denies the individual the fulfillment of normal emotional needs or wishes. Many older people who have no close satisfying personal relationships often lavish their affection and attention on pets. This investment of strong emotional feelings and attachments on animals becomes a sublimation or redirection of normal feelings whose expression may have been thwarted because of a lack of close human relationships.

6. *Regression.* In some adult behavior we see individuals utilizing ways of control that brought emotional satisfactions in earlier life stages. The man who must control others by telling them off or blowing his top is using the adult version of the child's temper tantrum. The executive

who could never make a decision without first talking it over and getting the support of his wife or secretary becomes, in old age, neurotically dependent, needing to retain a symbolic connection to a mother figure. If in the adolescent years the individual has not been able to free himself from the authority of his parents and internalize the authority in himself, he may as an older adult resent anyone who has power, position, or experience—his employer, the club leader, the executive of the senior center, or the director of the home with whose demands he must comply. He refers to the need to comply with group norms as being regimentation.

7. *Manipulation.* This is a healthy ego defense used by many older persons to secure the protection and help of a stronger individual when their egos are feeling weak and threatened. It takes the form of flattery, flirting or seductive conduct, complaints of helplessness, or displays of pain and stress. In these ways the older person strives to elicit the sympathy and attention of the authority figure. Constant complaining of aches and pains, monopolizing the attention of a nurse or staff member, and making excessive demands on children are all ways in which some older persons try to make others feel sorry for them and get their protection and favor. Some individuals make such excessive demands that they cannot be satisfied. They become so occupied with their insatiable demands that they are unable to appreciate and enjoy what they already have.

8. *Reminiscing.* The individual uses his experiences in the past as the frame of reference for a large portion of his thought content and much of his conversation. Through reminiscing he strives to maintain his self-esteem, work through personal losses, and reaffirm his sense of identity. Any sense of depression that may accompany reminiscing is neither deep nor chronic. Such thinking and talking of past experiences is not related to intellectual deterioration or a sign of senility. It becomes abnormal only if reality is distorted or if carried to excess.

Although each of these ego defense mechanisms has been discussed separately, they are, in fact, overlapping, interrelated, and directly related to the psychological stresses of change in old age rather than to any actual disorientation of the brain itself.

When defense mechanisms break down, the individual loses his ability to deal with the outside world

In times of waning physical and emotional strength even these coping mechanisms may often become inadequate to keep the ego related to reality. Such antisocial feelings as anger, hostility, hatred, anxiety, and fear can no longer be suppressed or dealt with directly. Because the older adult has so few persons from whom he can run the risk of experiencing disfavor and rejection, he withdraws from people and situations and clings to familiar patterns. The content of his conversation may become an endless repetition of stories about earlier life periods that gave him greater satisfaction. He may suppress and internalize these feelings and turn his anger in upon himself, thus retreating into psychosomatic illness or hypochondriasis. According to physicians, colitis, asthma, and rheumatoid arthritis are brought about by the intensity of emotional stress on the physical body. In hypochondriasis, the individual becomes narcissistically preoccupied with his physical functions and needs, making frequent visits to the physician and developing great confidence in patent medicines. Excessive anxiety out of all proportion to the reality of the situation results when feelings of depression are turned in on one's self, and suicide may follow. If the anger is turned on others, the individual may show paranoid behavior with unrealistic suspicions. He places blame on innocent persons and often retreats into fantasies of previous wealth, travel, conquests, and successes.

The mental health of any person at any period in life fluctuates greatly because of physical conditions, emotional moods, and the immediate events of his daily life. Among older persons this variableness of mental health within relatively short periods of time is more pronounced. For a younger person psychiatric care is indicated when the coping mechanisms break down and the individual is unable to function in reality situations. Most psychiatrists feel it unwise, however, except in extreme situations, to challenge the defenses of an older person and seek to reorient his consciousness to greater degrees of reality. The individual has developed certain coping mechanisms in an effort to tolerate the stresses that he is facing. These mechanisms keep him related in comfortable ways to a world that perhaps is becoming more and more intolerable for him. His defenses for coping with it should rarely be disturbed.

Conclusion

In this chapter the various patterns of personality organization and behavior, as well as the defense mechanisms individuals develop to cope with reality, have been reviewed. They indicate that there is no single formula for successful aging. Each individual finds for himself the pattern that best fits his own life situation. The ability of the older adult to continue to function as an adequate social being will depend on how successful his conscious and unconscious self has been throughout life in accomplishing the essential psychosocial tasks.

BIBLIOGRAPHY

Aging and Human Development: An International Journal of Psychosocial Gerontology. Robert J. Kastenbaum, editor, Wayne State University, Detroit, Michigan. Greenwood Periodicals, Inc., Box 51, Westport, Conn. 06880

Albrecht, Ruth, "The Social Role of Old People." *Journal of Gerontology* 6 (1951): pp. 138-145.

————— "The Parental Responsibilities of Grandparents." *Marriage and Family Living* 16 (1954): 201-204.

Allport, G.W. *Personality: A Psychological Interpretation.* New York: Henry Holt and Co., 1937.

Anderson, John E., ed. *Psychological Aspects of Aging.* Washington, D.C.: American Psychological Association, 1955.

Barron, Milton, et al. "Research on the Social Disorganization of Retirement." *American Sociological Review* 17 (1952): 479-491.

Birren, James E., ed. *Aging and the Individual: A Handbook of the Biological, Psychological and Social Aspects of Aging.* Chicago: University of Chicago Press, 1959.

Cavan, Ruth S. "Family Life and Family Substitutes in Old Age." *American Sociological Review* 14 (1949): 71-83.

Cavan, R.S.; Burgess, E.W.; Havighurst, R.J.; and Goldbamer, H. *Personal Adjustment in Old Age.* Chicago: Science Research Associates, 1949.

Clinard, Marshall B. *Role and Status Conflict in Old Age: Sociology of Deviant Behavior.* New York: Holt, Rinehart and Winston, 1957.

Cumming, Elaine, and Henry, William E. *Growing Old.* New York: Basic Books, 1961.

Duvall, Evelyn M. *Family Development.* Philadelphia: J. B. Lippincott Co., 1957.

Erikson, Erik H., "The Problem of Ego Identity." *Journal of American Psychoanalytic Association* 4 (1956): 56-127.

————— *Identity and the Life Cycle: Selected Papers by Erik H. Erikson.* Psychological Issues, vol. 1, New York: International Universities Press, 1959.

————— "Growth and Crises of the 'Healthy Personality.'" In *Personality in Nature, Society and Culture,* edited by C. Kluckhohn, H. G. Murray and D. M. Schneider, pp. 185-225. New York: Alfred A. Knopf, 1953.

Ford, Caroline S. "Ego-Adoptive Mechanism of Older Persons," *Social Casework* 46 (1965): pp. 16-21.

Freidmann, Eugene A., and Havighurst, Robert J. *The Meaning of Work and Retirement*. Chicago: University of Chicago Press, 1954.

Havighurst, Robert J.; Neugarten, Bernice L.; and Tobin, Sheldon, "Disengagement, Personality, and Life Satisfaction." In *Aging with a Future: Proceedings of the Sixth International Congress of Gerontology*, edited by P. Hansen. Philadelphia: F.A. Davis Co., 1964.

———— and Albrecht, Ruth. *Older People*. New York: Longmans, Green & Co., 1953.

Jung, Carl Gustav. *Modern Man In Search of a Soul*. New York: Harcourt Brace & World, 1954.

Kroeber, T. C., "The Coping Functions of the Ego Mechanisms." In *The Study of Lives*, edited by R. W. White, pp. 178-98. New York: Atherton Press, 1963.

Kuhlen, Raymond G., and Thompson, George G., eds. *Psychological Studies of Human Development*. New York: Appleton-Century-Crofts, 1952.

Lioz, Theodore. *The Person: His Development Throughout the Life Cycle*. New York: Basic Books, 1968.

Lowenthal, Marjorie Fiske, and Boler, Deetje. "Voluntary or Involuntary Social Withdrawal." *Journal of Gerontology* 20 (1965): 363-371.

Maddox, G. and Eisdorfer, C. "Some Correlates of Activity and Morale Among the Elderly." *Social Forces* 40 (1962): 254-260.

Maslow, Abraham H., *Motivation and Personality*. New York: Harper & Row, 1954.

Neugarten, Bernice L., ed. *Middle Age and Aging: A Reader in Social Psychology*. Chicago: University of Chicago Press, 1968.

———— *Personality in Middle and Late Life*. New York: Atherton Press, 1964.

————, Havighurst, Robert J.; and Tobin, Sheldon, "The Measurement of Life Satisfactions." *Journal of Gerontology* 16 (1961): 134-143.

————, and Weinstein, Karol, *The Changing American Grandparents*. Chicago: University of Chicago Press, 1962.

Phillips, Bernard S. "A Role Theory Approach to Adjustment in Old Age." *American Sociological Review* 22 (1957): 212-217.

Pussey, Sidney L., and Kuhlen, Raymond G., *Psychological Development Through the Life Span*. New York, Harper & Brothers, 1957.

Reichard, Suzanne; Lavson, Florence; and Peterson, Paul G. *Aging and Personality*. New York: John Wiley & Sons, 1962.

Riley, Matilda White, and Fouer, Ann. *Aging and Society*. Vol. I. *An Inventory of Research Findings*. New York: Russell Sage Foundation, 1968.

Shanas, Ethel, and Strieb, Gordon, eds. *Social Structures and the Family:*

Generational Relations. Englewood Cliffs, N.J.: Prentice-Hall, 1965.

———— *The Health of Older People: A Social Survey.* Cambridge: Harvard University Press, 1962.

Shanas, Ethel; Townsend, Peter; Pries, Henning; Miljh, Paul; and Stehonwer, Jon. *Old People in Three Industrial Societies.* London and New York: Routledge and Kegan Paul, Ltd.; Atherton, 1968.

Sussman, M.B. "The Help Pattern in the Middle-Class Family." *American Sociological Review* 18 (1953): 22-28.

Tibbitts, Clark, and Donahue, Wilma. *Social and Psychological Aspects of Aging.* New York: Columbia University Press, 1962.

Tobin, Sheldon, and Neugarten, Bernice L. "Life Satisfaction and Social Interaction in the Aging." *Journal of Gerontology* 16 (1961): 344-46.

Turner, Helen. *Psychological Functioning of Older People in Institutions and in the Community.* New York: National Council on the Aging, 1967.

U.S. Department of Health, Education and Welfare. Public Health Service. *Working With Older People: A Guide to Practice,* Vol. 2, *Biological, Psychological and Sociological Aspects of Aging,* 1970.

von Hentig, Hans, "The Sociological Function of the Grandmother." *Social Focus* 24 (1946): 389-392.

Weinberg, J. "Personal and Social Adjustments." In *Psychological Aspects of Aging,* edited by J. E. Anderson, pp. 17-29. Washington, D.C.: American Psychological Association, 1956.

8 / Psychological Aging as It Affects Intellectual Functioning and Motor Skills

THAT MAN HAS THE ABILITY TO DEVELOP new skills and learn and act on new information throughout his entire life has been well established by psychological research. This ability offers great challenge to each individual as he moves into the later years and is of paramount importance to administrators, teachers of adult education classes, and community planners concerned with providing opportunities for older adults that are commensurate with their skills. Stereotypes of aged persons as individuals whose mental capacities have deteriorated and whose interest in life is rapidly diminishing are no longer valid.

The brain has potentials for functioning effectively through all of life

Studies of intelligence and mental abilities of individuals in the eighth and ninth decades give some evidence of progressive loss with age. Decline in mental powers parallels the decline in physical powers unless a pathological physical condition exists. The decline begins to be evident after the twentieth and twenty-fifth years. The change is very slow until about the thirtieth year. From the thirtieth to the ninetieth year the brain drops in weight from 3.33 pounds to approximately 2.72 pounds. Biologists believe that this change in weight, which is a result of the loss of brain cells, accounts for some of the loss in mental functioning in older adults. Disease and accidents also may damage parts of the brain and nervous system and prevent its normal operation. The brain may also become functionally deranged by emotional factors and such interacting forces as heredity, nutrition, drugs, and social isolation. But

114

free of disease, accidents, and abnormal emotional stress, the brain has been found to be one of the body's most durable organs with a tremendous reserve for functioning effectively in the later decades.

This ability of the individual to maintain a high level of mental functioning is well documented in the lives and accomplishments of many men and women whose names are well known. Frank Lloyd Wright was still designing buildings when he died at eighty-five. Dr. Lillian Martin established the first Old Age Counseling Center in San Francisco when she was eighty. Konrad Adenauer was politically active in West Germany when he died at ninety-one. Ethel Barrymore, who lived to be almost eighty, made a movie, *Young at Heart,* when she was seventy-five. Helen Keller continued her lecturing and writing up to several years before her death at eighty-three. Cardinal Angelo Roncalli became Pope John XXIII at seventy-six, and Johann von Goethe wrote the second part of *Faust* at eighty. Michelangelo started his *Pietá* at eighty and worked on it until his death at eighty-nine. Jean Sibelius was still composing brilliant music at eighty-two, and Antonio Stradivari made violins until he was ninety-three. Imogen Cunningham, the renowned photographer, was awarded a prized Guggenheim Fellowship in recognition of the excellence of her work on her eighty-seventh birthday.

Psychologists differ widely on the precise effect of normal age-linked changes on the various aspects of mental functioning, such as learning, imagination, memory, abstract thinking, and association. They agree that in a physically healthy older adult these processes can not only be continued at a normal rate but some may even be developed in the later years. Research shows, however, that there is a sharp decline in intelligence just prior to death. Studies are now being made of the mental functioning of an individual when latent or active somatic disease is present with the possibility of forecasting the remaining time before death.

Losses in sensory acuity affect mental functioning

Intelligence is the capacity of the individual to act purposefully, to think rationally, and to deal effectively with his physical environment. Through the receptors of the five senses facts from the environment are received, assimilated, and then related to past knowledge. New concepts and patterns of meaning are thus formulated. Any loss in sensory acuity limits not only stimuli received from the physical environment but also from other people against whose ideas and opinions the individual tests his own reality. According to physiologists, visual acuity is attained at about eighteen years and then declines continuously until forty years when the eye can no longer accommodate to close objects. After age forty-two there is a sharp decline until approximately the middle fifties. After that the rate of decline decreases.

Maximum audio acuity is attained between ten and fifteen years of age. It then declines very gradually but consistently, becoming more marked in persons over seventy-five. In the seventh decade at least 20 percent of all men and 10 percent of all women show noticeable deafness. Because he needs to increase his sensory input in order to see and hear, an older person turns up the light or plays the radio at a greater volume. Like sound and sight, touch, taste, and smell begin to be dulled about the fiftieth year when the receptors in the skin, tongue, and nose become less effective. The decreasing number of stimuli reaching the brain from the sensory receptors account in part for what may seem to be a decrease in the intelligence of the older adult.

Intelligence in old age is difficult to measure by standardized tests

Because there are no valid projective tests to make comparative studies of the intelligence of aged individuals and that of younger people, it is difficult to know if, and how much, intelligence quotients of individuals change as they age. Such tests as the Wechser-Bellview Scale have been designed specifically to test the intelligence of school-age youth. Older adults show lower scores than youth when these tests are given to them. Such factors as lower levels of education that are found among older people, their lack of motivation, and their anxiety about exposing themselves to possible failure may be responsible for the differences in scores on intelligence tests. Longitudinal studies that measure the same individual throughout his total life span will be needed to give definitive evidence of any decline in intelligence with age, at what rate it declines, and under what conditions. The Terman Study of the Gifted Child holds promise of providing such data. This study was initiated in 1921 at Stanford University when 1,500 intellectually superior children were selected for study with respect to their physical, mental, and personality characteristics. These individuals are now in their fifties, and since 1921 they have been tested several times. The most recent tests, completed in 1959, give strong evidence that intelligence of the type tested by concept mastery tests continues to increase at least through the fiftieth year.

Individual differences in age, previous education, health, and the variety and extent of life interests all influence the learning ability of older adults. People with high intelligence quotients seem to have a biological advantage. They live longer and are superior in other ways. There is also good evidence to support the view that the greater the individual's intellectual endowment and educational attainments, the less rapid will be the decline in his intellectual ability. Many older adults who have had limited educational opportunities place a low value on learning as they grow older, while those who have attained a higher educational level have more positive attitudes. They value learning and knowledge as ends in themselves and seem to have more inner resources for continuing to be interested in life around them.

Although basic intelligence does not change, some changes take place in learning processes

Although there is a substantial retention of the ability to learn by the healthy older adult, there is a slowing up in the speed of perception and the rate of learning. An older person needs exposure to information over a longer period of time and can tolerate less interference from outside stimuli as he learns. Comprehension of difficult reading material shows little or no change with age, but there is a decline in the ability to remember random and isolated facts. Older adults think and reason by a simple association of facts rather than by an analysis and a checking out of facts. They tend to solve problems on the basis of already known facts rather than to experiment by trying new solutions.

In a test situation that gives choices for responses, a healthy older person is slower on the average than a younger one. If speed is not a factor, the scores of older adults are apt to be higher than those of a younger person in tests of vocabulary, general information, and reasoning problems. As a task becomes more difficult and necessitates abstract thinking or the manipulation of figures, an aged person will show a longer response time and a greater decline in the number of correct responses. If he is hurried he may become confused and give up or settle for approximate solutions. His poor performance results in a lessening of interest and motivation to finish the task.

There is also evidence of some deterioration in the ability to recall facts, even among healthy aged subjects, especially of complex material. This decrease in memory may be due to the fact that the older person did not initially learn or register the information efficiently. In the eighth and ninth decades the loss of the ability to recall seems to be for recent events rather than for earlier ones. The nervous system appears to be organized historically so that recent experiences and recently acquired patterns of adjustment are superimposed upon earlier ones. As memory becomes impaired the process is reversed.

Peer groups provide the best learning climate for older adults

Although the ability to learn new material does not change basically, the older adult's interest in learning does. Many older people become self-conscious and are unwilling to take risks of possible failure, especially when there are younger people in the group who are able to work at a quicker pace and show more efficiency in acquiring information and in mastering a skill. Older people develop self-protective attitudes and rationalize that they do not know enough about a subject to express a viewpoint or that, because they do not hear or see as well as formerly, they may be too slow or not compehend well enough to participate with younger people in group discussions.

Classes for older people that are also open to younger students often result in experiences that are discouraging and detrimental to the morale of the older person. Furthermore, unless the instructor has some understanding of the nature of the physical and psychological aging processes, his instructions may be too rapid or too general for the capacities of the older person.

Some psychomotor skills decline but new skills and dexterities may be learned in the later years

Learning new skills and dexterities, like learning new facts and concepts, is within the ability of physically well older people. There are, however, evidences of decline in the psychomotor performance of many older adults due to the loss of input through the sensory receptors as well as other physical conditions. The decline in these skills contributes to the high motor vehicle accident rate among older adults because driving involves many of the psychomotor skills as well as perception and judgment. Older and younger drivers have the most accidents, but of different kinds. The traffic accidents of older people are due to improper turning, starting, and stopping rather than to speeding. The failure to pass drivers' tests and the inability to renew licenses is a traumatic experience for the individual; however, because the proportion of accidents by older drivers is increasing, it has been necessary to tighten the regulations governing the operation of motor vehicles by older adults.

New motor skills may be acquired in the later years, and older adults can learn to use a tool and paint brush, to play a musical instrument, and to weave, knit, and throw clay on a potter's wheel. These motor skills are all dependent upon an interrelated working of sensory and muscular functions as well as memory, imagination, abstract thinking, and reasoning. As age changes bring some fluctuations in sensory and muscular functions, slower and poorer performance may result, but these changes can often be compensated for by glasses and hearing aids and by slowing down the pace of work. In learning new techniques adults often have to unlearn long-established patterns. Faced with this necessity they often become frustrated and discouraged and inflexible in their unwillingness to try something new. Developing old skills and learning new ones is especially satisfying to older adults when such learning takes place in a group from which they receive recognition and approval for their efforts.

Many challenging opportunities for learning new skills and facts are now being made available to older adults in senior centers, adult education classes, and university extension courses. Motivating the older person to take advantage of such learning opportunities is the critical problem. If an individual can be persuaded to take a first step and make an effort to participate, he will continue to do so if the experience gives him enough emotional dividends. Younger people are motivated to try new experiences and apply themselves to learning by parents and teachers whose aproval they value. Many aged people have few caring persons in their lives to encourage them to try something new. Helping older people to maintain an interest in continued learning and the will to expend their limited economic, physical and psychic resources in doing so is one of the roles of a senior center. The role of the staff members and teachers is to motivate and encourage those individuals who seem to lack the will and the interest. This is an important one for an adult child to play in relation to his aged parent.

Special methods and climate will be necessary to help older adults enjoy learning

For an older person to enjoy learning and for the experience to be personally satisfying, some thought must be given to methods and procedures as well as to creating a climate in which learning can take place.

The following guiding principles will be helpful for teachers and group leaders of older adults.

1. Quality work should be expected from older people but producing it will take longer than in youth groups.

2. The scope of the instruction should take into account the decreased speed and capabilities of the group members. Short units of work should be planned to give older adults a more immediate feeling of success and mastery.

3. Because learning flows primarily from a satisfying experience and a reward, every opportunity must be used to praise the older person. Errors should be minimized and sarcasm and ridicule should never be used.

4. Because the attention span of older adults is apt to be more limited than that of youth, it is important to have frequent short breaks in a class period. Recessing for a cup of tea or coffee or to see a short educational film related to the subject of the class can be helpful.

5. Unlike a school child, an older adult is a voluntary participant in a class. He has joined the group not only for what he hopes to learn but also to enjoy the companionship of other class members. He will soon drop out of the group if both of these expectations are not met. If older adults do not enjoy one another, they cannot learn together.

6. The content of any learning situation must be challenging and significant and not just busy work to fill time. Time becomes too precious a commodity to an older person to be wasted in meaningless activity.

7. Each individual in the group needs to feel that his opinions and thoughts are important and will be valued. He must often be encouraged to express them.

8. Older people learn better as participants than as spectators. Being a member of a class is a more effective and satisfying learning situation for older adults than learning alone.

9. Learning should produce immediate and visible satisfactions and tangible products that can be finished in a relatively short period of time. They must, however, be functional. Few older people are interested in making gadgets to clutter up their limited living space.

10. Older people are apt to comment that certain craft procedures are child's play. Materials used—especially scrap material—should be new or of good quality. Objects made should not be too simple but on an adult level.

Conclusion

Maintaining, utilizing, and developing mental functions and psychomotor skills are of paramount importance as individuals age. Through their constant use an older adult is able to relate to life in stimulating and meaningful ways. The progressive limitation of physical energy may eventually restrict an individual's mobility and involvement with other people. As long as he remains mentally well, even though he becomes isolated, he will be able to extend his mental and spiritual horizons and remain an intellectually vital person.

BIBLIOGRAPHY

Bayley, Nancy, and Oden, Melita. "The Maintenance of Intellectual Ability in Gifted Adults." *Journal of Gerontology* 10 (1955): pp. 91-107.

Birren, J.E., ed. *Handbook of Aging and the Individual.* Chicago: University of Chicago Press, 1959.

——— Butler, R. H.; Greenberise; S. W.; Sokoloff, L.; and Yarrow, Marion R., eds. *Human Aging.* Public Health Service Publication, no. 986. Washington, D.C.; Government Printing Office, 1963.

Bromley, D.B. *The Psychology of Human Aging.* Baltimore: Penguin Books, 1966.

——— "Some Effects of Age on Short-Term Learning and Remembering." *Journal of Gerontology* 13 (1958): 398-406.

——— "Some Effects of Age on the Quality of Intellectual Output." *Journal of Gerontology* 12 (1957): 318-23.

Bruner, J.S. "The Course of Cognitive Growth." *American Psychologist* 19 (1964): 1-15.

Fisher, Jerome, and Pierce, Robert C. "Dimensions of Intellectual Functioning in the Aged." *Journal of Gerontology* 22 (1967): 166-73.

Jones, Harold E. "Intelligence and Problem Solving." In *Handbook of Aging and the Individual,* edited by J. E. Birren. Chicago: The University of Chicago Press, 1959.

Kleemeier, Robert W. "Age Change in Psychomotor Capacity and Productivity." *Journal of Business,* 27 (1954): 146-155.

Lieberman, N. "Psychological Correlates of Impending Death." *Journal of Gerontology* 20 (1965): 181-90.

Peck, R.F. "Psychological Developments in the Second Half of Life." In *Psychological Aspects of Aging,* edited by J. E. Anderson, pp. 42-53. Washington, D.C.: American Psychological Association, 1956.

Terman, L.M., and Oden, Melita H. "The Gifted Child Grows Up," in Vol. 4, *Genetic Studies of Genius.* Stanford: Stanford University Press, 1947.

————, and Oden, Melita H. "The Gifted Group at Mid-life." in Vol V, *Genetic Studies of Genius*. Stanford: Stanford University Press, 1959.

Wechsler, D. *The Measurement of Adult Intelligence*. 3d ed. Baltimore: Williams and Wilkins, 1944.

Welford, A.T. *Aging and Human Skill*. (Published for the Trustees of the Nuffield Foundation). London: Oxford University Press, 1958.

Wesman, A.G. "Standardizing an Individual Intelligence Test on Adults: Some Problems." *Journal of Gerontology* 10 (1955): 216-19.

III — DEVELOPMENT AND ADMINISTRATION OF SOCIAL PROGRAMS FOR OLDER ADULTS

9 / The Multiservice Senior Center and Social Clubs for Older Adults

DURING THE PAST quarter century there has been a phenomenal development of programs and services to meet the needs of the increasing numbers of older people in all the populations of the world. These include housing projects and retirement communities, geriatric clinics and convalescent hospitals, residential and custodial care homes, housekeeping and shopping services, home health aides and meals-on-wheels, friendly visitors and telephone reassurance services, and senior centers and golden age clubs. There have been no set formulas for the development of these programs in local communities. The development has been spotty and slow moving in some communities, and in others it has followed a dynamic, well-designed, steadily unfolding plan. The recognition that the welfare of the total community is dependent on the well-being of all its citizens and the awareness of the many gaps in existing services for older people have led to the development of these essential new community programs.

Senior centers and other social activity programs planned exclusively and specifically for older adults are now recognized as essential community resources. This chapter will not deal with the autonomous social groups in which many older adults continue to be active after retirement. The focus will be on those groups organized by community organizations to provide opportunities for older adults to use the added years that longer life spans have made available in personally and socially meaningful ways.

Establishment of the first senior center in New York in 1944 marked the beginning of this development

Early in 1944 the staff social workers of the New York City Department of Social Services became aware that their clients had social and emotional needs that extended far beyond the subsistence needs met by monthly financial grants. They were convinced that any responsible public service should concern itself with the total needs of older clients, and they believed that opportunities should be provided to enable their clients, after retirement, to participate with members of their peer group in activities that were enjoyable and meaningful. They secured the use of a portion of an old Borough Hall in the Bronx, which they cleaned, painted, and renovated to serve as a center for all the older people in that neighborhood. This small beginning by a concerned staff of a public welfare department developed into the William Hodson Senior Center, the first project of its kind in this nation.

Three years later, in 1947, the second such project, the San Francisco Senior Center, was organized on the West Coast. During the past twenty-five years since these beginnings there has been a rapid development of such programs. Multiservice senior centers and social clubs sponsored by churches, synagogues, lodges and fraternal organizations, unions, and professional organizations have been organized in large and small communities across the nation. Public recreation and health departments, libraries, adult schools, and museums have extended their programs to include groups for older adults. Social activities have become an integral part of the services in housing projects, residential institutions, and nursing homes, and information and referral services have been established to help individuals learn about and use all of these opportunities.

Group programs for older adults, unlike many group programs for youths, have been grass-roots developments. Their structure and programs have not been determined by standards set by a national organization. Programs differ from community to community, depending on the vision of those who initiated the project, the facilities and financial support available, and the quality and skill of the leadership. Services range in size from small operations conducted by part-time volunteer directors to large agencies employing directors and interprofessional staffs of recreational leaders, teachers, and social workers. Although diversity has characterized the development through these years, the purposes and goals of all groups have been essentially the same: to provide opportunities for older citizens to enjoy meaningful activities with age mates and to continue to remain actively involved in the concerns of the community.

As the significance of these programs became apparent, funds for their development became more readily available. Tax monies through budgets of the municipal recreation, adult education, and health departments of the cities, allocations from united giving crusades, foundation grants, and more recently funds from the federal government through Title III of the Older Americans Act have all given great impetus to the development of senior centers. Enthusiastic response from older citizens and a high sense of commitment by staff and volunteers have characterized the projects as they developed.

In a field where there was no existing organized body of knowledge or experience it has been important for leaders to learn from one another. The first National Conference on Aging, called by the Social Security Administration in 1950; the White House Conference on Aging in 1961; national and international meetings of the Gerontological Society; a series of conferences sponsored jointly by the National Council on the Aging and the National Council on Social Work Education; and conferences sponsored by State Councils on Aging, universities, and national and state recreational and social welfare organizations have provided such opportunities over the years.

The senior center concept first started in 1959

With the wide variation in the quality and scope of programs, it soon became desirable to formulate guidelines for evaluating the existing projects and to set minimum standards to guide those communities looking toward the initiation of such programs. The first such set of goals and definitions for these dynamic new projects was undertaken by a committee appointed by the National Council on the Aging in 1959. From the meetings of this committee came a publication by Jean M. Maxwell, *Centers for Older People: Guide for Program and Facilities,* which states:

"The Senior Center may be a single purpose or multi-purpose agency established as a result of community planning based on the unmet needs of older people in any given community.

"The basic purpose of such centers is to provide older people with socially enriching experiences which would help preserve their dignity as human beings and enhance their feelings of self-worth." [1]

In 1964 this definition was refined and expanded by the President's Council on Aging, and the following derivative standard was formulated to guide communities in their development of centers:

A senior center is a physical facility open to senior citizens the year around, at least five days a week and four hours a day, operated by a

[1] Jean M. Maxwell, *Centers for Older People: Guide for Programs and Facilities* (New York: National Council on the Aging, 1964), p. 7.

public agency or nonprofit private organization. It provides, under the direction of paid professional leadership, three or more of the following services: recreation; adult education; health services; counseling; information and referral, and opportunities for community and volunteer service.[2]

These definitions have provided helpful guide lines, and centers of various types have been developed by local communities. Some of these centers are independent membership organizations that have their own buildings and are governed by incorporated boards of directors. Others are attached to a larger agency, which provides the space, staff, and program budget. The majority of centers are located in, or next to, public housing units, municipal parks, recreation agencies, or community centers. Some centers are lounges located in storefronts in downtown areas where older people may drop in to rest, use the toilet and washroom facilities, have a cup of coffee, read the newspaper, and meet and visit with friends. Others have been developed as day centers in conjunction with geriatric hospitals and extended care facilities. Here an older person who is living with his children and who needs close supervision is brought each day as his children go to work. He is picked up again in the evening following quiet group activities, simple crafts, a hot noon meal, and a rest period. Day centers offer specialized programs for physically and mentally frail older adults, and only a limited number have been organized.

There are other centers that are tent-like agencies. In addition to the activities for the center members, a variety of autonomous closed-membership clubs of retired men and women meet at the center. This plan is an excellent one if the status of the independent group and its responsibilities have been carefully worked out. Because it is the group and not its individual members who are affiliated with the center, conflicts and misunderstandings often result. We-they attitudes and competitive feelings develop between center members and those of the affiliated groups; the necessity to comply with certain center policies also results in points of conflict. The facility can become a senior center in fact when all groups serving older adults meet in one central place. The skilled administrator is able to accommodate these noncenter groups within the center facility by careful preplanning and a clear understanding of the mutual relationships.

The multiservice or multipurpose senior center is recognized today

[2] Subcommittee on Senior Citizens Centers, *The Senior Center—Its Goals, Functions and Programs,* (Washington, D.C. President's Council on Aging, 1964).

as the prototype desirable for future developments. These centers are membership organizations with stated procedures for joining and expectations that members will carry financial and leadership responsibilities. The programs offer a wide diversity of activities, as well as counseling for those older persons facing crisis situations. Many of the larger centers are now developing outreach programs to find and serve those older adults who, on their own initiative, do not join centers.

The image of the elderly person and of the senior center is changing

During the twenty-five years of pioneering in providing services for older adults, community attitudes have changed and a new image of old age and its potentials is emerging. The elderly person of tomorrow will have little except chronological age in common with those who joined the first centers over a quarter of a century ago. He will have, on the whole, a higher level of formal education and will be more interested in opportunities to continue learning. He will be healthier and continue to be more active and mentally alert into much later years. Despite inflation and its devaluation of retirement incomes, he will be economically more independent and have greater income protection than the retirees of 1945. With retirement from employment coming earlier, he will also be younger when he joins senior centers.

Senior centers will perform a disservice to older people if they become psychological refuges of safety, removing persons from the mainstream of community life that has suddenly become strange and threatening. Nor should they be located exclusively in the depressed areas of big cities and serve only the aged poor. The fact that most senior centers have, in their formative years, attracted physically and emotionally healthy older people has been a great advantage because their public image has not become that of a clinic or a hospital for the mentally and physically frail. The image of the senior center of the future must continue to be a positive one if all older people are to feel comfortable in identifying themselves with it and benefiting from its program and services. It must be highly visible to the total community—to the older people themselves, to their adult children, and more especially to youth who must be helped to become more aware of age and its potentials.

Members will become more involved in the
operation of the senior center of tomorrow

In the initial years of their development, the programs of many senior centers were limited to recreational activities. Members, by and large, became passive users of programs provided for them. The elderly person of tomorrow will be interested in being more involved in the decision making and management of the center. Because trained workers and funds to employ them were not initially available, the senior center movement in the early days was of necessity a volunteer one in many communities. As programs developed and the scope of services was enlarged, it became essential to employ professional staff to administer and direct them. Professional leadership will continue to be essential, but paraprofessional jobs are being developed to take over some aspects of staff responsibilities and new professional tasks are being defined. Programs for older people in the future will be effective only to the degree that those programs utilize the strengths and abilities of the members in leadership and management responsibilities and decision making. Because an experimental approach has always characterized the development of senior centers, they will be more able than many long-established community agencies to remain flexible and adapt programs quickly to the changing needs and interests of those who are old today, as well as of those who will be old tomorrow.

A separate agency to serve older adults
exclusively is essential and justifiable

Many citizens feel that programs and services designed specifically and exclusively for older people tend to segregate them and that it is unwise to fragment society into age groups. Most community planners, however, are in agreement that the social needs of the aged cannot adequately be met without at least one specialized agency whose program is specifically designed for them. It is, of course, true that not all emotional and social needs of older people can be met by peer relationships —they need to associate with people of all ages. Providing opportunities for older people to spend some portion of their day engaged in activities with age mates is not to isolate them from the rest of society or to deny them associations with individuals of other ages. No senior center, however diversified its program, occupies all of an older person's free time. An individual belongs to his family, has friends and neighbors, attends a church or synagogue, shops at neighborhood stores, and rides on public transportation. Some of these relationships are casual, to be sure, but many are meaningful and satisfying.

Friendship patterns of other age groups is with age mates. The child in his play groups and the adolescent in his after school activities associate with peer group members. In the adult years, although the age range of associates in work and in the community is wider, those in one's intimate group—a golf foursome or bridge or poker club—are the same age within approximately ten years or have similar social status, sex, marital status, and life-styles. These are the cohesive factors in human relationships. Individuals of different ages come together most naturally in hobby groups organized around common interests and skills. In such groups older adults can and do compete successfully with younger people because of their greater skill and experience. Every older adult, in addition to his association with his peers as a member of a senior center, should belong to at least one group whose members are of a wide age span. However, in a society where attitudes that reject older people are becoming more and more widespread, aged individuals are reluctant to go where they may experience rejection and negative reactions. The senior center provides for such older persons an accepting environment and a community of peers.

Specially designed facilities
are needed to serve older adults

The senior centers of yesterday were of necessity housed in whatever facilities were available. Too often these facilities were cramped and dark rooms that were down or up long flights of stairs and at the end of drafty halls. Moreover, they were poorly adapted for use by older people. Today in many communities new facilities are being designed specifically for senior center programs. Through Department of Housing and Urban Development programs, model cities are replacing the deteriorating cores of many large urban areas. Many of these redeveloped areas include housing and social centers for the aged that are situated in well-planned neighborhoods where the older person can shop or go to the library, church, or senior center without crossing traffic or climbing stairs. Curbings and walkways are so designed that older persons in wheelchairs are able to go wherever pedestrians can go. Such facilities as the library, craft shops, swimming pools, and health clinics are shared by the residents of all ages. The recreation areas are available to the aged when children are in school and to young adults and parents during evening hours. Central kitchens that are used to prepare snacks for the nursery school during the day become available for communal dining rooms for older adults in the evening. Craft, pool, and club rooms may be used in the daytime by older adults and are then available to children and youth in the after-school hours and for all ages during the evening hours. Such a plan assures maximum utilization of the facilities and develops the interdependence of the generations and the meaningful communication between them. In such planned communities older people have opportunities to serve as mothers' helpers and aides in the nursery school, and children are available to run errands and be foster grandchildren to the aged who live among them.

Today model cities that include housing for the aged within the same area as the housing for all other age groups are being designed in ways that recognize that the physical and social environments of the future must be planned to support, not negate, the capacities and potentials of older adults and their ability to function both for their own and for the community's welfare. Only with such planning will older people have a sense of security and of being a part of the total community. Communities will differ in who accepts the responsibility for developing a comprehensive master plan. In some it will be the welfare council, and in others the responsibility will rest in the various departments of municipal government. Church councils and other nonprofit corporations have taken the initiative in some communities to plan and arrange financing for multiservice senior centers to serve the older adults living in housing projects as well as those living in other neighborhoods; the latter will be served in satellite clubs related to the multiservice center.

Characteristics of a multiservice senior center

All component parts of the program of a multiservice senior center are closely related and interdependent. The program provides for its members opportunities not only for enjoyment and personally enriching activities but also help on personal problems. The center serves as a training center for volunteer leaders and as a living laboratory for research and demonstrations in social gerontology. Chart 4 pictures some of the essential component programs of a multiservice senior center and the professional leadership needed to operate it effectively.

Chart 4
A Multiservice Senior Center

A design concept showing the component activities and services,
the purpose and scope of each, and the staff roles and functions

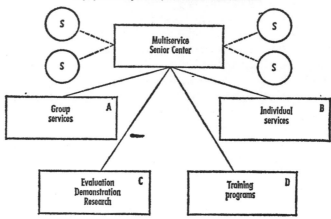

S = Satellite clubs meeting in the neighborhoods

A. *Group Services* (the core program)

Purpose

To meet the social and emotional needs of members by providing opportunities for meaningful activities and peer relationships.

Scope of the Group Program

1. Classes and interest groups in music, languages, needlework, dramatics, etc.
2. Recreational activities including table games, social and folk dancing, trips and outings, camping, birthday and holiday parties, etc.
3. Forums and lectures on world affairs, current events, health, legal and consumer problems, legislation, and social action, etc.
4. Service projects for the center and the community.
5. Membership councils and committees.

Staff

1. Director—Administrator
2. Caseworker—Counselor. Interviews and enrolls new members.
3. Social groupworker. Directs group programs and coordinates the leadership

of teachers, recreation leaders, nurses, health educators assigned for specific times each week by the municipal adult education, recreation, and health departments.

B. *Individual Services* (personal services for members and other older adults in the neighborhood)

Purpose

To help solve personal problems that prevent individuals from benefiting from the activity program.

Scope of the Service Program

1. Friendly Visitors to ill members.
2. Hot lunch program.
3. Library.
4. Information and referral to other community services.
5. Multiphasic health screening: chest X ray, glaucoma detection, etc., in cooperation with the medical society.
6. Counseling on personal and family problems, health maintenance, employment counseling, housing, legal aid, etc.

Staff

1. Caseworker—director of individual services. Coordinates services given by

staff of other community agencies assigned to the center for specific hours
each week to counsel on health, housing, social security, old age assistance
grants, medicare, employment, legal
problems.

C. *Evaluation, Demonstration, Research*

Purpose

1. To provide a plan and process for the
continuous evaluation of the program and to
help set goals for future developments.

2. Through demonstration to contribute
new knowledge to the growing research in
social gerontology.

Scope of the Evaluation and Research
Program

1. Maintains records and reports by which
the center and its service can be evaluated.

2. Identifies new problems and needs.

3. Secures government grants and funds
from private foundations for the development of new programs and services.

4. Provides population and setting for
university-based research studies, both
applied and basic.

Staff

1. Director with research and "grants-

manship" skills who supervises students
engaged in research studies and volunteer statisticians and analysts.

D. *Training Programs*

Purpose

1. To provide leadership training for
board and center members, community volunteers, students, and paraprofessional aides
for working with older adults.

2. To maintain a training library of current materials.

Scope of the Training Programs

1. To conduct courses for board members
and orientation workshops for new
staff members.

2. To train community volunteers and program aides to work in satellite clubs.

3. To train volunteers for friendly visitors,
meals-on-wheels, escort service, and
other reaching-out programs.

4. To provide a field work experience for
recreation, social work, nursing, and
other students in related professional
fields.

Staff

1. Training director who coordinates the
leadership of volunteer teachers, social
workers, and public health nurses as
they teach groups at the center.

Satellite centers in the neighborhood make the program available to more people

Decentralizing the program of the central multiservice senior center
into satellite clubs makes it possible to reach those older adults who
are psychologically and physically unable to leave familiar areas and
travel long distances to participate in a downtown area center. For
some older persons the smaller club meeting in a familiar neighborhood
church, school, housing project, community center, home for the aged,
library, or courthouse is more acceptable and accessible. The neighborhood club is more homogeneous in membership, and the individuals
are more apt to know and feel comfortable with one another. Many
older adults living on poverty-level incomes resist joining centers located in the more prosperous middle-class areas of the city because
they feel uncomfortable about their clothing. Difficulties of getting off

and on buses and the cost of bus fare are also eliminated in satellite centers.

Facilities used for neighborhood clubs should have high visibility; a storefront next to a grocery store or drug store where older people can look in and see what is going on is particularly appropriate. Where no suitable meeting place for a satellite club is available, a trailer or mobile unit located in different areas on specific days takes the program to the neighborhood and makes it possible to reach more people. This plan also makes feasible the sharing of expensive program equipment and supplies by a number of clubs.

The extensive and inclusive program described in Chart 4 will not be achieved immediately in any community. It will be a developmental process extending over a number of years with activities and services being added as budget and leadership become available. One of the most serious roadblocks in developing comprehensive services for older people lies in the operational patterns of some old-line agencies and their inability to adapt their procedures to provide their services in new settings. Innovative ways of providing essential services to older people have challenged traditional patterns in many communities. Coordinated planning between old established agencies and new ones, between voluntary agencies and tax-supported ones, and with governmental bodies at local, state, and national levels are all essential. Only through coordination of the existing services and the development of essential new services can the needs of older people be met without duplication of cost and effort. The development of centers in the future will be dependent on the ability of voluntary and public agencies to work in close cooperation and to compete with other pressing community needs for adequate financial support.

Clubs sponsored by altruistic organizations also provide social opportunities for older adults

In many communities, social activities for older citizens are provided by numerous social clubs sponsored by civic groups, churches, synagogues, recreation departments, and patriotic, fraternal, and service organizations. Operating funds, leadership, entertainment, and transportation are contributed by the sponsors. Such club groups are known as golden age or senior citizens clubs. Generally they meet weekly or semimonthly for three or four hours around the middle of the day. The groups are small and homogeneous in respect to social class and interests, and members are usually younger than center members. Most such clubs have a stated open membership policy. Most individuals would not feel free to join, however, unless invited by one of the members. The membership of such clubs becomes selective on the basis of the sponsoring group. A club sponsored by a welfare department is conceived by older people and by the community to be for welfare clients only. If the group meets in a public housing project, many conclude that it is only for the tenants, and if it is sponsored by a church, that it is for the members of that particular denomination. If the club meets in an institution for the aged, few nonresidents would feel free to attend unless individually invited to do so. Projects funded by the Office of Economic Opportunity usually attract only those individuals who live in a specific poverty area of the community. If these natural selective barriers are to be surmounted, special effort must often be made to interpret the purpose and inclusiveness of the group and to develop reaching-out processes to encourage all interested older persons to join.

The responsibilities that members carry for the group are also determined by the nature of the sponsoring organization. If the sponsoring group is one whose major emphasis is volunteer community service, then the group members, and not the older people themselves, operate and plan the program. One of the most significant contributions informal social groups make to older adults is the opportunity to experience the recognition, satisfaction, status, and approval that comes from carrying leadership roles and responsibilities.

With the limited meeting time, club programs cannot be as diversified as those of multiservice senior centers. The programs generally reflect the interests of social, activity-oriented individuals and are often limited to card playing, social dancing, parties, entertainment, and refreshments. These programs become defended and protected from change by the "in" group and only those older adults who enjoy these specific social activities join. In clubs where there is no nongroup member as the leader, conflicts inevitably arise over authority roles and personal relations among members often become hostile and disruptive. Unless such conflicts are skillfully handled they eventually disrupt the group and prove emotionally disturbing to the very individuals who need acceptance and understanding.

There are many more social clubs than multiservice centers. A weekly club meeting will be adequate for some older adults to break the isolation and loneliness that they begin to feel. For others the wider opportunities found in senior centers will be more meaningful. Each type of program makes its own unique and significant contribution to its members. In the years ahead, new organizational patterns and programs will be developed to serve many more older adults not yet being reached in large numbers by either clubs or centers. These will include many more members of minority and poverty groups, as well as those with special emotional and physical problems.

Opportunities for social activities are also recognized as essential for older adults living in retirement communities, housing projects, residential care facilities, and nursing homes. These programs will be covered in chapter 18.

BIBLIOGRAPHY

Cohen, Deborah B., ed. *Senior Centers: The New Look*. First Annual Report Massachusetts Institute on Senior Centers, Boston, Mass., April 15, 1966. Boston: Boston Commission on Aging and United Community Aid Service of Metropolitan Boston, 1966.

Cohen, Morris. "The Multipurpose Senior Center." *Centers for Older People Newsletter*. 2 (1969): 2.

Eckstein, Rebecca. *Senior Centers Today: New Opportunities, New Challenges*. Washington, D.C.: National Council on the Aging, 1968.

Frankel, Godfrey. "The Multi-Purpose Senior Citizens Center: A New Comprehensive Agency." *The Gerontologist* 6 (1966): 23-27.

Institute for Interdisciplinary Studies. *Senior Centers: A National Directory*. Prepared under contract with the Administration on Aging, U.S. Department of Health, Education and Welfare. Washington, D.C.: Government Printing Office, 1969; rev. 1970.

Kaplan, Jerome. *A Social Program for Older People*. Minneapolis: University of Minnesota Press, 1953.

———. "Functions and Objectives of a Senior Citizens Center." *Geriatrics* 17 (1962): 771-77.

Kubie, Susan H., and Landau, Gertrude. *Group Work with the Aged*. New York: International Universities Press, 1953.

Levine, Harry A. "Community Programs for the Elderly." *Annals of the American Academy of Political and Social Science* 279 (1952): 164-170.

Maxwell, Jean M. *Centers for Older People: Guide for Programs and Facilities*. New York: National Council on the Aging, 1962.

Morton, Malcolm, ed. *Senior Centers*. Chicago: American Public Welfare Association, 1968.

National Council on the Aging. *Challenges facing senior centers in the 1970's*. Alice D. Wolfson, ed. Fifth National Conference of Senior Centers. Proceedings of a conference held in Washington, D.C., 1969.

———. *First national conference of senior centers*. Ella Lindey, ed. Proceedings of a conference held in Chicago, 1964. New York (1965).

———. *The multi-purpose center for older people; new focal point for social services, social planning and action.* Papers presented at the National Conference on Social Welfare, 1966. New York (1966).

———. *The multi-purpose senior center.* National Council on Aging for the Community Action Program of the Office of Economic Opportunity, 1969.

———. *National directory of senior centers.* In cooperation with the President's Council on Aging, Washington, D.C.: U.S. Printing Office (1966).

———. *Planning today for tomorrow's older people.* Rebecca Ekstein, ed. Third National Conference of Senior Centers. Proceedings of a conference held in Detroit, Michigan, 1966. New York (1966).

———. *Resources for the aging: an action handbook.* In cooperation with the Office of Economic Opportunity. New York (1969).

———. *The senior center and the Great Society.* Leah Lauter, ed. Proceedings of the Second National Conference of Senior Centers, held in Washington, D.C., 1965. New York (1965).

———. *Social group work with older people.* Proceedings of the seminar on "Social Group Work with Older People," Lake Mohonk, New Paltz, New York, 1961, co-sponsored by the American Public Welfare Association, National Council on the Aging, National Institute of Mental Health, and National Association of Social Workers. New York: National Association of Social Workers (1963).

———. *Tomorrow's centers: a symposium of papers.* Centers for Older People—Exploratory Conference, New York City, 1962. New York (1963).

Note: unless otherwise indicated above, publications issued by the National Council on the Aging are published by that organization in New York City.

President's Council on Aging: Subcommittee on Senior Centers. *The Senior Center: Its Goals, Functions and Programs.* Washington, D.C.: U.S. Government Printing Office, 1964.

Sussman, Evelyn K. "A Golden Age Center." *Adult Leadership* 12 (1963): 13-14, 22.

Swenson, Wendell E. "A Multi-purpose Senior Citizens' Service in a Historical Setting." Final Report to AOA Mayo Clinic, Department of Clinical Psychology (mineographed). Rochester, Minn.: Mayo Clinic, 1970.

Vickery, Florence E. "A Multi-service Senior Center: Its Unique Role and Function." *The Gerontologist* 5 (1965): 246-249, 277.

Wolfson, Alice D. *Challenges Facing Senior Centers in the 1970's.* Report of the Fifth National Conference of Senior Centers. New York: National Council on the Aging, 1969.

Woods, James H. *Helping Older People Enjoy Life.* New York: Harper & Brothers, 1958.

Youmans, E. "Personal Adjustments of Older Rural and Urban Citizens," in *Social Change and Aging in the 20th Century,* Daniel Allejar, ed. (pp. 159-179). Report of the 13th Annual Southern Conference on Gerontology. Gainesville, Fla.: University of Florida Press, 1964.

10 / The Membership of Senior Centers and Clubs: Who Will Join?

EVERY TENTH PERSON IN AMERICA TODAY is sixty-five years and older. Not all will be interested in belonging to groups of age mates. Many will continue to lead active social lives with spouses, families, and friends and maintain their memberships in religious, patriotic, service, fraternal, and professional organizations. They will continue their life-long patterns of attending concerts and movies, adult education classes, and sports events. They will visit museums and art galleries and enjoy their longtime associations in card clubs, garden, and hobby groups. Other older adults, who will lose life mates and face other crises, will begin to feel themselves cut off from life and isolated. Loneliness and feelings of uselessness are human problems that cut across all barriers of social class, economic status, and educational, ethnic, and racial backgrounds. This chapter considers the reasons why some older adults join senior citizen organizations while others reject identification with their peers in organized groups.

The number of older adults joining senior centers is increasing

A decade ago, studies showed that a surprisingly small number of eligible older adults joined senior centers. In 1956 only one percent of the older adults in New York City [1] and five percent of those in Syracuse, New York, belonged to senior centers.[2] A study made by Peter Townsend in 1957 of a working-class district in London showed 12 percent of the older people there involved in community-sponsored

[1] Bernard Kutner, *Five Hundred Over Sixty: A Community Survey on Aging* (New York: Russell Sage Foundation, 1965), p. 225.
[2] Joseph Downing, "Factors Affecting the Selective Use of a Social Club for the Aged," *Journal of Gerontology,* 12:81-84 (January 1957).

social activities.[3] A more recent investigation on the effectiveness of senior centers in reaching those individuals who need them most, projected a formula for determining how many individuals should form the target population. The projected number was arrived at by dividing the number of senior centers in a community into its total population of people sixty-five years of age and over. This figure became the social indicator of the number of older adults who should be served. It was found that in 1969 senior centers were serving approximately 33 percent of this target population.[4]

A phenomenon described by sociologist Arnold Rose as "aging group consciousness" has developed over the past decade. A growing number of older adults think of themselves as members of the aging group in American society. They feel a great sense of group pride and a desire to associate with people of the same age, especially in formal associations. As centers have developed more sophisticated programs, membership in them has become a more acceptable social role and the percentage of older adults joining them has increased.[5] More women than men become members, and more women who have worked outside their homes become members than women who were only housewives. Approximately 50 percent join within two years after experiencing a major change, such as retirement, loss of a spouse, or moving to a new community. The percentage of members in each older age group declines progressively each succeeding decade. About one-fourth of the members drop out or are replaced each year for reasons of death, moving away, health, or lack of transportation. In the early years those who participated were not only of relatively high social and economic status but also generally active and well integrated in their other social roles.[6] As outreach programs have been developed, more hard-to-reach and socially deprived older adults are now found within the memberships of senior centers.

[3] Peter Townsend, *The Family Life of Old People.* (Glencoe, Ill.: Free Press, 1957), p. 216.

[4] Nancy N. Anderson, *Senior Centers: Information from a National Survey* (Washington, D.C.: U.S. Department of Health, Education and Welfare, 1969).

[5] Arnold M. Rose, "The Subculture of the Aging: A Topic for Sociological Research," *The Gerontologist,* 2:123-27 (September 1962).

[6] Ruth Storey, *Older People Tell Their Story* (Stanford: Stanford University Press, 1962), pp. 216-22.

Senior centers attract people who have always been joiners

Many socially adequate, emotionally healthy individuals who have been active in social groups all their lives readily join senior centers upon retirement. They are freer than ever before to choose how they will use their free time and are attracted by the social activities, trips, and classes that are scheduled. Some join hoping to find opportunities to be of service to the group and in the community; others are primarily interested in meeting new friends to replace those they have lost. After a period of mourning, many widows and widowers join groups of age mates to make new heterosexual contacts. All of these older adults are easy to interest in membership, and they come with little sense of inadequacy or of having personal problems that they themselves are unable to handle.

Among those who join groups on their own initiative are those who seem to have an almost insatiable need for social activity. They join three or four groups, attending a different one each day. Their overactivity has an almost frenetic quality, and few satisfying relationships with other individuals result. Such extreme patterns of busyness are often used by an individual as a defense against his anxieties around growing old.

Some groups serve only men or only women; both men and women are members of multiservice senior centers

Many club groups have memberships made up exclusively of women. Others, sponsored by unions, professional societies, and lodges, have only men. Multiservice centers with more diversified programs attract both men and women. The ratio of men to women members, however, is generally much smaller than in the population as a whole. In a 1960 study prepared for the White House Conference on Aging it was found that between the ages of forty-five and fifty-four years there were five percent more women than men, in the population. At age eighty-five this ratio had increased to 46 percent.[7] Men in general and specifically professional men and those who have retired from white collar jobs are a hard-to-reach group.

Most older couples continue to be active in the friendship groups of which they have been members during their middle-adult years. Many

[7] U.S., Department of Health, Education and Welfare, *White House Conference on Aging Chart Book,* 1960, p. 10.

thoughtful couples do join senior centers, recognizing that it is wise to be active together in a large social group as a kind of insurance against the time when one will be left alone. Other couples do not join groups because they are not secure enough in their mutual relationships to trust one another to participate in heterosexual groups.

Many older adults who are new in the community become members

Newcomers in the community find membership in a senior center of great help in meeting congenial age mates. On the death of a spouse, many older persons leave familiar surroundings and friends and move to new communities to join adult children and their families. They have not foreseen how lonely they will be in a strange city while children and grandchildren are at work and in school. In addition to new friends and interesting activities, membership in senior centers makes it possible for the older person again to establish his own identity and have an independent social life. Mrs. R's case is an example.

> *The case of Mrs. R.* Mrs. R, seventy-four years old, lived in the East for forty-six years. After the death of her husband she made her living baby-sitting. She had two married sons who were ready for retirement from the regular army in 1967 and 1968. One was stationed on the East Coast, the other on the West Coast. She lived in the home of her daughter-in-law and grandson in New Jersey after her husband died and paid her share of the household expenses. During this time she saved $1,200 and, when she quit work, had become eligible for $30 social security.
>
> After retiring from the service, her son in the East informed his mother that she could no longer stay with him and his family and stated that it was time for the other son to have her in his home. The son on the West Coast agreed that he could give her a room but could not support her otherwise because he had heavy expenses for the medical care of a child. Mrs. R paid her own traveling expenses and agreed to pay her son twelve dollars a month for board. She stayed in her room most of the time except at meals because her daughter-in-law resented her being in the home. She was distraught about her treatment in her son's home and apprehensive about what would happen when her savings were exhausted.
>
> Reading in a local newspaper about a senior center, Mrs. R applied for membership. She spent much of her time for the next six months at the center. She made friends and helped in the center's program in many ways, which made her feel useful and wanted. As a result, she

became emotionally more stable and self-assured, and the counselor encouraged her to look for a job. She found a live-in position caring for an elderly woman. Able to maintain herself independently, she would attend the center on her days off to see her friends and enjoy the activities.

Individuals who would benefit often do not join social groups

Some older adults who would benefit from and enjoy the programs of senior centers will not join. In 1952 the Community Service Society of New York made a survey of a neighborhood where a large number of older people lived. They found that in addition to the individuals in their sample who had joined a nearby center, another four percent of those interviewed knew about the center and said they needed the service but had made no effort to join. An additional four percent of those interviewed, who were assessed by the interviewers as needing the services, did not recognize their own needs and had negative attitudes about centers.

Increasing attention and outreach efforts are being focused today on those older adults for whom senior centers could provide therapeutic social and emotional experiences but who do not come easily on their own initiative. Among these are individuals unable to admit to themselves, much less to others, that they have grown old. Living in a youth-oriented culture, they feel that to be old carries the connotation of being of less value. These older adults resist any possibility that they may be so considered by other people. Unfortunately, to many people in the community senior centers carry the erroneous image of "the place where old people go to play." This attitude in the community keeps many who would benefit from the activities from joining. Such false and frequently heard stereotypes as "older people are just like children" or "he acts thus and so because he's in his second childhood" justify somewhat the reluctance of some individuals to identify themselves as members of senior centers.

Social experiences in earlier life periods have not been successful for some older adults

Certain older persons do not become members because they are shy and feel ill at ease with strangers. Socially insecure men have never joined social groups, and many shy women have depended on their husbands for their sense of security in all social situations outside the home. Such men and women often felt themselves failures socially when they were younger and fear risking themselves again in similar circumstances. Unless some effort is made to invite them specifically, they rarely join a group. If they do, they drop out after any experience that they interpret as rejection by other members and retreat more deeply into their feelings of failure, inadequacy, and loneliness.

There are some individuals who do not join centers because they have been hurt earlier in life by others and have never learned to trust enough to relate comfortably again to other people. They seem to have built up high walls of defense around themselves and never allow others to come emotionally or physically too close. They do not join groups that meet in the hotels, apartment houses, or housing projects where they live. To do so would then obligate them to be friendly with the members outside the group, in the halls, the elevators, or the lobbies where they chance to meet. Mrs. F is an example of such a self-insulated individual.

The case of Mrs. F. Mrs. F was referred to a center by a medical social worker who had placed her in a residential hotel after she was released from the hospital following a stroke. Mrs. F had been left with paralysis of an arm and leg, which made it difficult for her to walk or to care for herself. She was referred by the social worker to the center because of her increasing isolation. The referring worker thought that if Mrs. F could be encouraged to attend the group meeting in the same hotel, she could be helped to find new interests and new friends.

Mrs. F's anger and bitterness over her situation were alienating other hotel guests. No one would now speak to her and she was withdrawing more and more. She sat all day in her room watching television except when she went to the dining room for two meals a day. She would take no exercise. Her social worker felt that in time she would become completely mentally and physically incapacitated. Mrs. F was very critical of other residents and was pressuring her social worker to help her leave the hotel and take an apartment, in spite of the fact that she would be unable to care for herself.

After some careful planning in view of Mrs. F's hostile behavior, the hospital worker introduced the center's outreach worker to Mrs. F. Mrs. F said angrily to the hospital worker, "I told you I didn't want to hear about the club or the center or any of these activities," and turned the television on to full volume. Conversation ceased on that interview. On subsequent weekly visits by the center's counselor, Mrs. F's television was turned lower and lower, which became a sign of progress in the building of a relationship. One day Mrs. F turned on the picture, but not the sound, so she could hear the worker. The next time she turned off the television. During these visits nothing more was said about the club, but the conversation was focused on Mrs. F's feelings about her current situation, her interests, satisfactions in her past life, and her current assets. On a later visit, Mrs. F said suddenly, "What's going on in the club today?" and began to take an interest in its activities.

Some homemade Christmas bells were taken by the worker to Mrs. F who, surprisingly, hung them on her door in spite of the fact she wanted to ignore the holiday season. Mrs. F said proudly on the next visit, "So many people have admired these bells and wanted to know how they are made. I want you to tell me how." After that, Mrs. F began leaving her door open so she could talk to the other residents as they went by. She no longer talked about leaving the hotel. During the last interview, Mrs. F said suddenly to the worker, "I am a woman of few words—but I want you to know that you have meant a lot to me." [8]

Some members are referred by their doctors and other concerned persons

Doctors often refer older patients to senior centers when they find that loneliness and anxiety, rather than pathological conditions, are the basis of an illness. Such older people often show great resistance to joining and may interpret referral as the doctor's attempt to get rid of them. Anxious older persons endow a doctor with magical powers and feel that, as long as they have his attention and care, nothing can happen to them. Many geriatricians recognize that senior centers can offer valuable supportive services in the treatment of their older patients, as was true for Miss S and Mrs. B.

> *The case of Miss S.* Miss S came to a center to inquire about membership at the insistence of her doctor. She had recently been released from a mental hospital where she had been a patient for three years. She was neatly dressed, precise in speech and manner, and very sensitive regarding the subject of age. Although she was not pressed, she did not want to tell her age, saying, "I want to forget my birthday. I would not think of celebrating it." When talking to the counselor, her first question was, "Are there many very old members in the center?"
>
> It appeared from the first contact that one of Miss S's emotional problems was her inability to face old age. She had been a secretary since she finished school. She had a married sister in a nearby community with whom she spent many weekends, but she needed something to occupy her time during the week. She said she attended concerts and

[8] F. Estelle Booth, *Reaching the Hard-to-Reach Older Person.* (San Francisco: San Francisco Senior Center, 1967).

symphonies during the week, but her doctor advised her that she "should learn to do something herself and not go so frequently to entertainments."

Miss S was introduced to one of the members who recognized her as a girl she knew when she was in high school. Miss S said she did not remember any of the incidents mentioned and it was clear that she wanted to discontinue the contact. Other introductions showed that Miss S was ill at ease when coming into contact with other members even though they were younger than she was. She showed some interest in the art work of the center and began attending the group, which might have been in an effort to follow her doctor's suggestion to learn to do something herself and still avoid close contact with others.

The case of Mrs. B. Mrs. B called the center for an appointment to talk about membership. She said she was calling on the advice of a psychiatrist. She had come to the community from the Middle West where she and her husband had lived for ten years. A few months before leaving the Middle West she had divorced her husband. The blow to her pride and prestige, together with the difficulties in arranging a property settlement, had caused a severe emotional breakdown. Over and over again she said, "I never thought there would be a situation I could not handle but now there is. I feel like a misfit in the world today. There is no color any more; everything is gray."

If an older person has sufficient ego-strength and self-esteem, he follows through confidently on a referral by a doctor, lawyer, banker, or other person trying to help him. If his self-image is poor and his motivation weak, he may follow through on the referral only in fear that if he does not, he may displease the one whose interest and concern give him some sense of personal worth and security. He will come once or twice, and then drops out, making various excuses about the lack of interest in the program or the unfriendliness of the people.

Adult children often bring their parents to a center. A sensitive older person, conscious of the reversal of roles that has taken place between himself and his child and feeling already rejected in some degree by his children, interprets his child's efforts to interest him in a social group of his peers as further rejection and an effort to be rid of growing responsibility and concern for him. Unless the aged parent is himself interested in joining, he soon becomes discouraged because of minor reasons and decides that any satisfactions he might have in being a member will not compensate for the exertion that he must make and the psychological discomfort that he may experience in relating to new people and participating in activities.

*Few centers are able to serve
emotionally disturbed older adults*

Frequently individuals applying for membership have obvious mental
and emotional conditions that would prevent them from relating meaningfully to other members or participating independently in activities.
They usually have been referred by doctors who do not understand the
nature and limits of the services and programs of a senior center or
by adult children who hope to use the center for day care for their
problem parents. Few senior centers are geared to serve senile, deteriorated older adults, but most recognize their responsibility to contact
the family or physician and work with them on an appropriate referral.
Centers are often able to accept an individual who shows signs of deterioration if his spouse also joins. The social and emotional needs of
the well member of the couple can often be met while he is also helped
by the counselor to understand and plan care for his deteriorating
spouse.

Men as a group are hard to reach

Although many men move easily from jobs into membership and participation in leisure organizations they are, as a group, hard to reach.
It is difficult for many men to change attitudes and interests that have
been work oriented to those that emphasize leisure and self-fulfilling
activities. Membership in social groups has not been of as much interest
to them as it has been to their wives. Whereas women are restricted as
to where they can go unaccompanied, men are more free to move
about wherever they will and enjoy informal social interaction with
other men. They fraternize on the street corner, at sports events, on a
park bench, at commercial recreation of all kinds, and in lodge and
fraternal halls. Some men resist becoming involved in structured social
groups, feeling that they do not have the conversational skills to fit
comfortably into a group where women predominate. Men miss the
"man's talk" they had on the job and do not enjoy arguing politics and
other public issues with women. In certain nationality groups, socialization of men and women in public is not culturally acceptable.

Men as a group will be older than women when they join a center.
They will have enjoyed a period of complete freedom from job routines
and will have fulfilled their immediate retirement dreams of going fishing, working in the garden, traveling, and visiting the children in distant
cities. After a time many men begin to feel in the way of the social and

homemaking activities of their wives and look for opportunities to be out of the house and with other men for portions of the day. For some men, recently widowed, to be with women may be too painful. For others, heterosexual groups offer welcomed opportunities to meet possible marriage partners.

Many men, in applying for membership in clubs and centers, acknowledge that they have known there were such organizations for a number of years but have felt no need to join them. Culturally it is more difficult for men than for women to acknowledge loneliness and a need to feel a sense of belonging. They often remark, when they come for the first time, "I was just passing by and thought I would drop in to see what was going on." Men do not disclose how many times before they have come and looked in to be sure that there were other men present but, lacking the courage to enter, have walked on. An informal, unstructured drop-in type program with a male worker in charge makes it possible for many men to be immediately at ease and decide to join.

The living patterns of men when they become widowed also influence their need to affiliate with senior clubs and centers. When men are alone, they are likely to move into the downtown small hotels on the fringe of the commercial districts where shops and restaurants are available and rents are low enough to be met by old age pensions and social security payments. Hotels have lobbies where they can sit and enjoy ready conversation with others and watch people go by. When women leave their homes where they reared their children, it is more often to smaller apartments. Here there are no lobbies comparable to those in hotels where they can spend large portions of the day socializing with other women. They find this opportunity at senior centers.

Men who have been isolates or social misfits all of their lives will not be attracted to social groups of their peers. For such men a lifetime pattern of social withdrawal has become a rigid personality defense that, in old age, cannot be changed. Men of this type are usually single and of a very low socioeconomic status. They have lived alone during all of their adult lives. They usually left home at an early age and drifted from place to place earning a living by strenuous physical effort. They have maintained no contact with relatives or friends and have developed no continuing intimate relationships with women. Their lifelong patterns of isolation, however, may protect them in old age from being as vulnerable as others to the hurts and feelings of loss of loved persons.

Special outreach is needed to serve the emotionally depressed older person

As the more physically and socially adequate older people fill centers to capacity, thoughtful administrators ask themselves if they are serving the people who need them the most. What is happening to the socially, economically, and physically disadvantaged person who does not join? Will the programs contribute enough to the social and emotional rehabilitation of a depressed aged individual to enable him to function again in the community? There are many older adults who find that they no longer have the physical and emotional strength to meet the increasing problems of everyday life. They lose hope, become depressed, and feel defeated when physical or mental illness, the loss of a spouse or children, and diminishing finances force them to move to new neighborhoods and similar stresses once again fill their lives. They do not expect that their situations can be improved or that they can again have any pleasures in life. They do not respond to newspaper invitations or even to personal notes and telephone calls urging them to become center members.

If such depressed individuals are to be served, carefully coordinated plans must be made for a home visit by the staff member of the social agency making the referral and a representative from the senior center. Only the individual who knows the older person best and in whom he has confidence will be able to persuade him to try a visit to a center. More than one home visit may be necessary before the aged person can be persuaded to try himself in the new situation. If he comes, he will carry with him negative expectations. His initial experience at the center must be one that puts him at ease and gives him immediate emotional rewards and a maximum sense of well being. With enough individual attention and support by the staff and understanding volunteers, such individuals can be helped to become members. If they are not reached by agency staffs and brought out of their isolation and depression, or if they have no continuing close relationship with another person who serves as confidant, they frequently must be admitted to mental hospitals. Membership in groups that make possible some meaningful emotional involvement with at least one other person is one of the best defenses against hospitalization.

> *The case of Mr. K.* Mr. K, sixty-nine years old, was born in a small community in the Middle West and never married. He was employed in a furniture factory and voluntarily retired in 1955 because his health was not good. Following an operation in 1957 he completely

lost his memory and became emotionally unstable. He was sent to a state hospital where he stayed a year. He carried a prepaid voluntary health insurance.

Living in one room in a small hotel, Mr. K had no known living relatives. He cooked his own meals and spent most of his time reading detective stories and taking long walks. He said he would get very lonely and not know what to do with his time. "Although I am not a drinking man, I often go into bars as they are places where I can speak to someone without embarrassment," he explained.

Mr. K became a member of a center where he took no initiative in getting acquainted but was friendly with those who approached him. He said it had been a good many years since he had danced, but at the invitation of two hosts on the social committee he attended two evening dances at the center and enjoyed them very much. The hosts introduced him to his partners. The fourth week one of the hostesses encouraged him to participate in a card game that he had never played before; the other three members at the table were friendly and willing to teach him. The day of the bazaar dinner he worked all afternoon carrying merchandise for the women who were setting up the booths.

Mr. K needed to be useful and have some responsibility. He needed to make friends and feel accepted by the group. A beginning had been made but the staff still had much work to do, both with Mr. K and the committee, to give him the security he needed to make meaningful new relationships.

Few older people of minority groups join centers

In addition to social and psychological factors that limit the participation of some older people, more subtle and less understood cultural factors deter many older adults of ethnic and racial minorities from participating in intergroup experiences with age mates. Most multiservice senior centers—along with schools, churches, recreation agencies, and the mass media—reflect the middle-class white core culture in their leadership, program content, and goals. Very few of the present generation of older adults from ethnic minorities are active in community sponsored senior centers. These older adults participate socially more often within their own cultural group rather than seek intergroup social experiences. Even after some assimilation has occurred, most individuals still have a feeling of identification with the culture and traditions of their own ethnic heritage and prefer to socialize within it. They do not find that social interaction with other groups is meaningful for them.

Will clubs and centers sponsored by specific nationality, racial, or economic groups to serve their aged be needed in addition to community sponsored multiservice organizations and their satellite groups? Little is known about how the problems of growing old may be compounded for an older adult of a minority group. It is not yet clear to what extent members of the older generation will become involved in the struggles of the young activists within ethnic and social groups who distrust the dominant middle class and its institutions. Will it be possible to make intergroup experiences in centers meaningful enough to overcome the negative and discriminatory experiences that older people of most minority groups have encountered throughout life in the white middle-class society?

Many of the older black men and women living in large cities have come from rural backgrounds. As they have moved into the ghettos of large cities they have become part of a street corner society of black people with friends and neighbors nearby. Is it realistic to expect that they can, or will, leave familiar places and accepting persons to travel to strange parts of the city and expose themselves to the possible rejection of a predominantly white group? The leadership of centers is often troubled by the failure of sincere and consistent efforts to involve older black people in the programs. "We invite them but they do not come! They don't take advantage of the opportunities offered them." Many white leaders are unable to realize that all the older black people hear them saying is, "Come and be hurt again." It is unrealistic to believe that the white middle-class membership of most senior centers will be more accepting of members of the black community than they have been in other settings throughout their lives.

Studies made by Margaret Clark at the Langley Porter Psychiatric Institute in San Francisco show that prejudice toward members of minority groups decreases in individuals twenty years of age and still further in those thirty years old. Among those who are forty years old, the number of individuals who believe in the superiority of their own ethnic group and feel contempt for other cultures again begins to climb. Prejudice reaches its peak among subjects sixty years of age and over. Elderly white subjects who live in neighborhoods that are deteriorating into ghettos are not only more prejudiced than the white population generally but grow increasingly isolated socially as their prejudice increases.[9]

[9] M. Margaret Clark, "Racial and Ethnocentric Prejudices Much Greater Among White Residents of the 'Geriatric Ghetto,'" *Geriatric Focus,* 6:2, 3 (September 15, 1967).

According to William Grier and Price Cobb, two contemporary black psychiatrists, white people in our society have been imbued with the belief that black people are inferior and are born to be subservient and perform menial labor. White immigrants to this country, these psychiatrists point out, have been made to feel welcome and have had black people to feel superior to. This oppression of black people has become incorporated into our folkways and has become a part of our national character to such a degree that certain stereotypes are not even recognized as prejudicial. Too many older Americans are among the white people who still feel no personal guilt or responsibility for the discriminatory treatment of black people in our society.[10]

Cultural and language barriers also keep many Oriental, Mexican-American, and American Indian older adults from joining community-wide senior centers. The inability to communicate with other members or to understand announcements and instructions makes the non-English-speaking older person feel isolated and uncomfortable. Some centers use younger people with bilingual skills and retired language teachers to serve as interpreters, but the psychological and social differences continue to make the integration of the older adults into the dominant English-speaking group very difficult. There is more expectation among some nationality groups than within the middle-class American family that the social needs of the older generation should be met by the family itself and by the nationality church. Older people within these generally low-income groups have more status within their families than do some older people with more affluent children. Old age assistance grants and social security checks make many such parents financial assets in the homes of their children.

In many communities there has been a proliferation of clubs and centers organized to serve specific groups of old people exclusively. Whether the program of any one center in a community can ever be administered broadly enough to be an effective integrating social instrument for serving all older citizens is a challenging question. To reach such a goal, the warm acceptance and sensitivity of the staff to older adults of minority groups and their success in maintaining impartial relationships with all members will be of critical importance. The policy-making group, staff and members alike, will find it essential to follow the six basic guide lines that are listed below.

1. It is necessary to plan a program that is sufficiently diversified to be relevant to and have meaning for the life-styles of all groups within the membership, for only then can there be meaningful continuity from

[10] William Grier and Price Cobb, *Black Rage* (New York: Basic Books, 1969).

the varied past life experiences of each member to the experiences of today. *What* is done in the program and the *manner* in which it is done must come out of the group rather than from the expectations and goals of the staff.

2. There must be adequate staff to help individuals become more accepting and sensitive to the differences in one another and to feel socially comfortable with one another in spite of differences.

3. In addition to many heterogeneous groups formed around various activity interests, a program to include large groups around spectator interests will be needed. This program would provide anonymity for those who are not initially comfortable in relating on a face-to-face basis to strangers who are different. Homogeneous groups based on nationality, language, and race are essential to help some individuals feel comfortable in their own group until they gain confidence to participate within a more diversified group. Trained workers are essential to handle hostile feelings and attitudes and to motivate individuals in their growth as effective members of groups.

4. There must be involvement in the planning, administration, and policy making of the project by representatives from the nationality, ethnic, or racial groups to be served. The dominant group in any community cannot plan *for* the older people of any minority group.

5. There must be significant promotion of the program and the interpretation of its goals to the potential members among minority groups to convince them that the club or center *is for them*. The richness that will be added to the program and in turn to the lives of the members as they share in one another's cultural heritage will make a senior center an inclusive fellowship of the community's older citizens.

6. City-wide councils composed of representatives from the membership of all groups should be formed. The staff of the senior center is the logical group in most communities to initiate a council organization. The responsibility of the council is the sponsorship of exchange programs among groups, holiday and patriotic celebrations, worship services, trips, community service projects, conferences, leadership training workshops, and joint projects of all kinds. In such groups all older people can come together across all nationality and racial lines in meaningful unity. From such occasions, if they are scheduled frequently enough, there can hopefully come the realization that experiences of

unity between people are more compelling than the fears, anxieties, and prejudices that have separated them.

A summary of principles concerning membership

1. The sponsoring group and the place of meeting often become selective factors in the membership of senior clubs and centers.

2. The more varied the programs and services, the more attractive senior groups will be to all the older people of the community.

3. There is little correlation between the accessibility of the center and those who use it.

4. The membership will represent a cross section of older adults ranging from the socially adequate and physically and emotionally healthy to the emotionally depressed and physically and mentally feeble.

5. The frequency of use of the center's program and services by individual members will differ widely. For some, attendance will be daily or at least three or four times a week. Others will maintain a more casual and tenuous relationship, attending only the special parties and social events. The older person who is facing a crisis may use only counseling and referral help and be unable to involve himself emotionally in the social program. Many older adults feel that they vicariously draw personal social status in being members of organizations that have prestige in the community and, therefore, maintain their membership even though they do not attend regularly.

6. For some, the group experiences with other members will be helpful in the maintenance of emotional and social health. These experiences will help to strengthen the individual's ability to continue to function effectively and independently in the community. For others, the personal stresses and deprivations of old age and the threatening experiences in the environment have been more than they have been able to cope with. Feelings of futility and loss of self-esteem have been inevitable. For those who are reached soon enough, membership in centers where they are in relationship with caring people and involved in experiences that give their days meaning may be *preventative*. Experiences and relationships with age mates will help to halt further disengagement and deterioration. For those who have become chronically depressed and withdrawn the program may even be *rehabilitative*. Required, however, is a staff that understands the dynamics of such behavior and is trained in rehabilitative and therapeutic techniques and procedures. More staff will be needed to work with hard-to-reach older people who need a rehabilitative experience. Some individuals have

such a need to receive that they find it hard to share the worker with others and often demand his full attention. While the counselor remains at the door to welcome members as they arrive and give special attention to those on the fringe of the group, the group leader carries the program activity.

BIBLIOGRAPHY

Anderson, Nancy. *Information from a National Survey,* Washington, D.C.: United States Department of Health, Education and Welfare, 1969.

Booth, F. Estelle. *Reaching Out to the Hard-to-Reach.* San Francisco: San Francisco Senior Center, 1969.

Downing, Joseph. "Factors Affecting the Selective Use of a Social Club for the Aged." *Journal of Gerontology* 12 (1957): 81-84.

Grier, William, and Cobb, Price. *Black Rage.* New York: Basic Books, 1969.

Kubie, Susan H., and Landau, Gertrude. *Group Work with the Aged.* New York: International Universities Press, 1953.

Kutner, Bernard. *Five Hundred Over Sixty: A Community Survey on Aging.* New York: Russell Sage Foundation, 1965.

National Council on the Aging. *Project: Find.* Prepared for the Community Action Program of the Office of Economic Opportunity, Washington, D.C., 1966.

Storey, Ruth. *Older People Tell Their Story.* Stanford, Calif.: Stanford University Press, 1962.

Townsend, Peter. *The Family Life of Old People.* Glencoe, Ill.: Free Press, 1957.

Vickery, Florence E. *How to Work with Older People.* Sacramento: Division of Recreation, State of California, 1960.

Woods, James H. *Helping Older People Enjoy Life.* New York: Harper & Brothers, 1958.

11 / Involving the Individual in the Group Experience

THE CHAPTERS IN PART II discussed the many personal and environmental factors that make aging for each individual a unique experience. If senior centers are successful in providing a setting in which the emotional and social needs of members can be met, then each member must be known as a person to each staff member. The well-defined social work process whereby this knowledge is achieved is called the "individualization process." Through it the staff learn to know each new member, his life-style, and the day-by-day stresses that confront him. Individualizing members also enables the staff to assess the individual's strengths and weaknesses, whether he will be able to accept leadership responsibilities, or whether he will need help in making friends and participating in the program. The dignity and concern with which the older adult is treated as he applies for membership can reinforce, support, and even change his image of himself as a person of worth.

The intake interview is the core of the individualization process

The degree to which a center is able to individualize each new member depends on the size of its staff and their skills. In small centers with a limited staff, and sometimes in large ones where many new members join each week, it is useful to have applicants meet as a group for a description of the center's program and the individual's responsibilities as a member. In those centers where there is a staff counselor or social worker, the intake interview—the core of the individualization process —is his responsibility. Where there is no worker with interview skills, those staff members who direct activities must assume the additional responsibility of talking face-to-face and establishing a personal rela-

156

tionship with each older person who joins. Many centers are successful in using community volunteers or other center members to secure essential objective information from the applicant. This information includes his name, address, telephone number, birth date, whom to call in an emergency, his current interests, and the center activities in which he would like to participate. This is adequate information and can easily be secured by another member or a volunteer if the objective of the program is limited to recreational activities. However, most older persons who join senior centers have personal problems and no one to whom they can verbalize their anxieties and fears. When children are not heard from, income checks fail to arrive, pains become more persistent, or loved ones who have been their emotional support are lost, many older adults become anxious and feel there is no one to comfort or to help. For such members the staff can offer a most important service. This supportive relationship, in which the individual is helped to mobilize his own strengths to solve his own problems, is a professional skill that staff members—not volunteers—are trained to handle.

The intake interview should be a friendly, informal, and flexible experience adapted to the older person's comfort and ease. It does not necessarily take place all at one time but may extend over a period of time. A casual chat as the new member waits in the lounge for his class to begin; a visit with him at the table while he is having a cup of coffee; a telephone call to tell him he has been missed during an absence— these all may be part of the intake procedure and produce in time all information necessary to know him as a person. A formal interview in an office across a desk with specific personal questions being asked is an anxiety-producing experience for some older adults and often results in understandable resistance. This reaction comes about especially if the elderly person has not initiated his own joining but has been referred by his children, doctor, lawyer, or a social agency. Such an older person sometimes feels he is being manipulated and sees the counselor as a party to a process that he is determined to resist. Other older adults are so anxious to become members that they take the initiative and ask when they will be told that they can join. Talking with a friendly, interested staff member helps some individuals to share readily their feelings of rejection, frustration, and loneliness. The interviewer must guard against permitting such older persons to talk too freely and share personal information that they later may feel they should not have revealed.

In some centers a medical consultant plays a key role in the individualization of members

In a limited number of large cities, the Department of Public Health is involved in the administration of the multiservice center. There is a physician on the staff and physical examinations, medical counseling and referrals are the primary services of the center.[1] The activities are supplementary and supporting to the main health-related function. In such centers the intake process includes a physical examination and a comprehensive medical history. The staff physician works closely with the center's counselor and shares any information about the new member's physical condition that would affect his participation in the activities in the center. Pertinent facts are then shared with the program staff. A medical examination will become an integral part of the intake and individualization procedure of more multiservice senior centers as communities become aware of the many physical conditions that limit and, if not detected and treated, eventually cripple older adults.

The intake interview provides essential information about the new member

The counselor has the following three objectives for each intake interview.

1. To secure enough factual information about the individual to enable the staff to know him as a person. Through visits with him informally the counselor learns many of the facts included on the personal data card (see Form 1). He records this information on the card after the applicant leaves the office.

2. To give the new member information about the center and what his responsibilities as a member will be. The counselor describes the program and seeks to motivate the person to become active in it. The motivation process is a highly individualized one and requires that the counselor make a careful diagnosis of the individual's physical and emotional health. Only then can he know whether the older person is ready for high level activities and close personal relationships or if he will be able to function only as an observer for a period of time with no pressure to relate to other members. His tempo, gait, facial expressions, coloring and affective responses are all indices of his potential

[1] The Adult Health and Recreation Center sponsored by the Department of Public Health of Philadelphia, Pennsylvania, is an outstanding center of this kind.

Form 1

Individual Personal Data Card

Confidential			No. _____

Surname	First name	Birth date	Place of birth	Date applied
				Date of membership
				Referred by
Address		Tel.	Own home ( ) Apt. ( ) Furn. room ( ) Lives with	Relationship
Sex Marital status Death of spouse Occupation present or past			Is a retired or days employed	Reason for retirement
IN	Physician		Address	Tel.
EMERGENCY and NOTIFY			Address , Relationship	Tel.
HEALTH Limitations, medical insurance, etc.				
LEISURE-TIME INTERESTS Hobbies; organizations, etc.; attitude toward group participation				CENTER programs preferred
PRESENT SITUATION, including REASON for COMING to the CENTER				
FINANCES (if volunteered)	EDUCATION (if volunteered)		RELIGION (if volunteered)	

for good or poor social functioning and his readiness for center membership.

3. To give the counselor an opportunity to express to the older person his concern and interest in him and to lay the ground work for further discussions in the future with the new member about his health and other worrisome problems. Some older persons who are without close friends and family quickly reach out to form a dependency relationship with anyone who shows an interest in them. Without the supportive help of a staff member, many crisis-ridden older people do not follow through on the initial interview and become active members. However, a counselor who becomes too supportive, too "mothering," and too needlessly anxious infantalizes the older person and increases his dependency. Every older adult, however frail or confused he may be, should be addressed and treated as a mature adult.

At weekly review sessions the intake staff member shares informtaion about new members with the program staff

Because it is the program staff that will be directly involved with the new member as he participates in the various activities, it is important that the counselor share such information as will help the staff to relate meaningfully to him. The counselor does so by writing short social summaries about the individuals whom he has interviewed and reviewing them at weekly staff meetings. The confidential nature of these summaries makes it imperative that they be kept in locked files. The summary includes something about the applicant's present life-style, living family members, his past work experiences, and his statement about his health. Also included is the worker's evaluation of how the program can be most helpful to the new member. Staff members are then assigned the responsibility to follow through on those individuals who have indicated an interest in the groups for which they are responsible. This staff follow-through includes welcoming the member the next time he comes to the center and introducing him to the leader and members of the group or class that he has chosen to attend. Group attendance records are important to enable the staff to know whether the member attends and is involved in the program. If there are extended or frequent absences, the staff member telephones or writes the member to assure him that he has been missed. Such individual attention often leads the older person to comment, "How good it feels to be missed" or "You make me feel that I really do count."

The personal summaries written by the counsellor should be concise and contain only pertinent information. The following are samples.

Mr. S. Mr. S is a loquacious little man of eighty-six years. He gives a first impression of being very pompous but as the interview proceeded I detected a sadness and depression in his remarks. He spoke of his "wonderful children" and how proud he is of them, but I think he is feeling rejected. They all live in other cities and he has little contact with them. Mr. S was a well-qualified engineer. He has been an evaluator for a railroad and lived in many communities in the West. He has been a widower for the past twenty years. His two sons are professional men in the East. A married daughter lives in a nearby community. Mr. S is scruffy in appearance. His suit was old, worn, and wrinkled. His alert mind belies his age. He receives a pension of seventy dollars a month from a railroad retirement fund in addition to ninety-one dollars social security. For the past four weeks he has been suffering from a heavy bronchial cold and cough and seemed frightened by this. He has not seen a doctor for twenty-five years. He told me that he will visit his daughter next week and will go to see her doctor while there. He indicated an interest in the Forum, learning Spanish, and Men's Day. He will need help in making initial contacts with other men. His acceptance by women will be even slower.

Mr. W. Mr. W, a solemn-looking seventy-two-year-old man, came to the center after reading an article about it in a local paper. He has been retired for only three months and seemed depressed and almost tearful. He was in business for thirty-four years. In order to conduct his business he had to be a member of a union. He is now drawing a union pension as well as social security. He feels he is in the way at home and tries to be away part of every day. When I asked about his wife and her interest in joining, he stated that she belonged to several clubs, had many friends, and was not interested in joining. Mr. W likes music and showed an interest in the Symphony Preview Group. He would like to go with the group from the center to the next concert if a group ticket can be obtained for him. He also indicated an interest in the Men's Club. He wants to sample several groups and then pick those he wishes to attend. My impression is that Mr. W has some leadership ability.

Mrs. B. Mrs. B, accompanied by her daughter, visited the center when they were shopping in the neighborhood. She is a short, mousy-looking woman of sixty-five years but appeared much older than that. She was born in Europe but has lived in the Middle West for many years. Her husband died three and one-half years ago. She remarked that she had done nothing but cry ever since. Her doctor advised her to find some new interests. She keeps house for her daughter who is employed as a secretary. Mrs. B has arthritis, but other than that says her health is good. She belongs to no organizations, does not like to read, and spends most of her time watching television. On the whole she seemed rather listless until she mentioned her childhood in her native country and I told her I had visited that country. She really livened up when we visited the craft room and she saw the weaving. It reminded her of her childhood when she had done a great deal of weaving. She almost crawled under the loom to see how it worked. Mrs. B wants to join the creative stitchery group and attend the Forum. She will need much encouragement from the staff to become active and make friends.

"Did You Know?" forms enable the staff of a large center to share with one another pertinent information about members

If the membership is not too large, personal information about members can be easily shared by staff in direct conversation. In a multiservice center with a large membership and a large staff, however, it is often difficult to keep the staff informed about day-by-day crises that members are facing. The counselor is not the only staff member with whom members form a close relationship. Each older person has his favorite staff member to whom he feels closest and shares his concerns. Such pertinent information, unless given in strict confidence, should be shared with other staff members so that they can relate meaningfully to the member the next time he comes to the center. A brief statement on the situation is recorded by the worker who received the information on a "Did You Know?" form. These are placed in a designated box easily accessible to the staff. It is the responsibility of each staff member to record and share what he has learned about any member and to read the recordings of fellow workers.

An annual rating of the involvement of new members in the program is a part of the individualization process

The final step in the individualization of new members is the annual review to determine how well each is being served by the program. Using a five-point scale, the staff, meeting as a group, objectively rates each new member. A rating of (1) is given to those individuals who completed their membership enrollment and paid their initial dues but did not become further involved in the program. The member whose participation has been spotty and who has made only tenuous relationships with other members is rated at the (2) step. Those whose attendance and participation have been consistent and regular are rated as (3) on the scale. Step (4) is given to those who have assumed more than average responsibility and leadership and who have been enrolled in at least two weekly classes or groups. The highest rating of (5) is given to those who have not only participated in center activities and served on its operating committees but have also volunteered for service projects in the community.

On the basis of these ratings the staff determines what next steps should be taken to enable each individual member to experience greater satisfaction from his participation in the program. Although no older person should be encouraged to assume responsibilities beyond his energy, ability, or interest, the staff should encourage those who have been on the fringes to become more active. The counselor has the responsibility to follow up on all who have been rated (1) or (2) to determine whether the member's nonattendance was a result of his inability to find what he desired from the program or if there were other reasons he did not attend. Those members who are rated (3) and (4) form a group from which the members and chairmen of member committees can be selected for the next year. Those who have the highest rating become potential candidates for membership on the board of directors, representatives of the center at state and city wide meetings, and leaders of neighborhood clubs.

These four well-defined procedures—the intake interview, social summaries of new members, "Did You Know?" forms, and the annual review of the level of the new members' participation—all help the staff to know each member as a person. They enable staff to be effective in helping, in the same setting, older people with widely different needs, interests, and abilities.

The hostess committee helps
to individualize new members

As important as the staff's individualization process is, it has no practical value unless it serves as a bridge to relate the new member to his peers. Most older people move easily into groups and make new friends without help from the staff or hostess committee. Others are timid and will need help to feel accepted. Some older people who have been members over a period of time develop proprietary and possessive attitudes about the group and sometimes in subtle ways reject the newcomer and make him feel unwelcome. Members of the hostess committee stationed at strategic spots to welcome shy newcomers help to minimize this possibility. Committee members have the responsibility to introduce the new member to one or two other members who that day are assigned the role of "special friend" for the new member. Members who serve on the hostess committee must, of course, be warm, friendly individuals who are able to cope with the negative feelings of new members, who may be feeling unsure of themselves and anxious about being accepted by the group.

The program is an important part of the individualization of members

The program itself is of primary importance as the setting in which the individualization of each member can take place. A wide diversity of groups in terms of size, program, and degree of homogeneity is essential in order that the older person can choose those activities he is interested in and in which he feels accepted and comfortable. The following are typical of the kinds of groups found in most multiservice centers:

1. Sheltered groups where there is maximum attention from staff and no pressure for the older person to be active;

2. Mass activity programs, such as movies, where one can sit alone in the dark and be in the group without having to relate intimately to anyone;

3. Small, intimate, homogeneous friendship groups and large heterogeneous interest groups;

4. Educational classes for mental stimulation and learning new skills and recreational activities for fun and relaxation;

5. Activities that take place away from the center, such as camping, trips, and community service projects;

6. Committees and councils through which members assume management responsibilities;

7. Drop-in lounges where members can sit, read, or observe the action around them.

Other ways to encourage the individualization of members include having new member parties and birthday parties to which individuals are invited by personal letter; wearing name tags while at the center; sending sympathy cards when an illness keeps the member away from the center; having an award assembly in which certificates of appreciation are given to those who have served on committees and as teachers; and putting an article in the monthly center newspaper designating a member who has given outstanding service as the member-of-the-month.

How members are addressed by the staff can indicate whether they are receiving individual recognition or whether they are being seen as "just one" of many members. To identify each older adult by name and to be able to recall it each time he is addressed is a challenge to the staff. The practice of using surnames, first names, or nicknames when speaking to members will differ person by person. Some older adults feel complimented and fully accepted when addressed informally by their first names. Others will resent this practice, particularly by younger people. They feel it an affront to their dignity not to be addressed as Mrs. X or Mr. Y by staff members whom they think of as "hired help." Which practice is acceptable to individual members and makes for warm reciprocal relations can be determined only through experience by staff members who are innately sensitive to the feelings of the members.

The way in which the death of a member is recognized helps to increase the individual's sense of worth

The way in which the death of members is recognized and dealt with by the staff and other members becomes for some older people a subtle indication of how valued they are as individuals. It is important that members themselves be involved in the action that the center takes at such times. Societal and cultural practices will influence their expectations. Their suggestions will include the request that verbal announcements be made of each death, that contributions be collected and a floral tribute sent, and that a delegation represent the center at the funeral or memorial service. Those members who are without family and have few friends to mourn them are usually most adamant about the importance of these traditional practices, reflecting their unconscious fears that their own deaths may go unnoticed and their funeral services be unattended by mourners. A skillful and sensitive staff member can help the group be more objective and realistic in its expectations. The collection of funds for flowers and enlistment of representatives to attend funerals can occur frequently and place undue emphasis on death in an organization whose purpose is to enrich the days of the living. Here again, sensitive staff can help members give meaningful recognition to the loss of one of their group without having each occurrence interrupt the normal course of the program.

Members should also be helped to recognize that the staff who have the responsibility to operate the center are not free to attend funerals.

Centers and other groups serving older adults have found several appropriate ways to recognize the death of members; these include posting an announcement of the death on a specially designed board giving the time and place of the service so that those who wish may attend, carrying an "In Memoriam" column in the center's newspaper with the names of any members who have died since the last issue, and sending a condolence card to the family in the name of the members and staff of the center or group. Many organizations have Memory Funds to which family and friends of the deceased member send contributions that will provide a living memorial—a special piece of equipment or an additional service for the members who remain. Such memorial contributions should be reported in the center's newspaper.

Procedures for care in emergencies also demonstrate the center's concern for the individual

The procedures followed for caring for members in case of accident or serious illness while at the center also demonstrate the center's concern for them as valued persons. In the case of such emergencies the member's family is called and their instructions are followed. If the individual has no close family or the family cannot be reached, his doctor is notified and an ambulance is called to take the ill or injured member to the hospital. If the emergency was caused by an accident, a report describing all of the attendant circumstances should be sent immediately to the company that carries the center's liability insurance. It is essential that all administrative and supervisory personnel be familiar with the explicit procedures to be followed and that emergency telephone numbers be plainly posted.

The individualization of older adults in a depersonalizing society is essential

Organizations serving older adults will develop their unique and varied ways of making members feel that they are important persons who are accepted and respected by others in life and in death. Individualizing each member can help to combat the depersonalization that older people experience so often in their daily lives in modern society. Organized programs that help them continue to feel valued as persons make a significant contribution to their mental health and, in turn, to the mental health of the total community.

BIBLIOGRAPHY

Cohen, Ruth G. "Casework with Older Persons." *Social Work* 2 (1957): 36-40.

Hollender, Marc H. "Individualizing the Aged." *Social Casework* 33 (1952): 337-42.

Jones, Maxwell. *The Therapeutic Community.* New York: Basic Books, 1953.

Klein, Wilma H., et al. *Promoting Mental Health of Older People Through Group Methods: A Practical Guide.* New York: Manhattan Society for Mental Health, 1965.

Lokshin, Helen. "Casework Counseling with the Older Client." *Social Casework* 36 (1955): 257-63.

Reynolds, Rosemary; Powell, Amy S.; and Zelditch, Morris. "Symposium: Casework and the Aging Population." *Journal of Social Casework* 30 (1949): 58-65.

Riesman, David. "Some Clinical and Cultural Aspects of the Aging Process." *American Journal of Sociology* 59 (January 1954): 379-383.

Turner, Helen. *Psychological Factors Affecting the Social Functioning of Older People.* New York: National Council on the Aging, 1967.

Vickery, Florence E. "A Multiservice Senior Center: Its Unique Role and Function." *The Gerontologist* 5 (1965): 246 50.

12 / The Role of Members in Self-Government and Leadership

STUDIES OF LIFE SATISFACTIONS in the older adult years suggest that those activities that provide status, recognition, and achievement help to build morale and produce feelings of self-worth. Activities that do not fulfill these basic emotional needs contribute little to an individual's sense of fulfillment and meaning. To provide roles that give recognition and status to individual members is an important goal of senior centers. Responsibilities for the operation of the center and for the leadership of its groups and classes provide such roles. The self-government roles in which members may be involved will differ in different settings, depending on the size of the membership, the responsibilities assigned to staff, and the physical and emotional health of the group members. Even for those individuals who are frail and live in protected settings, some opportunity to make choices and help plan the social activities that take place there are important. Involvement of ill older people in planning and making decisions will, of course, be limited, but some part in the process is important for the maintenance of their emotional social well-being. This chapter will describe some of the leadership roles of the socially adequate older adults who belong to senior centers and clubs.

Groups differ in the leadership responsibilities that members are expected to carry

Senior centers and clubs differ in organization and underlying philosophy concerning the roles played by those who participate in the programs. Some centers are autonomous membership organizations, and those who join are expected to carry responsibilities for the planning and operation of the program. As members, they have a stake in what happens; their skills and abilities are recognized and used; and their views of themselves as able persons are strengthened rather than diminished. Other centers are units within larger organizations, such as community centers. Here, an older adult may participate in activities within his club as well as with younger center members in programs planned by an overall center committee. The programs of still other senior centers are planned, financed, and operated by sponsoring organizations. Those who join are participants who enjoy the activities provided by the sponsoring group but carry no responsibility for planning them.

The self-government structure should be simple

The needs of a particular group will determine how elaborate the self-government structure should be. A constitution and by-laws, officers, and committees are the usual component parts of most self-government structures. The involvement of members in carrying management responsibilities does not imply that staff is not needed. A high degree of professional skill is required in order to involve as many group members as possible in significant ways in self-government and program operation.

Constitution and bylaws. Groups of older adults want enough organization and regulation to assure order, direction, and protection of the rights of each member. The constitution and bylaws provide the structure for an orderly operation of the business of a center, state its purpose, and provide for the self-government positions and the responsibilities of the members. The structure must be simple and its tasks not so demanding that those who assume them have limited time to enjoy the activities. Many older people have little patience with involved rules of order, motions, and amendments which confuse and stalemate group functioning. Involved business meetings take too much time from the activities and cause members to lose interest and fail to attend. It is in the business meeting that members have a voice in electing officers and representatives to the governing council after nominees have been selected by a nominating committee appointed by the council chairman. In business meetings members feel free to discuss any concerns they have and take action on recommendations that are presented by the council.

The officers. When groups are first organized, officers are often elected and committee members appointed before the group knows what leadership it will need and the leadership potentials of the members. The individuals who become the officers before the members have had an opportunity to become acquainted with one another are usually the self-assured articulate members who are able to manipulate the group to elect them to positions of leadership. Such individuals then often strive for power and seek to identify with the staff rather than with peers. Self-government structures the responsibilities of members, but it does not turn over to them any of the authority of the staff. The authority vested in the staff by their employers cannot be delegated to members. Conflicts sometimes develop between the members who have been elected to the offices and the staff. To minimize the possibilities of such conflicts, it is advisable to have written job descriptions for members who are elected to leadership roles, including the length of their term. Those elected then know the limits of their responsibilities and will not feel resentful or threatened when they are replaced at the end of their term. Some centers have found it helpful to invest the self-government function in a larger, more flexible structure—such as a council, senate, or assembly of elders—rather than placing the control in the hands of a limited number of officers.

Membership councils. Self-government councils usually consist of the chairmen of standing committees and representatives from the total membership elected at a business meeting. Overlapping terms of council members assures the participation of experienced members who give continuity to the deliberations and help orient new members as they are elected. This plan increases the number of different individuals who will have an opportunity to be a member of a high-status group, which elects its own chairman every six months. The chairman of the council becomes the presiding officer at business meetings of the membership and at special events. The council formulates policies, makes decisions related to the program, and deals with problems reported by the members concerning program operation.

In centers operated by nonprofit organizations of municipal departments, a group of nonmember citizens constitutes a commission or board of directors. This group makes all administrative decisions and carries the legal responsibility and the financial accountability to the community for the center. Its bylaws should provide for representation from the council members to serve on the board or commission. These representatives of the active members thus become a part of the policy-making group operating the center and participate in important decisions that affect all members.

Committees are important

Activities, of course, form the core program of any senior center. Equally important, however, are the committees that involve members in planning the activities and making decisions that affect them. The number of committees needed will depend on the size of the membership and the scope of the program. Some committees will be responsible for planning activities or "happenings," such as classes, interest groups, trips, social activities, volunteer community services, and social action projects. Membership, hostess, attendance, visiting, and "sunshine" committees will be concerned with the quality of the "encounter" or interaction of members taking part in activities. In order to keep as many members as possible involved as chairmen and as members of committees the staff will need to maintain an inventory of the leadership jobs and of the manpower available. The staff worker or nonmember leader will be responsible to meet with committees to help them plan realistically. The leadership of the staff with the committees is as important as its direction of any other part of the program. These small committee groups are most important because it is through them that members have the opportunity to grow in self-confidence and leadership ability.

Committees are also needed to help make the center a friendly place where the members know and enjoy one another. In a small community, where individuals are already acquainted with one another through other relationships, fewer committees will be needed than in large metropolitan centers that have heterogeneous memberships. Committees help newcomers feel welcome and keep in touch with those who are absent.

Program committee. With staff assistance, program committees plan all activities. In centers with a large membership there are a number of committees that are responsibile for different aspects of the program, such as social activities, educational classes, service projects, and social action. If the range of members' interests is more limited, fewer committees will be needed. The function of the program-planning committee is to provide members with a wide choice of activities and to keep the planning and evaluation of the program member centered.

Membership committee. This committee is responsible for orientation meetings and parties held each month for new members, where newcomers are formally introduced and receive their membership cards from the executive director. Refreshments and entertainment make the occasion a celebration and give dignity and significance to becoming a member of a senior center or club. The membership committee also keeps in touch with those who are absent. In a small center the individual's friends share pertinent information with the staff about illnesses and other personal problems, but in a large, heterogenous membership it is important to have some plan for knowing who is absent and who needs help so that no one is overlooked. A friendly telephone call to assure the absentee that he is missed and to inquire if there is any way in which

Form 2
INDIVIDUAL NAME CARD and ACCUMULATED
ATTENDANCE RECORD CARD

INDIVIDUAL NAME CARD

No. 72

Jones, John

ACCUMULATED ATTENDANCE RECORD CARD

No. 72   ATTENDANCE RECORD _____ CENTER

NAME ___Jones, John_____ Date of Joining_____
(Name)

Last   First

MONTH	WEEK 1 S M T W Th F S	WEEK 2 S M T W Th F S	WEEK 3 S M T W Th F S	WEEK 4 S M T W Th F S	WEEK 5 S M T W Th F S
Jan.					
Feb.					
Mar.					
Apr.					
May					
June					
July					
Aug.					
Sept.					
Oct.					
Nov.					
Dec.					

the center staff can be of help gives the ill older person a sense of security and reassurance.

Sunshine committee. The membership committee gives the names of ill members to this committee, which sends get-well cards from the center and places notices on the bulletin board so that individual members may also send cards. If the ill member would like to see his friends, members of the *Friendly Visiting Committee* call on him. If his illness is such that it will be difficult for him to continue to use public transportation to come to the center, the *Homebound Committee* provides transportation in a private car so that he may attend a center homebound party. The personal information about each member obtained by these committees during their home visits is reported to the staff counselor. Any significant information and the action taken is entered on the member's confidential record card and a permanent record is thus maintained. Sometimes telephone committees find that members have become busy with other interests or have joined other groups and may request to be dropped from the center's membership. This information is reported to the membership committee and the records are adjusted. This plan helps to eliminate from the membership roster individuals who are no longer using the center's program and services.

Attendance committee. Calling the roll or having members sign in each time the group meets is a time-consuming task in large centers. Some groups have found that a do-it-yourself method is more efficient. The name and membership number of each person is printed in large letters on a three-by-five index card and placed alphabetically on a rack located at the entrance to the center. The member draws his card from the rack as he arrives and drops it into a box on the attendance committee desk. Here a committee member checks each member present on his master file card and replaces the name card on the rack. In this way both a cumulative record of the participation of each member and a statistical record of total daily attendance at the center are kept. Sample record forms, Form 2, are presented on page 172.

Members of the *Host and Hostess Committee* have the responsibility of greeting and talking with visitors to the center. If a visitor is interested in becoming a member, the host or hostess takes his name, address, and telephone number. The following day the counselor telephones and makes an appointment for an intake interview. If the host feels that the individual who is inquiring about membership appears highly emotional, hostile, or timid, he immediately finds a staff member—who is not with a group at the time—to talk with the visitor. A member of this committee also welcomes all members when they arrive, directs those who are not sure where groups meet, and finds partners for those who want to join card games.

In some centers the opportunities for
leadership roles for members are limited

The number of members who carry responsibilities for self-government and committee leadership roles is one reliable index of the effectiveness of a center's program. In too many centers volunteers from the community or the sponsoring agency, rather than the members themselves, are responsible for leadership functions. In a national survey of 1,250 senior centers made in 1969 by the Institute for Inter-Disciplinary Studies for the Administration on Aging, it was found that in 1,002 of the centers an average of twelve members only assumed the responsibilities of serving on advisory committees, conducts programs or activities, helping with clerical or maintenance tasks, and offering suggestions. Because some members may carry more than one responsibility, the actual unduplicated count of those assisting with the planning and conduct of center programs is lower than the twelve member average. The survey showed that members carried more responsibility in those centers that had small professional staffs and operated on limited incomes.[1] These findings indicate that in too many centers the staff and community volunteers plan *for* members, rather than enable them to plan for themselves.

Many members must be encouraged to
carry responsibility for the group

The expectation that each member will carry some responsibility for the center's operation must be established in the initial interview. The new member is informed that if he joins, he will be expected to take his turn in performing some service for the center. Whether to serve and how he will serve must be the individual's own decision. Stimulating interest in serving on committees and as teachers and leaders of groups and classes is a skilled staff function. Many older adults will need to be reassured over and over again that they are able to take positions of leadership and that the staff is available to help them. The recognition that is given by the staff and members to the individuals who have served motivates others to take their turn.

[1] Nancy N. Anderson, *Senior Centers: A National Survey* (Washington, D.C. Administration on Aging, 1969), pp. 44-45.

The underlying motivational force that encourages older adults to carry responsibilities is the recognition, status, and approval that comes from staff, age mates, and the community. This recognition is made possible because committee members wear identification tags that specify their functions, and their names are listed on the bulletin board or in the center's newspaper. It is good practice to introduce members who assume special responsibilities at membership meetings and honor them with certificates of appreciation at a special ceremony or party when their terms end. It does not matter what procedures are used for saying "thank you for a job well done," but there must be some plan for focusing the attention of all the members on those who have carried responsibilities for the smooth operation of the center's program.

The administration and management of the program might be easier and more efficient if the staff gave all directions and made all decisions, but this method would take from the individuals one of the most meaningful opportunities that center membership provides,—the opportunity to use one's leadership skills and abilities for the good of all. Membership participation enriches the program. If staff is committed to the importance of helping individuals maintain the independence and self-determination of which they are capable, then ways must be found in centers, homes, and other institutions to keep individuals involved in leadership roles and decision making.

Not all members will be able to carry leadership roles in self-government or as teachers

Some older adults cannot serve as committee members or chairmen or as teachers and group leaders. They may have physical limitations, such as the loss of hearing, poor eyesight, and unsteady hands and gait, or they may be too mentally or emotionally frail to be leaders. Others, who have lost status in some relationships and have developed feelings of inadequacy and inferiority, resist trying new experiences that involve responsibility. They put protective walls around themselves and become dependent on the more capable members, happy to let the willing few do all the work. If these older persons can be helped to become involved, there are marked changes in their attitudes and feelings about themselves.

There are some older adults, as there are individuals of any age, who find it difficult to give up ego goals for group goals, and for this reason they do not make good leaders. They become hostile when they cannot impose their wishes on others. Others are unable to accept all of the differences in attitudes, appearance, and behavior that are present in a heterogeneous membership and reject and become highly critical of certain members. Some individuals become easily discouraged when things do not happen as they think they should. They resign from the committee and even drop out of the center's membership. Other persons are so authoritarian in manner that they create friction and hostility in the group and are not acceptable as leaders by other members.

Many older adults prefer to carry individual responsibilities rather than function as a member of a committee. The staff will need to be creative in defining jobs that are challenging to individuals and contribute to the welfare of the total membership. Checking on supplies for the canteen, pouring coffee, keeping bulletin boards and magazine tables current, operating a movie projector, arranging flowers, serving as librarian, watering plants, checking on lights and ventilation, and checking coats and packages are essential jobs that can be assigned to individuals.

Serving on a committee or in any leadership capacity must be a voluntary decision if the experience is to be a positive one for the older person. No one should ever be asked to assume tasks that are beyond his ability or that do not interest him. After the member has agreed to serve, he is sent a letter from the staff member who supervises that committee to confirm the appointment, describe the job, and state the length of time he will be expected to serve. Such a letter will help to avoid misunderstandings and confusion. He should also receive a letter, acknowledging his help, when the assignment is completed. This second letter gives the member a sense of being appreciated for a job that he has been willing to carry. Even if the older person fails in some degree in the assignment, he should never be belittled or criticized before his peer group. The staff member who has served as the consultant to the committee on which the older person has served should discuss with him the problems he has experienced and help him handle any feelings of personal guilt or inadequacy. To be praised by the staff in the presence of other members may be embarrassing to some older persons, and the group may not be ready to accept the leader's high opinions of the person lauded. For a staff member to give the impression that he thinks one of the group members is better than the others reinforces the feelings of rivalry that may already exist within the group. Constructive criticism and worthy praise are both important but sometimes are best given in private.

It will be necessary to keep within the membership a balance between able and less capable individuals if a center is to have enough members with leadership potentials. This balance can be assured if the intake staff

is aware of the leadership needs. The stronger members will be able
to assume leadership roles and help those who are frail and less alert
to develop new interests and a willingness to help where they are able.
When an older person helps others in a setting where he himself has
come for help, heightened feelings of adequacy and usefulness are experienced.

The role of the staff in helping members to carry leadership responsibilities is a professional skill

Helping older adults to function as leaders of groups of their peers requires the skilled assistance of professional staff or nonmember volunteers acting for the staff. In addition to consulting with the committee or
council chairman before the meeting to help him work out the agenda,
the staff member attends the committee meeting and helps facilitate the
interaction of members. His role is to ask questions rather than to give
directions or to manipulate group decisions. He encourages the slower
member to express himself and the critical one to be more patient and
accepting of the opinions of others. The staff member anticipates difficulties before they arise and acts to prevent them. Once the group has
made a decision, he does not change it.

Older adults sometimes reject the staff member who is assigned to
supervise the group. As members of all other age groups do, they test
out a new leader and have subtle ways of refusing to accept him. They
fail to attend meetings, complaining that the meetings are no longer fun
or that they themselves are too busy. Some young students, who are in-
experienced and unsure of their authority roles as staff in relation to
older people, often have a difficult time being accepted by the group.
Members will comment that the young leader does not know anything or
that he is patronizing and talks down to them. The insecure staff member responds to this rejection and aloofness of members with his own
reactions about the stubbornness and rigidity of old age. Other young
workers, who listen and then proceed slowly in expressing their own
ideas, being careful not to force their authority on the group, have no
difficulty in being accepted. Most older adults are complimented by the
interest and attention of a younger person who evidences sincere concern
and respect for each group member. They are happy to have his help in
carrying out their assignments.

Training is essential for center leaders

Training sessions for member-leaders is essential if they are to be effective in their jobs and experience real satisfactions. In these training workshops practical information must be given on how to prepare an agenda for a meeting, how to conduct the meeting in an orderly manner, and how to summarize the discussions and action taken. Officers and council and committee members are helped to understand their roles in relation to the roles of the staff and board as well as to the functions and limitations of the center itself. Through demonstrations, discussions, and role-playing techniques, member-leaders gain an awareness of the interpersonal relations involved in good group functioning and learn to help the members of their committees work together to achieve their goals. In training sessions, discussions of their problems as leaders are encouraged. A sense of fellowship develops and a democratically administered and vital senior center results.

Guidelines for involving individuals in carrying responsibilities for the group

1. In senior centers older adults have opportunites to use their skills and leadership abilities in new social roles. Negative attitudes and stereotyped thinking about the uselessness and dependency of older people in society may thus gradually be modified.

2. Older people are able to maintain existing leadership skills and develop new ones if encouraged and guided by skilled staff members.

3. Group programs, to be meaningful in helping older adults to maintain a sense of well-being and high morale, must provide opportunities for self-government and leadership roles.

4. Committee structures should be flexible and geared to essential tasks rather than to unnecessarily mechanical tasks. Every member has the potential, at some time and in some situation, to be a leader in his group.

5. Committee assignments must be geared to the ability and interests of those asked to assume them. In the intake interview the staff learns of the past experiences, interests, and capabilities of those applying for membership; it is then able to recruit members for jobs they can do or can be helped to do.

6. Each committee member must be helped to feel personally responsible for doing the job assigned to him or for reporting to the chairman if he is unable to do the job.

7. Leadership roles and committee responsibilities must be carefully defined for those asked to serve in order to minimize friction within the group.

8. Committees should meet regularly at the same time and place.

9. Terms of committee membership should be established when individuals are asked to serve so that they will not feel threatened when their terms are completed and new persons are asked to take over the assignments.

10. When an assignment has been completed it is important to thank the member and acknowledge his service before the total membership group.

11. The staff will need to be aware of the domineering, aggressive individuals who strive to dictate the group's action. Such older adults must be helped so that the group is not damaged by their attitudes.

12. Frequent and regular training sessions will be essential to help members learn the skills of group leadership.

13. Older adults living in protective care settings and some members of senior centers will be unable to carry demanding or extended responsibilities or make important decisions. Even these older adults, however, must be involved, to the degree that they are able, in decisions that affect them.

14. Carrying leadership responsibilities in groups of their age mates provides significant social roles for older adults and replaces in some degree those they have previously carried.

BIBLIOGRAPHY

Anderson, Nancy. *Senior Centers: A National Survey.* Prepared by the Institute for Inter-disciplinary Studies for Administration on Aging, U.S. Department of Health, Education and Welfare, April 1969.

Cooley, Charles H. *Social Organization.* New York: Charles Scribner's Sons, 1909.

Hare, Paul; Bergetta, Edgar; and Bales, Robert. *Small Groups.* New York: Alfred A. Knopf, 1955.

Olmsted, Michael. *The Small Group.* New York. Random House, 1959.

Sprott, W. J. *Human Groups,* rev. ed. Baltimore: Penguin Books, Inc. 1964.

Tine, Sebastian; Hastings, Katherine; and Deutschberger, Paul. "Generic and Specific in Social Group Work Practice with the Aging." In *Social Work with Groups, 1960: Selected Papers from the National Conference on Social Welfare,* pp. 86-99. New York: National Association of Social Workers, 1960.

13 / Professional and Nonmember Volunteer Leadership of Older Adult Programs

THE RAPID GROWTH OF SOCIAL PROGRAMS for older adults was made possible by the vision, commitment, and leadership of many volunteers. They became aware of, and concerned about, the increasing number of retired men and women, seemingly with nothing to do, sitting dejected and alone in the lobbies of downtown hotels and department stores, in parks and public buildings. Clubs and centers were organized to provide a friendly and comfortable place where such lonely older people could meet their peers and enjoy the entertainment and refreshments provided for them. In these programs well-trained volunteer hostesses gave adequate leadership. Many volunteer and member-led groups proved successful in keeping participants active and happy as long as the groups remained small and the interpersonal relationships remained harmonious. In most instances, when new individuals joined and groups became large and more heterogeneous, dissension and conflict developed. Members soon grew tired of static, monotonous programs based on the lowest common denominator of interest.

As centers developed, volunteer leaders realized that employed staff would be needed to give continuity to programs and to help develop wider goals than merely meeting the recreational needs of members. The volunteers became aware that staff trained in group leadership would be essential if the goal was to provide a group experience in which each member could be helped to solve his problems of loneliness and his feelings of uselessness and continue to grow as an adequate and interesting human being. Only with trained leadership could new ideas be introduced into the program for individual members—as well as for the group—to be enabled to develop new interests and to move continually

180

toward new goals. The successful operation of multiservice senior centers today requires three levels of leadership to direct the activities and services: (1) the professional and subprofessional staff; (2) the nonmember volunteer leaders, and (3) the active members who carry leadership roles as a part of membership responsibilities.

Volunteer boards of directors or committees of management, legally incorporated, also play essential and unique roles in conjunction with the professional staff. Formulating general policies within which the activities and services are carried out, these volunteers secure and maintain the physical facilities, employ the executive director, plan for adequate financial support, and interpret the program and services to the community. The board may function through various committees: finance, personnel, publicity, program evaluation and development, and building and maintenance. The board represents the center in the community and members are often able to recruit their friends to serve as volunteers in the program.

The skills of professional staff are learned through formal educational courses and practice

Being an older adult himself does not necessarily prepare a person to work successfully with his age mates. The necessary knowledge, skills, and attitudes are learned. Formal education courses, based on scientifically acquired facts about the growth and development of human beings, the experiences and relationships that make for mental and physical health in the later years, and the techniques of group leadership, form the core of the professional knowledge needed. The skill of guiding the interaction among members so that each may find meaning and satisfaction at the center is further developed with practice under the supervision of an experienced staff member.

Because work with older adults is one of the newer helping professions, opportunities for professional education have been limited. Presently, in an increasing number of universities and professional schools, courses are being developed to prepare professional staff for the rapidly developing field of social gerontology. Undergraduate courses for training paraprofessionals and aides in recreation, occupational therapy, and social work are being offered in junior and community colleges.

The size of a center or club, its program goals, and the scope of its services will determine what professional staff will be needed. Not all social projects for older adults will require—or will have funds to employ—all of the trained staff discussed in the following paragraphs. As programs and services develop, it will be necessary to add the appropriate staff.

The roles of staff members overlap and are interdependent

Unlike some other agencies, senior centers offer staff leaders multifaceted roles that do not fall into neat professional categories. Leaders must be flexible in their practices and develop respect for one another's skill and competency. The recreation specialist will become involved in counseling individuals and making referrals to community resources. The social group worker, who is often responsible for the intake of new members, will work to develop program leadership and do group counseling. The executive director, in order to have firsthand contact with members, may lead an activity group. The nurse will function as a friendly visitor when she calls on members who are ill. This ability to function as a team will require each staff member to subordinate professional pride and status and work with the others for the excellence of the program and the welfare of each older person. The functions of each staff member will be interdependent and of equal importance.

All of the various leadership functions are essential

The professional and volunteer staff positions needed to operate a multiservice senior center will include: executive director, program director, program aides and students-in-training, teachers, group leaders, recreation leaders, skill specialists, and program consultants. The service aspects of the program will require a caseworker or counselor, nurse, nutritionist, and, in some centers, a doctor. Statisticians and research workers also will be needed at times to make studies and design demonstration projects. Secretarial, clerical, bookkeeping, and maintenance personnel will be essential.

There may be in the membership retired office workers who are willing to volunteer their help in answering telephones and performing useful office tasks. Members performing such functions should not have access to staff correspondence, records, and reports that deal with confidential information about members or employed staff. Difficult situations may be avoided if confidential records and correspondence are handled only by an employed or nonmember volunteer secretary.

Responsibilities of various staff
positions must be clearly defined [1]

Executive Director. The executive director performs management functions and correlates the overall program of the center. He shares in center program development, works with board and member council committees, and supervises the work of professional staff. In consultation with the board finance committee, he prepares the budget and controls income and expenditures. He interprets the needs of older adults to the community, and advocates pertinent legislation and essential services. While performing these administrative and community related tasks, he must also find time to develop a warm one-to-one relationship not only with the staff, board members, and volunteers but also with as many members as possible. The executive director may be an employed leader but he will not be so in fact unless he can develop a "we" feeling and a sense of community with all the people involved in the center. Even though he may not supervise them, the volunteers will look to him for recognition and approval. His authority is invested in him by the board, and he must be able to carry out his role without assuming an authoritarian approach. Professional education and experience in social work, counseling, religious education, rehabilitation, recreation, or education are helpful backgrounds against which to develop the administrative skills needed to be an effective executive director of a senior center.

Program Director. Program directors are usually recreation leaders, social group workers, ministers, or teachers who have had experience working with younger age groups. A qualified volunteer can assume the responsibilities of this position if he can give the required time on a continuing basis. The program director works with staff and with planning committees made up of members, to develop classes, clubs, interest groups, trips, and special events of all kinds.

Program Leaders. Specialists with all kinds of creative skills and individuals with extensive knowledge in intellectual, cultural, and social subjects are often willing to serve as short-term nonmember volunteer program leaders. Other volunteers having special hobbies may be enlisted to share their interests with center members for a single program. In many communities, teachers from the adult education divisions of the public schools are made available for instruction in creative arts and for lectures, forums, language classes, and discussion groups. Librarians

---

[1] See samples of job descriptions for executive director, program director, and counselor at the end of this chapter.

assist by giving book reviews. Using paid or volunteer teachers from the community helps to keep the program creative and develops in the members higher levels of skill performance.

Using the talents and skills of the members as teachers is most important. Although activities should not be limited to those for which member-teachers are available, volunteers should not be recruited to teach classes that members themselves have the skills and the experience to teach. Serving as a group leader or as teacher of one's peers can become a difficult assignment for some older adults. In the class he teaches, the member serves in place of staff and relates to class members with the authority delegated to him by staff. When he participates in other activities in the center, it is as a learner, and he must relate to his age mates as a fellow member. The transition from participant to teacher to participant may become confusing. As a group member, an individual's reactions are on a subjective level—how he personally thinks, feels, and enjoys or dislikes what he experiences. As group leader or teacher, the member must be sensitive to the reactions of group members and consciously gear his responses to their needs and interests rather than to his own. Only then can he maintain an impartial relationship to each member. Simply because he is an older person himself, a member-leader does not necessarily understand all other older adults. Remaining objective requires a high degree of self-awareness, which is an acquired skill. Many older adults have the skills to *teach* groups of age mates but may not have the insights to *guide* the interaction of the individuals in the group to positive ends for all.

Confusion in role and identity also arises when an older adult who is not a member volunteers for a leadership role. He may find it difficult to teach his skill to the members of the group without becoming emotionally involved and partial to those whom he personally enjoys. An interesting experiment in using older adults as paid leaders was made possible at the San Francisco Senior Center through a project funded in 1968 by the United States Department of Labor. The center was enabled by the grant to employ a limited number of social security recipients for not more than twenty hours a week. These aides were supervised by a professional staff member and served as friendly visitors, canteen workers, recreation assistants, and office and statistical clerks. They freed the staff to perform professional tasks related to training and supervision of volunteers. Because such older adults were themselves facing some of the same personal problems as the individuals they had been employed to help, they sometimes strongly identified with their clients. They did not respect the confidentiality of information, and difficult situations arose when they tried to handle problems themselves rather than refer them to the professional staff. Resentment toward these aides who were being paid for their services was frequently expressed by center members who had been working as volunteers, especially if they too had applied for such assignments and were not selected. In spite of these difficulties the project demonstrated that aides can perform needed and valuable services if supervised by skilled professional staff.

Counselor. A trained social worker or counselor will be needed in multiservice centers to interview all new members and provide short-term supportive help for some when crises arise. The counselor accepts referrals for membership from doctors, clinics, adult children, and social agencies and refers members to community resources when continuing help is needed. Only trained personnel are able to help older adults who have deep-seated emotional problems, and in a center with a large membership staff time is usually too limited to carry individual cases over a long term. In such cases the counselor refers the member to a family service agency, a mental health clinic, or a geriatric screening center. A group that meets in a church or synagogue generally has access to a priest, rabbi, or minister who either has had training in pastoral counseling or who knows how to utilize community resources for casework treatment. Nonmember volunteers can help in a supportive way by being good listeners, but they are not trained to handle crisis situations or give long-term help. In addition to having a one-to-one relationship to members, the counselor serves as a resource for programs and speakers in such areas as employment, health, housing, nutrition, wills and other legal matters, social security, and Medicare. He will be an ombudsman for those individuals who have no family members or close friends, and he will help members find resources to deal with legal matters, such as making wills and funeral arrangements.

Nurse. Some centers employ a nurse as a full-time staff member. Other centers have the services of a public health nurse who is assigned to the center for specific hours by the public health department. The nurse serves as a consultant to the staff and to members concerning health problems and care during illness. He counsels adult children about physical changes he notices in their parents, and, after consultation with a doctor, advises on plans for care. When illness occurs, the nurse refers individuals to their own doctors or recommends the center's medical consultant or doctors in the neighborhoods where the members live. He demonstrates the uses of prosthetic devices and clarifies for the older patient the explanations and instructions of his doctor. The nurse also visits the ill member at home or in the hospital and helps him and his family, in consultation with his doctor, to make whatever plans are needed for his continuing care. The uniformed nurse helps to create in the center a positive image of a person and profession ready to give help when needed. The center nurse also carries the responsibility for programs of health education and calls on health educators to supply educational materials.

When a counselor notices unusual behavior and marked physical and personality changes in an older person, he makes an opportunity for the nurse to talk with the member about his health, living situation, meals and eating habits, and the medical attention he is receiving. If he is not seeing a doctor and requests help in locating one, the nurse provides a list of doctors from which the member can make his choice for a diagnostic appointment. The nurse or the counselor will request from the doctor pertinent information that will enable the program staff to help the individual understand and adjust to his illness when he returns to the center.

Medical Consultant. Some centers employ a medical doctor as a consultant. The doctor is available by telephone to advise the nurse or counselor and may occasionally attend staff meetings to discuss general health problems of older adults and observable danger signs that indicate the need for referrals for medical care.

Psychiatric Consultant. Among the members of senior centers there will be those whose personality structures and emotional needs make it difficult for them to function in a group. Their behavior can often be sufficiently modified to enable them to function and get along with other members through the planned intervention of the staff under the guidance of a consulting psychiatrist. Many senior centers receive this consultation through community mental health services. The psychiatrist, who helps the staff grow in their understanding of the psychosocial needs of all older adults, also aids in the understanding of behavior that is negatively affecting a member's adjustment to the center and his acceptance by the group. The counselor convenes staff meetings with the psychiatrist and prepares case presentations of individuals who are having difficulties. In the discussions that follow the presentations, staff members add their observations of these individuals based on their participation in the activities they supervise. The psychiatrist raises questions about the dynamics of the members' behavior, the possibilities for effecting change, and the steps necessary to bring it about. Through these meetings, the center becomes for the psychiatrist a real-life laboratory where he can gain insight into the importance of social interaction with age mates for optimum social adjustment and high morale in the later years.

Each staff member is perceived differently by the members

In addition to carrying the specific responsibilities of his staff position, each professional leader will play many roles in his relationships with individual members. Each older person will perceive the staff in various ways depending on his individual emotional and dependency needs. Staff members will need to know when to give warm emotional response to one member and when to withhold approval of the actions of another, from whom it is important to accept a gift, and from whom personal invitations must be refused. In order to understand individual behavior, staff will need to listen patiently to what seems important to the member even though it may seem repetitive and petty. If the older person senses that staff members are impatient with him, he will become guarded and say only what he believes staff members want to hear and not what he really thinks or feels.

Some younger persons find it difficult to work with older adults because they have not completely resolved their own adolescent conflicts with parental authority. An unconscious fear of older persons persists, and if they are challenged, they may become unsure of themselves and fearful of discussing any controversial issue with members. Among the center members there will be older adults who strive to play authority roles and are overly sensitive to younger people in positions of leadership. The insecure staff worker either responds negatively to the member striving to compete with him and acts in an authoritarian manner or he capitulates and permits the member who is challenging his role to take over the leadership of the group. In general older adults who are unable to accept younger people in position of authority do not join senior centers.

It is often difficult for younger workers to function from an older person's perspective—their insights are limited by their own experiences and they unconsciously transfer their own values and attitudes to older adults. Because they cannot identify completely with an older person or feel in advance what it will be like to be old, they must have the capacity to establish a meaningful rapport with center members.

Some staff members infantalize and patronize older adults, encouraging dependency because they enjoy and need the feelings of personal power and importance that such dependency and flattery bring. Emotionally healthy older persons resent such treatment and show hostility toward these workers. Most group leaders are extroverts and are at ease with individuals who are like themselves. They may have difficulty relating warmly to and being accepted by shy, timid older adults. Leaders need to *listen* to an older adult. The morale of members will be dependent upon the leader's ability to establish a noncompetitive atmosphere and to maintain an impartial relationship with all members—the attractive and likeable, the hostile and angry, the shy and depressed. The staff member's ability to maintain this relationship will depend on his own maturity and his consciously controlled use of himself to help each individual in the group feel accepted and wanted.

> ### The attitudes and skills of the staff member
> ### are determining factors for involving the
> ### hard-to-reach older adults in center programs

Skilled leadership will be needed to involve those depressed, socially and economically deprived older adults who are forced to leave their homes and live in the deteriorating downtown areas of big cities. The role of the professional staff member in motivating these hard-to-reach individuals is described by F. Estelle Booth, director of the Downtown Senior Center in San Francisco, who writes:

> The friendly attitude of the worker who "likes you for yourself" is probably the single most important factor in involving the unmotivated person. It is to this attitude that the hard-to-reach person responds. Most workers with groups are welcoming and kind but in reaching out a *plus* quality is needed. A continued demonstration of interest and concern, and a willingness to go the second and third mile in building a relationship, is essential. It is this relationship with the worker which brings the hard-to-reach individual into the group, particularly the discouraged, resentful, depressed and frail older person whose energy level is low. Where the relationship is good the depressed person may begin to feel there is a new factor in the situation—the worker—and the hope that perhaps after all things can change and become better.
>
> In working with depressed, angry, unmotivated persons, the worker will need much patience and an ability to accept hostility and disappointment. Disappointment is frequent. The hard-to-reach person will seem ready to attend the group, all arrangements will be made and, when the day comes, he will not be present.
>
> In going the second mile and beyond with an unresponsive, openly hostile or apathetic person no longer able to love, the worker in a

sense "primes the pump," lending her energy and her affection to enable the isolated person to relate again . . . The sources of his emotional satisfactions have dried up and he has nothing left to share with others. If the worker can give to such individuals evidences of her liking—such as listening to whatever he has to tell her, appreciating his strengths, getting him small things he needs—he can start to give again of himself, probably first to the worker and then to the other members of the group.

The worker needs to have strong convictions that:

1) The will to live, in human beings, is more powerful than the death wish and one can capitalize on this drive for physical and mental health.

2) Older persons can develop and contribute up to the last day of life.

3) There is a satisfaction in small gains for both the hard-to-reach person and the one working with him. For instance when he is able to pick up a pencil again on his own and start drawing after months of just sitting and staring; or when he is able not only to enter a room where there are other people but to be able to sit down and talk with a group for the first time.

If the staff person is convinced that each hard-to-reach person has an unrealized potential of some kind, she can convey this to him. If she can feel the excitement of helping a vegetating individual achieve some of this unrealized potential for becoming a self-actualizing person on the last time around, she can give him hope. There is real satisfaction in helping a depressed person surrounded by emptiness fill his days with some new interest, or hear him say, "I did not know *we* could do this," and to know that he had been able to achieve the "we" feeling of the group.

The staff worker must be able:

1) To individualize and find the answers for such questions as: How is the bent, fragile, white-haired little lady with non-distinctive clothing different from the one who just came in? What are her abilities, her interests, her lifetime of experiences? What are her problems? What are her strengths? What is she seeking from joining the group? What skills and personality strengths can she share with the other members of the group?

2) To accept persons who are different from the rest of the group and from one's self.

3) To go slowly with kindly patience and make no demands. After living alone for a long time the elderly person may become confused by many unaccustomed stimuli in the group and, when it is suggested that he do this or do that, he may think only of escape.

4) To express warmth and concern toward the hard-to-reach per-

son. An individual with a poor self-image and many feelings of inferiority needs much reassurance that he is liked and tangible evidences of this liking.

5) To give hope. This is one of the most important skills in working with persons who have given up hope that life can ever be any better. Without hope, there can be no change.[2]

Member and nonmember volunteers play unique and needed roles in the center's leadership

Although professional staff is essential, the volunteers—both member and nonmember—are essential for the operation and management of multiservice senior centers. In serving as an extension of the professional staff, the volunteer leaders with their individual interests and skills make possible an enriched and varied program. They also perform an important public relations function. Because they see the contributions that the program makes to the mental health of its members, they become its most effective interpreters in the community; they are able to recruit others to volunteer as program leaders and to support the center's fundraising events.

Some volunteers are able to relate more warmly to certain members than to the staff itself, especially if the volunteers are of the same age range as members and have had similar experiences and life-styles. Volunteers from high schools and church youth groups, with their eagerness and enthusiasm, make their unique and valuable contributions to older people. Getting to know individual young persons helps to counteract the negative attitudes about youth that are part of the current scene. The young people themselves increase their understanding of the elderly through their interaction with older adults. Both groups gain mutual respect.

Training courses for volunteers are the responsibility of the staff

The staff is responsible for making the volunteer's experience a satisfying and meaningful one. Not every individual who offers his services will make a good volunteer, and the staff must interview each one to assess his maturity and his ability to relate positively to members. The specific assignment being considered by the volunteer and the time it will take must be clearly stated. Each person should be screened care-

---

[2] F. Estelle Booth, *Reaching Out to the Hard-to-Reach Older Person* (San Francisco: San Francisco Senior Center 1966).

fully and then given an appropriate assignment and asked to serve for a stated trial period. If he is not successful in his teaching or in relating to the members meaningfully, it will not be difficult for him and the center to terminate his assignment. Some volunteers may not be able to work directly with members but will be able to carry other assignments in the center.

Every volunteer should know something about the history and goals of a multiservice senior center as well as some basic facts about the psychological, physical, and social aspects of the aging process. Only then will he be able to understand the needs and the behavioral dynamics of those older adults with whom he will be working.

Because volunteers, as a rule, are recruited one at a time and lose interest if they are not given immediate placement, they often begin their assignment before they have had an opportunity to participate in a training workshop. To help orient a volunteer to a center before his training, manuals should be prepared that briefly describe the center and its program, the administrative routines and records, and the responsibilities of a volunteer.

Workshops for volunteers should be held on a continuing and regular basis. Informal conversations between staff members and the volunteer leader after his group has met and regular supervisory conferences will help to uncover problems the volunteer may be having. Volunteers identify with the center and its goals if they are included in staff meetings when programs are being planned and members' problems are being discussed.

The staff should plan specific ways to say "thank you" to volunteers and let them know their help is appreciated and valued. A morning coffee or afternoon tea party to which members of the board of directors and other community people are invited may be appropriate. Certificates of appreciation and feature articles in center bulletins and community newspapers introducing different workers as the Volunteer-of-the-Month give volunteers needed recognition.

Certain attitudes and personality traits characterize the successful leader of older people

Before accepting responsibility to be a leader, an individual needs to evaluate himself and his motives for becoming involved. Is he really interested in using himself and his skills in working with older adults? Does he honestly believe that older adults have equal claim with children and youth for the community's concern and support? Certain personality characteristics make some people more effective than others in their leadership. One must have a sincere liking for older people and believe in their potentials to develop new skills, learn new knowledge, and expand their mental and spiritual horizons. The friendly, warm person with a positive outlook on life transmits these attitudes to those with whom he works and enables the center to become a setting in which truly creative encounters can take place between leaders and members and among members themselves.

Basic principles of leadership

1. Interested, skilled, and trained professional staff is the most important factor in determining the effectiveness of programs for older adults. Without such a staff, a group will fall apart or stagnate in a monotonous, uninteresting routine.

2. Knowledge of the social and emotional needs of older adults is needed in order to work successfully with them.

3. Volunteer leaders should be carefully screened and should receive orientation to the agency, its program, and goals before starting to work in the program.

4. A volunteer leader should know his specific responsibility with a group and the staff worker who will be his supervisor.

5. When active members accept volunteer leadership roles, it is a part of their *membership responsibility*. They are not an extension of staff.

6. Members accept directions from a member-teacher in a teaching situation but not in other relationships.

7. Leaders of older people must be able to accept each individual at his level of socialization and offer him opportunities to enlarge and enrich his scope of interests toward greater self-fulfillment.

8. Willingness to serve and interest in older people and their problems do not necessarily make a person a good leader. A leader must have a skill in working with people—the ability to relate meaningfully and yet remain objective in relationships with all individuals in the group.

9. A trained nonmember volunteer is able to provide excellent consultative leadership in small, homogeneous groups of self-directing individuals in a club or interest group situation. The professional staff gives guidance and consultation to this volunteer.

10. Volunteers who tend to take over the group and do things for the members do not make good leaders even in a nursing home situation.

Although their intentions are altruistic, they only increase the dependency strivings of the elderly people with whom they work.

Job descriptions are helpful tools for the selection and evaluation of staff and volunteers

A description of each staff position should be written by a personnel committee of the board and executive director. Job descriptions list the responsibilities and tasks of each job and help prospective staff know whether they are qualified and interested in applying for available positions. They also enable the staff and the executive director to evaluate the employee's progress and performance. Because so many positions in a senior center are multifaceted, some centers have developed check sheets, rather than job descriptions, listing the areas of responsibility rather than stating the specifics of the job.

The following job descriptions give qualifications for and functions of three key staff positions: the executive director, the program director, and the counselor.

EXECUTIVE DIRECTOR

Definition

Under the general direction of an agency or of the center's board of directors, the executive director administers the total program of a multiservice activity center for older adults; supervises professional and clerical staff and volunteer workers; and performs related duties as assigned.

Examples of Duties

Plans, develops, and supervises a comprehensive program of activities which will promote the continuing development and the social and emotional adjustment of older persons.

Meets with groups of older persons who come to the center; encourages them to participate in program planning; and assigns them leadership roles in carrying out various activities.

Identifies the interests, capacities, and needs of the older persons who come to the center; evaluates the center's program and expands the program as needed.

Recruits, assigns, and supervises all personnel serving the center.

From U.S., Department of Health, Education and Welfare, *Guide Specifications for Positions on Aging at the State and Local Levels,* October 1965, pp. 57-58.

Develops a staff training program to insure that maximum use is made of each staff member's skills.

Cooperates with other agencies and organizations in the community to encourage the use of the center, learn how the center can attract older persons, and induce such agencies and organizations to make their resources available to the center.

Develops a public relations program which will promote community understanding of the center's purposes and programs; contributes to the success of the center's fund-raising efforts; and attracts older persons not now aware of the opportunities.

Advises the board of directors and sponsoring groups on the center's operations; the community's changing needs; and policy and program changes to meet the needs.

Prepares the center's budget; interprets the budgetary requirements to the board of directors and to the center's allocating agencies.

Administers the center's operations by exercising fiscal control, establishing and maintaining personnel standards, and developing operating procedures; provides for adequate maintenance of the center's physical facilities and equipment.

Minimum Qualifications

Education. A Master's degree from an accredited college or university in social work, education, recreation, gerontology, or a related field.

Experience. Five years of responsible full-time paid employment in group work which may have been in the field of adult education, recreation, social work, religion, rehabilitation, or a related field of which one year must have been in work with older persons, and of which two years must have been in an administrative, supervisory, or consultative capacity.

Substitution. An additional year of graduate work in one of the fields listed above may be substituted for one year of general experience.

Knowledge. Thorough knowledge of group dynamics and of the techniques for working effectively with groups.

Thorough knowledge of human development, including the processes of aging.

Thorough knowledge of the motivation and capacity of older persons for participation in multipurpose activity centers, employment, and in recreational, social, and educational activities; knowledge of a variety of activities which can be established.

Thorough knowledge of current research and demonstration projects relating to senior centers.

Considerable knowledge of how adults learn and of the various training media.

Considerable knowledge of community organization and resources for older persons.

Abilities. Ability to organize and provide leadership for group activities.

Ability to work with older people, either individually or in groups, and to encourage their participation in planning the center's program.

Ability to speak and write effectively.

Ability to coordinate the efforts of individuals and groups in achieving an effective program.

Ability to conduct formal and informal meetings.

Ability to work with community agencies; and to exercise leadership.

PROGRAM DIRECTOR

Definition

Under the general direction of the executive director, administers the activities program of the center; supervises member and nonmember volunteers, students and aides serving as teachers and group leaders; and performs related duties as assigned.

Examples of Duties

Program. Carries responsibility for over-all direction, guidance, supervision and correlation of all program areas. These areas include group work, recreation, adult education, community volunteer service projects, social programs and food service.

Works with committees that plan and carry out regular program activities and special events.

Directs center-wide events and mass activities.

Program leadership. Recruits, trains and supervises volunteer and employed group leaders and teachers.

Coordinates work of a counselor and nurse (as related to program), community consultants, music, art and crafts specialists.

Administrative responsibilities for program. Serves as consultant to a program development committee of the board of directors.

Assists in preparation of the annual budget.

Prepares reports, studies and recommendations for the executive director.

Prepares proposals for research demonstrations and training projects.

From the *Personnel Manual* of the San Francisco Senior Center, San Francisco, California.

Carries out special assignments as a principal associate of an executive director.

Community leadership and participation. Represents a center on appropriate community committees and participates in conferences and workshops on aging problems and programs.

Conducts or delegates responsibility to a hostess committee to conduct individuals and groups through a center to observe the program.

Works cooperatively with other agencies; e.g., adult education department of the public schools, municipal recreation department, volunteer bureau, heart association, cancer society, hearing society, and others.

Performs related duties as assigned by an executive director.

Minimum Qualifications

Master's degree in social group work, recreation or education. Some previous experience in working with older adults, as an employee or volunteer.

Ability to work cooperatively with members of a staff, other professional workers in public and private agencies and with volunteers.

Ability to carry out the duties and responsibilities outlined.

COUNSELOR

Definition

Under the general direction of the executive director, administers the individual services program; is responsible for intake of new members; counsels with members around personal problems and makes referrals to other agencies when appropriate; and supervises volunteers and students who give direct personal services to members.

Examples of Duties

Individual services to the members of the center. Interviews all applicants considering membership; gives each a visitor's card; introduces applicant to a member of the membership committee; talks again with applicant after his third visit, if he decides to join the center; completes confidential card recording such information as will help the staff in working with the individual; introduces member-applicant to the finance committee for payment of his dues.

Confers with members: on personal problems, referring them to appropriate community agencies for continuing help; with individuals who are having difficulties being accepted in and adjusting to group activities; helps resolve conflicts among center members.

Confers with others about members: talks with relatives or friends of an older adult who are interested in having him become a member; talks with children or relatives of older adults needing out-of-home care; confers with nurses and doctors about patients whom they feel will benefit by the center's program; confers with members who need part-time employment; confers with other welfare and health agencies about clients and patients whom they feel will benefit from membership in the center.

Services to groups. Serves as trainer and adviser to a center's visiting, homebound, membership, hostess and attendance committees.

Is staff consultant for a board of directors commitee on individual services.

Maintains liaison with psychiatric consultant and acts as chairman of psychiatric consultation staff meetings.

Meets with groups of nurses and social work students on visits to observe the program and learn of its value to older patients or clients.

Is supervisor of social work students assigned to a center for field work training.

Participates in in-service training of staff and orientation and training of volunteers.

Responsibilities to program staff. Works with program staff to help integrate new members into the program.

Advises with program staff about developing new groups to meet special needs related to analysis of members' needs revealed in records of intake interview.

Prepares and reviews for staff meetings pertinent information about each new member that will facilitate his individualization in center program.

Participates in research and demonstration projects.

Participation in the community. Represents a center in appropriate community committees.

Participates in such workshops and conferences to which experiences of the center can make a contribution in understanding needs of older adults and action to meet them.

Records. Supervises clerical workers in keeping membership files and all individual records current; i.e., membership, attendance, dues, statistical.

Records case studies that could be used for teaching materials.

Minimum Qualifications

Master's degree in social work or equivalent education in another profession related to counseling and personal problem solving.

Five years' experience in social work, preferably casework, in a family agency or department of public social services.

Ability to supervise professional, student and volunteer staff.

Ability to work cooperatively with members of other professions and other agencies.

Ability to carry out duties and responsibilities outlined.

BIBLIOGRAPHY

Bassett, E. C., "Some Impressions of Programs for Training Practitioners in the Field of Aging." *Gerontologist* 5 (1965): 30-33.

Danford, Howard G. *Creative Leadership in Recreation.* Boston: Allyn & Bacon, 1964.

Forman, Mark. "Conflict, Controversy and Confrontation in Group Work with Older Adults." *Social Work* 12 (1967): 80-85.

Kansas State Department of Social Welfare. *Activities in Nursing Homes: A Handbook for Volunteers.* Topeka: Division of Services for the Aging, Kansas State Department of Social Welfare, 1960.

Kraus, Richard. *Recreation Today—Program Planning and Leadership.* New York: Appleton-Century-Crofts, 1966.

Lowy, Louis. *Training Manual for Human Service Technicians Working with Older Persons, Part 2.* Boston: Boston University Bookstore, 1968, pp. 39-50.

Maxwell, Jean M. *Centers for Older People: Guide for Programs and Facilities.* New York: National Council on Aging, 1962.

Oregon State Board of Health. *Oregon's Handbook for Volunteers Serving the Aged: A Guide to Assist Volunteers, Communities, Organizations, Groups, Nursing Homes and Homes for the Aged.* Portland: Oregon State Board of Health, 1962.

Shapiro, Robert, and Shura, Saul. "Effective Use of Volunteers in Group Work and Recreational Programs." *The New Outlook for the Blind* 53 (1959): 361-66.

Shivers, Jay S. *Leadership in Recreational Service.* New York: Macmillan Co., 1963.

Tead, Ordway. *The Art of Leadership.* New York: McGraw-Hill, 1935.

U.S. Department of Health, Education and Welfare, Administration on Aging. *Demand for Personnel and Training in the Field of Aging.* Publication no. 270, 1969.

U.S. Department of Health, Education and Welfare, Administration on Aging, *Guide Specifications for Positions in Aging.* 1965.

Welfare and Health Council of New York City, Central Volunteer Bureau. *Organization and Administration of Agency Volunteer Service Program.* New York: Welfare and Health Council of New York City, 1954.

Zander, Alvin; Cohen, Arthur R.; and Stotland, Ezra. *Role Relations in the Mental Health Professions.* Ann Arbor: University of Michigan Center for Group Dynamics, Institute for Social Research, 1957.

14 / Programs of Social Groups for Older Adults

PROGRAM IS MORE THAN SCHEDULED ACTIVITIES. Program is the planning of activities and the interaction that takes place among individuals when they participate in them. Activities, however enjoyable, have little value in helping individuals cope with persistent feelings of loneliness, uselessness, and depression. These are primarily important because they provide the settings in which members may experience acceptance by others, the feeling of belonging to a group, and recognition as individuals of worth. Such feelings strengthen the older adult's self-image and help him feel good about himself. Program then is not only *what* happens and *when* it happens, but *what meaning* it has for each member as he participates.

Interests of members will differ

Members will be men and women from widely diversified social, economic, racial, and cultural backgrounds. Ranging from sixty to ninety years of age, their interests will be as varied as their total life experiences. Members choose to participate in activities that have personal appeal, and what will be meaningful for one individual will be a chore for another. Some will want to play cards and scorn the service projects that interest others.

While most activities will interest both men and women, some planned exclusively for men will serve as psychological substitutes for former jobs. Activities that interest a sixty-two-year-old member may be too active or too rapidly paced for the eighty-five to ninety-year-old, who will enjoy smaller groups and more passive activities. The extroverted, secure older person with many interests will need to select from the variety of activities available. The timid, withdrawn person, like Mrs. B, will participate vicariously by watching others.

Mrs. B was a widow for more than twenty years before joining the center. She has no children or close relatives and lives in a tiny room in the rear of the laundry where she has worked for many years. She speaks English haltingly and therefore talks to very few people. The first thing she does when she arrives at the center is to come directly to the director's office and say, "Hello! I just wanted to be sure you were here." Then she goes into the big social hall, finds herself a seat along the side of the room, and spends several hours watching the activity in the room. Her history of living alone and doing hard physical work, along with her lack of facility in English, have made her a withdrawn, passive kind of person. The staff has often tried to interest her in participating in some of the small group activities, but with a winsome smile she will say, "I just don't feel like it today."

To force such an individual into a socialization pattern woud not be meeting her needs. Her participation is on a simple level, but her satisfaction is meaningful, if one can judge from her regularity of attendance, her expectation that she will receive some recognition from the staff, and the cheery disposition she shows to all who stop to visit with her.

The program must be diversified to meet differing needs

The program will have different meanings for different members. For most it will provide opportunities for personal enjoyment and enrichment. For others facing crisis and loneliness, the program's value will be the emotional support it gives. For the depressed and for those who have experienced mental illness, the center will be a therapeutic community where friendly relations with others will help in social rehabilitation. Within limitations imposed by physical facilities, size of staff, and budget, the program must be as diversified as possible. Alternative choices of activities for fun, creative self-expression, education, service, and social action will be necessary to assure a balanced program that will hold something of interest for every member.

Physical facilities limit the diversity of the program

The buildings in which some senior centers are located impose practical limitations on the diversity of program. When only one large room is available, it is difficult to schedule interest groups, classes, committee meetings, social activities, and table games all at the same time. Some groups have found it successful to schedule classes, interest groups, and committee meetings in the morning; other members join in for a noon coffee hour, with a speaker or program; and in the afternoon the room is used for social activities. Where the facilities are large enough, the interest groups and the classes are often held in the same room as the social activities in order to expose members to possible new interests and motivate their participation.

The time when the group meets is also determined by the facilities that are being used. If the rooms are shared with school-age youth, the morning, midday and early afternoon hours assure groups of older people the longest periods of undisturbed time. If the facilities are available for long periods, many leaders believe that the hours from nine to five are desirable because they approximate the workday hours; the program then becomes a natural substitute and may offer some of the compensating values of a job routine. Occasional evening social activities and Sunday afternoon musical programs can be scheduled, if facilities are available, to enrich the regular daytime program.

Leaders must find ways to
learn members' interests

Some leaders believe that Is is easy to plan activities for a group because all one needs to do is ask, "What would you like to do?" Such a query will bring no response from many individuals, and from others merely a reference to activities in which they are already engaged. Older adults often say, "I didn't know what else to want." Because most people express interests in terms of known experiences, the leader will need to *lead;* he must arouse curiosity and stimulate interest in new experiences. A successful approach is to use interest inventories. Each member checks his preferences and the program committee schedules those activities in which most members have indicated an interest. (See Sample of Interest Inventory, pp. 222–223.)

Through informal conversation with the group, the skilled leader can stimulate new interests by asking such questions as, "Did you read—?" "Did you know—?" "Wouldn't it be fun to—" "Did you hear that a senior club in another city—?" Some of the best leads for programs can be secured during the intake interviews by asking applicants to tell what they always had wanted to do if they had had the time. The leader will need to keep a file of program ideas that he can pull out at opportune times to help the group move ahead in developing widened interests. In the file he can accumulate ideas for programs, names of speakers, places to go, subjects for discussions, stories and poems for birthday ceremonials, new members' parties, and bulletin boards. Programs will sometimes be determined on a trial and error basis. Activities that are enjoyed and include many members will be requested over and over again by the group. Popular activities soon become accepted as an established part of the program. They become so sacred that certain members become extremely angry when newer members suggest that they be dropped. Nevertheless, the memberships of groups change, and activities, too, must change in order to be relevant to the interests of current members.

It is not possible to list all the activities enjoyed by older adults. Those described are typical of the kinds found in many senior centers and clubs. Few organizations are able to include at any one time all of those mentioned. Additional suggestions can be found in the resources listed.

Fun and Games

Older adults need fun and gaiety in their lives. Therefore those activities whose sole purpose is entertainment and diversion will be among the most popular in senior center programs. Becoming totally absorbed in a bridge game, matching wits against another in a charade, helping a team win a walking relay, and laughing uproariously over the entries in a funny hat contest can be truly therapeutic experiences. Not all older adults enjoy playing games. Some will feel that playing is not adult behavior; others are self-conscious about participating in activities that make them appear conspicuous, awkward, or ridiculous. Other adults have such poor self-images that they do not feel themselves worthy of feeling happy and engaging in joyful activities. It is often good strategy for the staff to participate enthusiastically with the members in games and contests. The fact that a staff member enjoys them and considers them an appropriate part of an adult's life gives reticent members tacit permission to enjoy them also.

Games and contests are effective techniques for helping new members become acquainted. Games that start with the early arrivals and gradually include others as they come help to create a happy mood and a welcoming climate. Active games should not last too long, but should be stopped while the enjoyment is at its height and before the group becomes fatigued. A leader responsible for such programs will find it helpful to keep a file of games and contests, adding new ones occasionally.

Card and table games. Informal card and table games rank high in popularity among older adults. Classes in bridge, canasta, chess, cribbage, dominoes, and other table games give members an opportunity to learn new games. Occasional tournaments add excitement to the program. In addition to the fun of the game, members who play together form intimate social units that lead toward closer friendships outside the center. If members of foursomes are carefully selected for skill and congeniality, a card game in which one must relate to only three other persons provides an easy way for a new member to begin to feel acquainted. Card games and the necessity to shuffle and deal may also offer a degree of physical therapy for members with arthritic fingers.

Card and table games, on the other hand, have within them the potential for becoming seriously divisive factors in a group and the locale of hostile behavior and misunderstanding. When the same partners always play together and never feel any responsibility to include the newcomer in their game; when their interest in the club is limited to this one activity and they are unwilling to assume any responsibility on committees; when they are resentful if this activity is terminated in order that the room can be used for another one—then card and table games become a disintegrating force in the club rather than providing a means for easy socialization. If limited space is absorbed by this one activity, those older adults who do not enjoy card playing do not join the center. The members' council must be responsible for setting limits as to where, and for how long, card games may be played. Other table games for two, such as dominoes, Chinese checkers, and double solitaire, are often taught at centers. They, too, keep minds alert and responsive and can be played at home as well as at the center with just one other friend.

Bingo. Bingo continues to be popular in most groups of older adults, but it holds little interest for those who play a good game of bridge because it requires no skill and little concentration. Leaders seeking an easy way to keep members occupied may be too dependent on it. Some members, however, do enjoy playing bingo and are motivated to participate by the small prizes offered. It is an excellent game for groups of older people with visual and hearing handicaps and for parties for the physically and mentally frail members. Writing numbers on the blackboard as they are called and using cards with large figures make it possible for such handicapped older people to play a game with others.

Outdoor games and exercise classes. Outdoor games, such as lawn bowling, roque, bocci ball, shuffleboard, and croquet, are popular activities in those centers that are situated in park settings or where there is space for such activity. Although some women do participate in such games, they are essentially of interest to men and, for that reason, are highly desirable activities to include in center programs.

Exercise classes, popularly called geriatric-calisthenics, interest those older adults who recognize the importance of physical activity as the body ages. They are generally individuals who have included some exercise in their daily living for many years. In exercises for older adults the movements are often performed while the individual is seated on a straight-backed folding chair. They are interspersed with frequent periods of rest and relaxation and are designed to maintain muscle tone and to provide movement for stiffening joints. Instructions are given for proper breathing, posture, and tension and relaxation of the body. Tai Chi Chuan, a series of ancient Chinese exercises in physical sensitivity, is highly adaptable to use with older adults. Participants frequently describe the great sense of freedom and physical and emotional well-being that results from exercise classes and the help the classes give them in remaining mobile.

Parties and celebrations. A party for older adults, as for young people, is a high occasion. Holidays, anniversaries, birthdays and receptions for new members, are marked by appropriate celebrations. Each center develops traditional ways of observing special events that are soon invested with deep feelings of fellowship and group loyalty. In most centers birthdays are celebrated at monthly parties. For an older person who no longer has an intimate family group with whom to celebrate, a birthday may be just another day and best forgotten; it becomes too painful to recall the happiness that once surrounded the anniversary. For many older people, the group can be a substitute for their former family and friendship circle, and the celebration of birthdays by the members becomes a very meaningful experience.

In some groups, a record of each member's birthday is kept by a birthday committee chairman, and a greeting card is sent to him at the appropriate time. Enclosed with the card is an invitation to be a guest at a party that will be given in honor of members who celebrate their birthdays during a particular month. The celebrants are seated at a special table that has been decorated by the birthday party committee, and at each place is a rose bud and a small candle. Sentimentality has no place on an occasion such as this, but older people do respond appreciatively if the leader gives a short talk that is sincere, warm, and inspirational. At the conclusion of the talk, the leader lights the small candle of each celebrant, and the group greets the guests by singing "Happy Birthday to You." Then the celebrants lift high their candles to form a circle of light, while the group sings, "The More We Get Together the Happier We'll Be." As the song ends, the candles are blown out.

Then follows the most significant part of the celebration. The leader introduces each guest with some comment that calls attention to his contribution to the group. The guest then stands and tells where he had his first birthday, and makes any other comments he wishes. When he had his first birthday is never asked, though of course many proudly tell the year. A box of candy is given to the woman and to the man who have had the most birthdays, and the ceremonial is over—but not the celebration! Members surround the celebrants with their personal words of greeting and congratulation! The celebrants often comment, "I haven't had a birthday party for thirty years. There is no one else who even knows when my birthday is." Birthday celebrations are important and popular activities in programs for older people and should be made as meaningful as possible for each guest.

Educational Programs

Continuing research is finding convincing evidence that if pathology is not present, mental decline can be slowed down and even reversed by learning new knowledge and skills. In support of this fact, educational classes of all kinds are found in many senior center programs. In most communities, adult education departments of the public schools are alert to the challenge and responsibility of providing opportunities for making learning a lifelong process, and many elderly people enroll in school classes along with students of all ages. They study English to qualify for citizenship and many take pride in completing requirements for high school diplomas. School-centered classes, however, are not easily available for many older adults when they are scheduled at night or held in rooms reached only by climbing long flights of stairs. Therefore, many communities also provided teachers for classes at senior centers.

Classes held in senior centers are characterized by an informal educational approach in which students can come to know one another intimately. Many older adults welcome the opportunity to widen their intellectual horizons, and in the process have opportunities for meaningful interpersonal relationships with age mates. Educational experiences, however, must be relevant to needs and interests. Formal schooling, travel experiences, and the extent of one's social contacts will determine the degree of member motivation to learn new concepts, information, languages, and skills.

In this culture, learning has always been important as a means to make a living rather than as a value that should continue throughout life. Therefore, the terminology that is used in scheduling activities will affect the individual's desire to participate. Some people associate classes with a school situation and with pedantic methods and goals—and sometimes with failure. Because they have not attended school for many years they have often lost confidence in their ability to learn. A craft studio, a Spanish conversation club, and a round table discussion may help to give a recreational tone to learning situations.

Young people accept the discipline of mastering a specific body of knowledge because they are preparing for specific vocational goals. Older people enter into a learning situation only if it appears to have immediate value and interest and hold little potential for failure. The sense of mastery that comes in completing one's first ceramic bowl or woven mat, the chance to present one's ideas during a discussion group even though they may not be accepted, the ability to speak a phrase in a new language even though it can be understood by no one but fellow classmates—these are all experiences that add zest to the day and bolster feelings of accomplishment and adequacy.

Lectures and films on a variety of subjects of social concern followed by discussions or question-and-answer periods are better learning situations for older adults than formal presentations by a teacher. Many older people who live alone rarely have anyone who serves as a listener before whom they can express themselves and test their ideas. Informal learning experiences give them this opportunity. Some individuals at forums and discussions verbalize their comments and questions easily, but the silent participation of others is equally significant. The shaking head, the wandering eyes, and the tight lips prod leaders to search for ways to reach and open minds so that understanding may be increased. The possible areas of interest that can be dealt with in educational programs are unlimited and should include world problems, community problems, current legislation, politics, comparative religions, and problems of youth and age.

Information on all aspects of health maintenance is of great interest to most members. Doctors and representatives from health agencies are usually very cooperative in speaking on various aspects of health and alerting their audiences to the initial signs of conditions that might develop into chronic illnesses. Public health nurses, members of smog control boards, and representatives from safety councils and the traffic bureaus of police departments are also popular and highly appreciated speakers.

A series of talks on health is often climaxed by a Health Fair for members of the center and other older adults in the community. Exhibits are set up by heart, cancer, arthritis, and other health organizations; informational literature is distributed; and glaucoma and diabetes screening, some inoculations, and chest X-rays are offered to all who attend.

Talks on defensive driving and the prevention of traffic accidents can be culminated by a Traffic Education Day. A report of such an event follows:

> The chief of the traffic division of the police department became concerned over the increasing number of traffic fatalities among citizens sixty years of age and older. He appealed to the staff and members of the senior center to help him with an educational campaign for older adults. A committee of members was appointed and a staff member was assigned to work with them. Representatives from the police department, safety council, municipal railway, state automobile association, and taxicab company met with them.
>
> The group decided to stage a traffic pageant and demonstration in a downtown park and called it "Walkers-Aware." All older adults of the city were invited. The mayor greeted them and assured the group of the city's interest in them and in their welfare. Then followed a pageant which demonstrated the increased power of the modern motor car over the "surrey with the fringe on top" and the Model T Ford. Pedestrian safety factors, car-stopping distances, traffic signal controls and their operation, and techniques for crossing the streets safely were demonstrated and discussed by safety officials.
>
> After these demonstrations, the group was led by the school band and a Boy Scout troop to a nearby high school, where safety movies were shown and door prizes of taxicab scrip books were awarded. Led by the center glee club, the entire group joined in singing the Walt Disney song, "I'm No Fool, No Siree! I wanna Live to Be Ninety-three." The planning committee agreed that if just one traffic fatality was prevented, Walkers-Aware Day was well worth the effort.[1]

In addition to discussions of such subjects as social concerns, consumer problems, nutritional needs, health questions, and safety and prevention of accidents, older adults are interested in and need help in understanding the emotional problems of aging and in developing a positive philosophy about growing old and the inevitability of death. Much of the available information about the aging process and the adjustments that must be made is not geared or directed to older adults themselves but to those with whom they live or who direct programs and give services to them. Small groups, staffed by a skilled leader, that provide a climate of security and maximum freedom of expression help group members look at themselves and explore their feelings about

[1] From the author's booklet *How to Work with Older People,* published by the Division of Recreation, State of California (1960).

growing old. Group members are encouraged in discussions to relate to one another honestly and to share their own experiences rather than to talk objectively about old age and its potential problems. A climate of mutual trust is developed and dilution therapy takes place as individuals become aware that others in the group have similar feelings, fears, and hopes.

Resource materials for educational programs

United States Office of Education: Adult Education Section, Washington, D.C. 20036.

National Education Association, 1201 16th Street N.W., Washington, D.C. 20036.

Adult Education Association of the U.S.A., 1225 19th Street N.W., Washington, D.C. 20036.

The association offers general infomation services receiving and distributing educational information, encourages and assists agencies to develop adult education programs, and sponsors preretirement programs through local affiliates.

American Association of Retired Persons and National Retired Teachers Association, 1225 Connecticut Ave. N.W., Washington D.C., 20036.

In addition to its many services to individual members, its monthly publication, *Modern Maturity,* has excellent articles of educational interest.

Food and Drug Administration, U.S. Department of Health, Education and Welfare, Washington, D.C. 20204, or the district office of the F.D.A.

In conjunction with its efforts to enforce laws governing foods and drugs, the Food and Drug Administration also provides a broad educational program, which offers general information and professional consultations. Information is made available to interested persons or groups. Consumer information services include the preparation and distribution of pamphlets, periodicals, films, radio and television scripts, booklets and visual aids for teachers, and radio and television spot announcements.

U.S. Department of Health, Education and Welfare, Administration on Aging, Washington, D.C. 20201.

Project Money-Wise Seniors: Consumer Education for Older People was developed by the Administration on Aging in cooperation with the Bureau of Federal Credit Unions as a program of consumer education and action.

Consumer Interests of the Elderly,
U.S. Senate Special Committee on Aging,
Senate Office Building,
Washington, D.C. 20510.
This subcommittee of the Committee on Aging was set up to investigate quackery, frauds, or deceptions that exploit the elderly and to study special consumer problems affecting older people.

Federal Extension Service,
U.S. Department of Agriculture,
Washington, D.C. 20250.
Educational materials of all kinds for groups meeting in rural areas are available through this agency.

National Safety Council—Home Department,
425 N. Michigan Avenue,
Chicago, Illinois 60611.
Films, discussion guides, and helps on planning conferences on accident prevention and traffic safety are available. A film, *A Matter of Seconds,* is loaned free of charge.

American Optometric Association,
7000 Chippewa Street,
St. Louis, Missouri 63119.
In addition to its normal information service, which makes available various publications, the association provides exhibits and programs through state associations for fairs, senior citizens' groups, conferences, public health exhibits, and so forth.
    Available printed information: A textbook, *Vision of the Aging Patient;* and pamphlets, *Mature Vision and Its Care, Driving Tips for Senior Citizens, Getting Used to Bifocals, How Healthy are Your Eyes, Answers to Your Questions About Glaucoma, Answers to Your Questions About Cataract.*

American Podiatry Association,
1301 16th Street N.W.,
Washington, D.C. 20036.
This association has had a long interest in the foot health of the older person. Through its Committee on Aging it stimulates, guides,

and assists states and local communities to develop general education programs regarding foot care. It also assesses the needs and resources to provide for adequate foot care. A free leaflet on foot care is available.

U.S. Department of Health, Education and Welfare,
Washington, D.C. 20201.
This federal agency has free pamphlets available on most all aspects of health, chronic illness, and health care.

Outings, Trips, and Camping

Bus trips. Interest in going to new places and seeing new sights persists throughout all of life. Members often lament that now that they have retired and have time for travel, they have little money to spend and too often have no one with whom to go. Because so few older people—especially those who live in large cities—continue to own and drive their own cars, trips by chartered bus to nearby points of scenic, historical, and cultural interest, at costs they can afford, are popular activities. They contribute significantly by helping to broaden interests and horizons and by giving older individuals something to look forward to.

Careful planning of every detail must be done in advance of the event; the thought and care put into preparation will make all the difference between a relaxed and enjoyable trip and one filled with uncertainties, frustrations, and disappointments. The wisdom of sending groups of older people off on trips and excursions without a responsible, nongroup member accompanying them is questionable. Many older persons would be as effective in an emergency situation as a younger leader, but a bus trip can be a lonely experience for some older people if no one in the group is responsible for helping all the travelers feel included and involved in this joint experience.

A committee of members working with a staff leader plans the trips and makes the regulations that govern them. Misunderstandings and unreasonable demands for preferential treatment can be eliminated if the following suggested regulations are followed.

1. Bus seats are reserved in the order reservations and cash deposits are received. Refunds cannot be given unless an emergency occurs or the member cancels the reservation three days before the trip. Members wishing to sit together must make their reservations together.

2. No reservation can be made by phone.

3. Reservations cannot be transferred by one member to another. Cancellations must be filled by the staff from a waiting list.

4. Trips are for center members. If there is additional room, guests may be added if the request is cleared with the staff.

5. All persons going on overnight trips must pay a stated amount for group accident insurance and must have a medical form filled out and signed by a doctor not more than ten days prior to the trip.

Armchair trips. Limited mobility becomes an increasing reality in the lives of many older adults. Center programs should provide many opportunities for those who cannot go on trips and outings to experience these pleasures in other ways. Travel slides, movies, talks, television programs, and travel book reviews are all enjoyable substitutes. Beautiful colored and sound movies on trips to all parts of the world are available from most major airlines.

Camping. The importance of preserving open spaces and natural resources for public use is recognized. Local, state, and national governmental bodies as well as voluntary associations are working to develop more park areas in cities and counties and camping areas in state and national parks, monuments, and forests. School, church, and agency camps are making camping experiences possible for more young people and for families. Recognizing the values of camping experiences, a growing number of senior centers are now providing camping for members.

Camping as an integral part of a center's program opens up a whole new world to older adults who live alone and rarely travel far from their neighborhoods. Camping is more than a vacation and a break in routine. It offers opportunities to live with age mates for a short time in a beautiful outdoor setting, to enjoy being a member of a camp family group, and to experience the daily adventures that only camping can provide. It has a quality of experiences and relationships that no other part of the center program offers.

The American Camping Association, which is interested in developing and setting standards for camping for older people, has a committee on camping for senior citizens. This committee has formulated four objectives for camping for older adults. Programs and living arrangements should (1) foster simple and wholesome living, (2) provide an enriching experience not obtainable in urban areas, (3) develop peer friendships, and (4) give opportunities for personal growth. The committee recommends that the camps used should not be more than seventy-five miles from the home community and should be located where a physician is not more than fifteen minutes from the camp and a medical facility is easily accessible. Health examinations should be required and accident insurance should be carried by the center to cover campers and staff.

Public recreation and park departments have taken the lead in developing camping for older adults. Facilities and programs are scheduled in municipally-operated camps at stated periods or as part of family camp periods. Few nonprofit organizations serving older adults own camps. Most centers use either the program of the public recreation and park departments or the established, well-equipped facilities of churches or youth-serving agencies before or after regular camping seasons. Other centers rent a beach cottage or cabins at a mountain resort. Some reserve group camping areas in state or national parks and forests where a more primitive experience is possible, but few older adults enjoy sleeping on the ground or on camp cots or cooking outdoors unless they are experienced campers. Physical safety and comfort are primary considerations for older people, and sites used should have adequate areas of level terrain with paths that are level and well lighted at night. Heated cabins with running water and toilet facilities are more appropriate for older people than dormitory arrangements.

Camps for older adults are often organized as a unit within a family or children's camp. This plan takes from the center staff the responsibility for food service, health services, water safety, and camp maintenance. An arrangement of cabins set apart from the mainstream of activity with their own dining room and lounge area provides a quieter and less active environment for older campers. This arrangement makes possible a balanced community with opportunities for some joint programs and interchange between young people and the elderly. The adult campers should have their own activities schedule with a member of the center staff serving as the director so that continuity of relationships and program with the center is maintained. Specific planning is the responsibility of a council of campers made up of representatives from the various living units working with the camp director.

The daily program should have some regularly scheduled activities but for the most part should remain flexible and should be carried out at a leisurely pace with adequate time for rest and quiet. The campers will want to continue some of the activities that they enjoy at the center, such as table games, crafts, group singing, and dancing. Carefully supervised outdoor activities, such as nature walks, fishing, boating, and evening campfires, will make the whole experience a special adventure. Participation in the camp activities should be voluntary. The program at camp, as at the center, must be kept person-centered rather than activity-centered.

A camp setting where the staff leaders live as well as play with the group provides a unique opportunity for a deeper and more intimate relationship with individual members than does the center. Counselors and program leaders must therefore be carefully selected and should have had some previous experience in working with older adults.

It will not be possible to interest all older adults in a camping experience. They will not want to leave the familiar place that is home and go with people they may not know too well to an unknown place. Will it be safe? Will they like the food? What will it be like to sleep in a strange place? What will happen if they become ill? The anxieties around these questions are intense, and many older people are unable to accept the risks they imagine. Precamp meetings at which pictures of the campsite and activities are shown and questions are answered by the staff and those who have camped in previous years help to allay such fears and apprehensions.

Financing such a vacation is also difficult for many older people. Even though "campership" funds are available to supplement the minimal charges paid by the campers, many individuals do not have even this much margin to spend on a vacation.

Residential camping as a part of a year-round program has been achieved by very few senior centers. With budget and staff limitations, outdoor programs have had to be restricted to day camps in park settings accessible by public transportation. Sheltered areas with picnic tables and benches, with easily accessible toilet facilities, drinking water, and some level ground, are minimal requirements for a day camp setting. Here campers bring their own lunches and spend the day. Although this experience does not approximate that of an out-of-town camp, it does have some advantages. It is available to more members, the cost is minimal, and the setting makes possible certain activities that cannot be enjoyed at the center. In addition, volunteers are often willing to work in a day camp setting that does not require them to be away from home for an extended period. With some experienced volunteers, a staff member who serves as program director and a nurse may be the only full-time staff members needed.

Recreational areas in rural settings, suitable for use by groups of older adults, are being developed through the innovative credit program of the Farmer's Home Association authorized by Congress in 1962. Through this program loans can be made to farmers and nonprofit associations of rural residents to develop income-producing recreational projects and community recreational facilities, picnic and camping areas, golf courses, and vacation farms. As more nearby facilities are developed and funds become available, camping and outdoor activities will become integral parts of the programs of greater numbers of multiservice senior centers.

Resources on Camping

The American Camping Association, Inc.,
Bradford Woods,
Martinsville, Indiana 46151.

> The association has a national committee on camping for older adults. A pamphlet, *Camping for Senior Citizens,* by James M. Fuhery, is available for 75 cents.

The Christian Church Camp and Conference Office,
222 South Downey Avenue,
Indianapolis, Indiana 46219.

> A film, *Camping is Ageless,* is available (sale price $5.00).

National Council on the Aging,
1828 "L" Street N.W., Suite 504,
Washington, D.C. 20030

> Pamphlet, *Camping for Older People,* by Geneva Mathiasen.

Creative Activities

Arts, crafts, creative writing, drama, and music. The interests, skills and experiences of members in creative activities will differ widely. Some will have developed skills over the years and be able to teach classes, others may have never had the time or opportunity to develop their latent interests and talents. They seek opportunities to do so after retirement. The latter may derive deep satisfaction from participation in creative activities. Still others have no interest in this kind of personal enrichment and expression.

Only a few of the creative activities enjoyed by older adults are discussed in the following section. A wider variety is included in the programs of some centers, but in others, because of limited facilities, equipment, and teachers, few opportunities to enjoy creative activities can be made available. Many books describing techniques for various art projects are found in libraries and art stores.

Crafts. The leader of the crafts program must be interested in helping older people feel a sense of satisfaction and accomplishment in what they make rather than being concerned with the perfection or even the beauty of the finished object. The emphasis must be on the joy of creation in companionship with members of the class, rather than on the excellence of the product. Standards of workmanship, good design, and harmonious colors can be expected and achieved with guided help. Goals should be flexible enough to permit each student to attain his own potential; otherwise he will feel frustration in trying to compete with the achievements of more skilled members.

Although demonstrations are often given in the general club rooms as a technique for stimulating interest in a class, a separate, well-lighted area is essential for a successful craft program. It should be large enough to give all students ample room for working without feeling crowded. Adequate storage space where unfinished work can be safely kept is needed, especially if the building and equipment are shared with other groups. If funds are limited, programs can include only those crafts that need a minimum of equipment, but such expensive items as looms, power tools, ceramic kilns, and potter's wheels are often provided by service clubs and other interested community groups. Attractive craft articles can be made of scrap material but older adults, after they have learned the process, should have quality materials with which to work.

Projects should be functional and not too expensive to produce. Older people enjoy knitting, but it is an unrewarding activity if there is no one to knit for. There is a limit to how many milk mugs will be needed as gifts for great-grand-children. If the group has a bazaar where a mug can be offered for sale or a hobby show where it can be displayed bearing the name of the potter, then there is added purpose and meaning to the activity. The men in the workshop enjoy the whir of the machinery and repairing card tables and making needed equipment for the group; but the hum of the machinery, as well as the interest of the men, take on new tempo if an order has just come for play equipment for a nursery school for retarded children, bed trays for a hospital, or easels for a painting class.

Older adults who enjoy creative arts are often reluctant to enter other activities, preferring to spend all of their time in the craft studio. This practice can create an administrative problem when popular classes become too large to admit new students. When new members must be told that classes in which they are interested are closed, they often lose interest in joining the center. Some centers have met this problem by requiring students to reregister every three or six months, letting new members register first. Feelings of rejection, resentment, and disappointment are inevitable if individuals to whom the activity has great interest are excluded. However, those students who have developed a high degree of skill can be encouraged to enroll in more advanced classes in adult schools and colleges, and in some centers there are advanced and beginners classes in various crafts scheduled on different days. A student may enter only one class but he may also participate in a weekly informal studio program in which he is free to work on a special project.

In addition to providing the satisfaction of participating in a creative experience, most art and craft activities are excellent programs for older adults because they require little gross mobility and only slight physical exertion. Because many of the movements can help to keep fingers and arms flexible and joints limber, a teacher who has had some training in occupational therapy is an especially good leader for an arts and crafts program for older adults.

Woodcraft. Woodcraft is essentially a man's activity, and in those centers in which buildings have been designed specifically for programs for older adults well-equipped wood shops are usually provided. Because of concern about safety, hand tools, rather than power tools, are often used. For a man to whom working with wood has been a job skill or long-time hobby—unless, of course, he has been a woodcarver—hand tools are inadequate and too slow. Power equipment is expensive and there are some risks involved, but staff can take precautionary measures to minimize dangers. The power tools must be checked regularly by a safety engineer and the shop supervised by someone with experience in operating the equipment. There is usually some member whose job experience or hobby interest qualifies him to assume this assignment. Caution must be used by the staff in screening members who use the shop to determine that they have no physical handicaps that might preclude the use of power tools.

The woodshop is the scene of many different kinds of activity. Many men design and work on their own projects; some make articles to sell at the center bazaar; others repair the center's card tables and chairs and build bookshelves and storage cabinets for other members. All participate in service projects for children's hospitals and nursery schools. The number of men who work in the woodshop will be relatively small, but for many of them the shop approximates a work environment and is the one place in the center where they feel completely at home and at ease.

Creative writing. For many older adults writing becomes a satisfying medium for creative expression and in center programs members find outlets for their literary efforts. Gathering in poetry groups, they read their original verse and write articles for the center's newspaper and magazine, plays for the drama class, and ceremonials and songs for special occasions. Members of the creative writers group are usually amateurs, and there is no expectation that they will achieve such excellence in their writing as will make it acceptable to the general public. Older adults write in the style and idiom of their day, which is appreciated and enjoyed mostly by their contemporaries.

Drama and puppetry. The fun of participation, rather than the perfection of performance for a viewing audience, should be the emphasis of a drama program. The program should include reading and writing as well as the acting of plays. It is difficult to find appropriate plays with characters that do not seem incongruous when played by an older adult, and initially the choice of dramas will be determined by the taste, level of experience, and identification of the participants. Plays contemporary with the young adult years of the participants or even earlier periods are more acceptable than modern plays because members identify more easily with that era. Dramatics are often more successful if the group writes its own plays based on life experiences, and, because memorizing lines often places too much stress on older adults, play reading is an excellent activity. It gives a great deal of freedom and flexibility, minimizes the anxiety, and adds to the enjoyment and increases the number of those who wish to participate. Play reading can be just for the pleasure of the participants or can be presented as a program for an audience.

The development of puppet theaters by groups of members not only stimulates interest in play writing but also in production and manipulation of the puppets. Recording the script alleviates the need for memorizing and makes for a smoother performance. Many older adults enjoy and are more comfortable in this kind of dramatic activity than in regular play performances.

Drama groups can provide some of the most enjoyable creative experiences within a senior center program. Their success will not depend upon the availability of a stage, scenery, and a skilled coach who expects actors to learn lines and participate in numerous rehearsals. The success will be determined by the fun and escape from personal problems that each actor experiences as he projects himself into his role and provides enjoyable entertainment for others.

Resources for Plays for Production by Older Adults

Two plays about problems faced by older adults written by Nora Sterling are available through local Family Service Agencies or The Family Service Association of America, 44 East 23rd Street, New York, N.Y. 10010. *A Choice to Make* is designed to help older people and their relatives understand aging and the use of inner strengths in making the most of the later years. *Ever Since April* deals with the problems of retirement and how to make constructive use of new leisure. These plays are most effective when followed by open-end discussions on how the situations presented could be resolved.

Plays recommended for play-reading groups include:

Henrik Ibsen. *Ghosts, Enemy of the People, The Doll's House.*
Eugene O'Neill. *Beyond the Horizon.*
James Barrie. *The Old Lady Shows Her Medals, Twelve Pound Look,*
    Alice Sit by the Fire.
Bernard Shaw. *Candida* and other one-act plays.
Alice C. D. Riley. *Five Minutes by the Clock.*

Dancing. Dancing of all kinds—social, folk, and square—provides moderate physical exercise for the participant as well as sociability and a happy time. Generally speaking, older adults prefer dance steps they enjoyed in their early adult years: waltzes, schottisches and two-steps, as well as some of the slower-paced folk and square dances. Some center members belong to folk dance societies and are able to perform the more intricate faster-paced dances. For most older adults, especially those who are just learning, dances with simple, slow-paced steps should be taught. For someone who has not danced for a period of years, the coordination of learning and movement is not easy. Watching a demonstration of steps by those who are familiar with them helps the learner master the dance more rapidly and with less embarrassment and awkward effort. Participation in dancing helps to improve the physical tone and posture of the aging body and also provides incentive for the older person to use care in manners, cleanliness, and in speech. The music and dancing provide emotional outlets even for those who sit on the sidelines and watch. Feet tap and heads nod in time to the music and rhythm, and eventually some of the most timid individuals can be encouraged to try the next dance.

Music. Listening to music, producing it, and sharing talents with others is another creative activity that gives enjoyment to many center members. It holds interest for those members who have studied and developed some musical skills, as well as for those who have never before played an instrument or participated in a choral group. Group singing is a part of most membership events and strengthens group morale, solidarity, and loyalty. Although the old familiar songs are popular, older adults enjoy modern folk songs and selections from light opera and musicals. Some of the modern ballads from jazz and country music groups are singable and help to interpret the ideas and social concerns of modern youth to members of the older generation. Song books and song sheets printed in large type are essential if new, unfamiliar songs are used. It is necessary to secure permission from copyright owners before music or words may be duplicated.

Glee clubs or choral groups are found in most senior centers. Their membership is not limited to those individuals who have excellent singing voices but is open to anyone who enjoys singing with others. When the group is preparing for a special performance for center members, to sing at citywide hobby shows, to appear on television, or to sing at a Christmas party in the geriatrics section of a hospital, there is added meaning in the activity and interest and participation are high.

The opportunity to enjoy and produce instrumental music is also part of the program in many senior centers. Those who already know how to play instruments often form an orchestra to play for center dances and entertainments. Interest in learning to play the organ was stimulated in many centers by a project sponsored in 1965 by the National Council on the Aging and the Baldwin Piano and Organ Company.[2] It was found that the organ was an instrument that an older adult could learn to play quickly through simplified teaching techniques. In the early stages of learning, the organ pupil acquired a gratifying sense of accomplishment that encouraged sustained effort. The organ is particularly suitable for playing the hymns and early American folk songs especially enjoyed by older adults. The project found that in those centers where organs were placed the enjoyment of group singing was increased. In those centers that own organs, many members now enjoy learning to play for personal pleasure and for group singing.

Ringing English handbells is a skill enjoyed by many older people who have had some training in reading music. These beautifully fashioned bells, each tuned to a note of the musical scale, are played by the individual ringing his bell when his note occurs on the musical score. The concentration and alertness necessary for each player to contribute his note to the beauty and harmony of the whole selection make bell ringing a stimulating aesthetic experience. For adults who cannot read music, a rhythm band, playing with recorded music, can offer fun and relaxation; many adults, however, will not participate because they associate rhythm bands with children's programs. Rhythm orchestras may be appropriate when used as entertainment and for the purpose of involving physically and emotionally frail older persons in nursing homes and extended-care facilities.

Music appreciation groups for listening to fine recordings, familiar symphonies, and opera are enjoyed by many center members. In some communities tickets for concerts and operas are made available at reduced cost to groups of center members. Programs scheduled before performances to hear the scores of the symphonies and the stories of the operas make these experiences more enjoyable.

[2] This project has been described in a pamphlet, *Music in Autumn*, a publication of the National Council on the Aging, Washington, D.C.

English handbells, organs, and stereo reel-to-reel recording units are all expensive equipment but they give members experiences of dignity and deep meaning. (Good quality recording and play-back cassette units, however, can be purchased in a $50-$100 price range, and are easy to use.) Televisions, which are also expensive, are often found in senior centers. Their use is limited and questionable because television programs are available to most older adults when they are alone in their rooms, and programs at the center should involve members one with the other.

Resources for Musical Activities

English handbells: Schulerich Carillons, Inc., Carillon Hill, Sellers-ville, Pennsylvania

Handbell Ringing by Scott Parry. Carl Fischer Co., New York

Public libraries are excellent sources for borrowing records and tapes of all kinds.

Food Service and Refreshments

Food and occasions when it is shared with others have emotional overtones and social significance. Giving and receiving food has become a symbol of giving and receiving love. Center and club groups now approximate for many older adults a family, and eating together becomes an experience of belonging and sharing. No program day is ever complete without freshments of some kind being prepared and enjoyed with others. Perhaps it is tea or coffee served to supplement the sandwich and salad that the older person has brought from home; ice cream and cake for all on the occasion of the monthly birthday party; a potluck lunch when each member brings some contribution for a communal meal; or a hot, nutritious luncheon that helps to supplement the limited and inadequate diets that many members eat on the days when the group does not meet.

Well-designed and well-equipped kitchens are essential parts of new facilities built for senior activity centers. In such facilities a hot noon meal becomes a part of the daily program. Meal preparation requires the employment of a part-time kitchen manager and enough storage space and refrigeration to make it possible to buy in quantity lots. Adequate maintenance personnel will be needed to assure sanitary standards in kitchen and storage areas. For members who may be in a higher-income level, a hot nutritious meal at the center is more of a convenience than a necessity, but for the many members who have limited incomes and live isolated and deprived lives, the daily lunch is the one balanced meal of the day and is made more enjoyable because of the atmosphere of sociability and companionship. Living in hotels or rooming houses without cooking or refrigeration facilities, lacking the financial means and physical energy to shop and prepare meals, or finding cooking and eating alone day after day an oppressive experience, these older adults often exist on quickly prepared snacks. They fail to have adequate nutrition and benefit greatly from a hot meal at the center.

All centers may not have well-equipped kitchens, but by using electric hot plates, they can provide nutritious soup at minimum cost. All members can still sit together as a family at attractively set tables and enjoy a hot meal. Some centers have been able to develop food service programs, taking advantage of the Commodity Program of the United States Department of Agriculture, which distributes surplus foods. Senior centers can receive foods on the same basis as other institutions, depending on the number of needy persons in the membership. The food must be served at the center as an integral part of the program. In September 1967, the United States Department of Agriculture issued procedural instructions to cooperating agencies in each state responsible for the distribution of surplus foods, clarifying the policy on the eligibility of senior centers and providing a simple method for determining the number of needy older adults in a center.[3]

In some communities, service agencies are being developed to prepare low-cost hot meals for older adults. The meals are prepared in central kitchens often located in housing projects or retirement residences. The senior center contracts with the service agency for the delivery of the meals to the center at regular times and days.[4] In addition to providing a nutritious meal, the hot lunch serves to motivate many isolated older adults to join centers. The staff is then able to reach out to them and help with personal problems and interest them in other areas of the center program.

Guidelines for program planning

1 To interest older people from various backgrounds and life experiences, a diversified program of activities must be offered.

2 Enrichment and interest can be added to the program by capitalizing on the background of the members and celebrating their customs, traditions, and religious holidays.

3 Individuals enjoy different activities. As wide a variety as space, leadership, and facilities permit should be included in the program.

4 A center program must provide opportunities for the older adult of limited educational background and limited income, as well as for those who have had educational, cultural, or social advantages.

5 No one type of activity should be overemphasized to the detriment of others.

6 The program should never become so static that a change of schedule meets resistance of the members. If new members are to have an opportunity to participate in the program planning, the process must be a continous one. The details of program probably should not be announced for more than two or three months ahead.

7 One of the conscious goals of the leader is to enable the individual to move from one kind of activity and develop interest in a new one. Only thus can the older person experience the satisfaction that comes through creative growth and the development of his interests and skills.

8 The activities are not ends in themselves but settings for interpersonal relationships among members that will produce feelings of approval and recognition.

9 The program should provide a noncompetitive environment in which no member will feel embarrassed, threatened, or inadequate or made to appear foolish.

10 The reticent member should be permitted to sit and observe until he decides to participate in a more active way.

Interest Inventories

Interest inventories similar to the following are helpful in determining the kinds of activities that members of centers will enjoy. They serve as a guide to staff and committees as they plan programs.

A GUIDE FOR PROGRAM PLANNING

To the member: Check the activities in which you would like to participate.

WHAT PARTIES WOULD YOU ENJOY?
___Monthly birthday parties
___Holiday parties
___Potluck dinners
___Progressive card parties
___Dancing parties – social and folk
___A party with grandchildren

IN WHAT WOULD YOU LIKE TO PARTICIPATE?
___Glee club
___English handbell choir
___Center's orchestra
___Play-reading group
___Puppet theatre

---

[3] U.S. Department of Agriculture. *Report of the Consumer Marketing Service,* Commodities Distribution Division, Washington, D.C., 1969.

[4] Such a program has been developed in San Francisco by the Northern California Presbyterian Homes, Inc.

WHAT SKILLS WOULD YOU LIKE TO
LEARN?

__Weaving   __Spanish
__Woodworking   __German
__Ceramics   __Social
__Leatherwork   dancing
__Woodcarving   __Folk & square
__Copper   dancing
  enameling   __Bridge
__Basketry   __Canasta
__Photography   __Chess
__Millinery   __Home
__French   nursing

ABOUT WHAT WOULD YOU LIKE TO
HEAR?

__Social Security program
__Conservation of sight
__Deafness and lip reading
__Good grooming and charm
__House plants: how to care for
  them
__1-meal on 1-burner for 1-person
__World affairs
__Services in the community for
  older adults
__State and federal legislation that
  benefits older citizens
__Talks on maintenance of good
  health in the later years
__A philosophy for the later years
__Wills and legal affairs
__How to invest in stock market
__Ecology

WOULD YOU LIKE TO HEAR?

  Recordings of new musical plays
__Recordings of semiclassical music
__Book reviews
__Play readings

WHOM WOULD YOU LIKE TO HELP?

__Visit members who are ill
__Serve on homebound party com-
  mittee

ABOUT WHAT WOULD YOU LIKE TO
TALK WITH OTHERS?

__Most interesting place I have
  visited
__My hobby
__Most interesting thing I remember
  about my childhood
__How to be a successful grand-
  parent
__Should older people live with
  their children?
__What I think about the youth of
  today
__What I would do if I were presi-
  dent

WHAT WOULD YOU LIKE TO SEE?

__Travel slides and movies on for-
  eign countries
__Educational slides on aging
__TV programs
__A jet airliner
__How a newspaper is produced
__Entertainments and programs by
  children

WHERE WOULD YOU LIKE TO GO?

__Interesting industrial plants
__Visit the State Legislature
__Nearby historical spots; places of
  interest
__Parks and scenic spots
__Ball games
__A play
__A live TV show
  A radio broadcast
__Visit a neighboring community

HOW WOULD YOU LIKE TO HELP THE
CENTER (CLUB)?

__Preside at meetings
__Make others feel at home
__Purchase and sell craft supplies

___Make articles needed by Amer. Cancer Society

___Make layettes for visiting nurses

___Make and repair toys for nursery schools

___Help community agencies with mass mailings

___Adopt a ward at children's hospital

___Make tray favors for geriatrics hospital

___Make afghans for wheelchair patients

___Make articles for center's bazaar

___Tutor a newcomer to the country needing help in learning English

___Play musical instrument

___Participate in dramatics

___Prepare and serve refreshments

___Make posters and signs

___Take care of supplies

___Do secretarial work

___Type

___Lead songs

___Arrange a room

___Instruct in crafts

___Have charge of Bingo game

___Write for center's newspaper

___Keep center's scrapbook

___Be center's librarian

___Keep records

BIBLIOGRAPHY

Games and Contests

Allen, Catherine. *Fun for Parties and Programs.* Englewood Cliffs, N.J.: Prentice-Hall, 1956.

Eisenberg, Larry, and Eisenberg, Helen. *How to Help Folks Have Fun.* New York: Association Press, 1954.

Kohl, Marguerite. *Games for Grown-Ups.* New York: A. A. Wyn, 1951.

National Recreation and Parks Association. *Games for Quiet Hours and Small Spaces.* Washington, D.C.: National Recreation and Parks Association, 1956.

Stafford, Virginia, and Eisenberg, Larry. *Fun for Older Adults.* New York: Association Press, 1956.

U.S., Department of Health, Education and Welfare. Children's Bureau. *Handbook for Recreation.* Publication no. 231. Revised 1959, Washington, D.C.

Card and Table Games

Crespi, I. *Social Significance of Card Playing as a Leisure-time Activity.* American Sociological Review 21 (1956): 717-21.

Outdoor Games and Exercise Classes

King, Frances. *Golden Age Exercises.* New York: Crown Publishers, 1968.

Educational Classes

Kalson, Leon. "The Therapy of Discussion." *Geriatrics* 20 (1965): 397-401.

Lowy, Louis. *Adult Education and Group Work.* New York: Whiteside, 1955.

Middleman, Ruth R. *The Nonverbal Method in Working with Groups.* New York: Association Press, 1968.

Whitaker, Dorothy, and Leibeman, Morton. *Psychotherapy Through the*

Group Process. New York: Atherton Press, 1964, chapters 12 and 13.

Camping

Bowen, Georgene. *Summer Is Ageless.* New York: National Recreation Association, 1958.

Derringer, Le Roy. "Senior Citizens Go to Camps." *International Journal of Religious Education* 39 (1963): 10-11.

Hockheimer, Rita. "How Senior Citizens Enrich Camp Programs." *Camping Magazine,* February 1963.

Kamaiko, Jack. *"Camping With the Elderly Person." A Report of a Twelve-year Experience at Camp Salomon of the Educational Alliance.* New York: Educational Alliance, 1965.

Kaplan, Jerome. "The Maturing of Golden-Age Camps." *Recreation,* June 1953, pp. 175-76.

Margolin, Lillian. *Residential Camping Service for Older Adults: New Prospectives in Services to Groups.* New York: National Association of Social Workers, 1961, pp. 133-40.

Mathiasen, Geneva. *Camping for Older People.* New York: National Council On the Aging, 1955.

McClain, Martha, and Scholer, E. A. "Camping for Older Adults." *Adding Life to Years* 14 (1967): 3-6.

White, Gertrude M. "A Day's Camping for Youngsters over Sixty." *Recreation,* 45 (1951): 221-22.

Woods, James H. "Camping for Oldsters." *Recreation,* March 1950, pp. 573-75.

Arts and Crafts

American Craftsman's Council, *Crafts for Retirement: A Guide for Teachers and Students.* New York: American Craftsman's Council, 1964.

Gross, Selma Woodrow. *Opening the Door to Creative Experience for the Aging Through an Art Program.* Baltimore: Commission on Problems of the Aging, 1963, pp. 9-10.

Leeming, Joseph. *Holiday Craft and Fun.* New York: J. B. Lippincott Co., 1950.

Drama and Puppetry

Batchelder, Marjorie. *Puppet Plays.* New York: Harper & Row, 1947.

Batchelder, Marjorie. *Puppet Theatre Handbook.* New York: Harper & Brothers, 1947.

Benyon, Helen. *Puppetry Today.* New York: Watson-Guptill Publications, 1966.

Buch, Philo; Gassner, John; and Alberson, John. *A Treasury of the Theatre: An Anthology of Great Plays.* New York: Simon and Schuster, 1940.

Cerf, Bennett A. *Plays of Our Time.* New York: Random House, 1967.

Musselman, Virginia. *Informal Dramatics.* New York: National Recreation Association, 1952.

Dance Programs

McKay, Jack. *Dances for Senior Citizens.* San Francisco: San Francisco Council of Churches, 1962.

Musselman, Virginia. *Mixers to Music for Parties and Dances.* New York: National Recreation Association, 1954.

Music

Kaplan, Max. "Music in Adult Life." *Adult Leadership,* January 1957.

Shapiro, Alex. "A Pilot Program in Music Therapy with Residents of a Home for the Aged." *The Gerontologist* 9 (1969): 128-33.

Zanzig, Augustus D. *Starting and Developing a Rhythm Band.* New York: National Recreation Association, 1954.

Food and Refreshments

Booth, Estelle. *A Meal in a Bowl* (mimeographed). San Francisco: San Francisco Senior Center, 1968.

Williams, Joseph Terrance. *Good Meal Planning on $7.00 a Week* (mimeographed). San Francisco: San Francisco Senior Center, 1968.

General References on Program

Anderson, Harold H. "Psychological Aspects of Geriatrics Recreation: New Programs or New Approach." *Geriatrics* 14 (1959): 742-47.

Du-Covny, Amran. *The Billion $ Swindle Fraud Against the Elderly.* New York: Fleet Press, 1969.

Engel, Sophie. "The Adult in Older Adult Programming." *Journal of Jewish Communal Service* 35 (1958): 183-92.

Klein, Wilma, and Associates. *Promoting Mental Health of Older People Through Group Methods.* New York: Mental Health Materials Center, 1965.

Lucas, Carol. *Recreation Gerontology.* Springfield, Ill.: Charles C. Thomas, 1964.

National Council on the Aging. *Resources for the Aging: An Action Handbook.* Prepared for the Community Action Program, Office of Economic Opportunity, 1969.

Novotny, Geraldine, and Kent, Donald P. "Physical Activities and the Older Adult." *Journal of Health, Physical Education and Recreation* 31 (1960): 23-25.

Pantell, Dora Fuch. "Methodological Implications of Day Center Teaching Experiences." *Gerontologist,* 2 (1962): 41-45.

Pierce, Milton. "How to Organize a Cultural Program in an Adult Center." *Adult Leadership* 15 (1966): 120-21.

Rachles, David. *Mini-cost Programs and Services for the Aging Poor.* New York: National Council on the Aging, March 1969.

Wilson, Gertrude, and Ryland, Gladys. *Social Group Work Practice.* "The Creative Use of the Social Process." New York: Houghton Mifflin Company, 1949.

15 / Center Members Serve the Community–Community Services in the Center

IN ADDITION TO PROVIDING ACTIVITIES for self-enrichment, senior centers must also provide opportunities for members to continue to contribute to the community and its welfare. Volunteer community service corps and social action committees are organized in many centers to provide channels for older adults to be related to community needs.

Members of senior centers are a ready source of potential volunteers

As community groups become aware of the large numbers of older people meeting in centers and clubs they conclude that the elderly will be a ready source of volunteer workers because they have "nothing else to do." Many older adults can be counted on to make contributions in many different ways to the welfare of the total community; however, people who join centers and clubs do not necessarily have unlimited uncommitted time. They may serve as volunteers within the center itself, visit ill members, care for sick spouses, shop and prepare food for homebound friends and neighbors, feed the paralyzed, and read to the blind. Others continue to carry the volunteer assignments in community agencies, churches, and lodges accepted during their middle-adult years. Some centers officially recognize their members for these services by asking them to list all their volunteer assignments on a Volunteer Service Record card. These records are compiled and the member who has given the most hours of service receives a certificate of recognition as volunteer-of-the-month.

Serving as volunteers in nonprofit and welfare agencies can be a meaningful activity for older adults after retirement. Opportunities in most communities are many and varied, requiring all kinds and levels of skills and abilities. A careful matching of people and their skills with the jobs to be done is essential. Most older adults who join centers are able to carry assignments in which they give direct help in personal ways to other older people or to small children. Few have the group work or recreational skills to be effective as leaders of youth groups or in assignments requiring a high level of professional skill. Many older women with clerical and stenographic competence welcome an opportunity to keep in practice. Unless they have served during their middle-adult years, older adults will not necessarily be helpful as members of boards of directors or agency committees. However, community committees studying needs and planning services for the aged should have, without exception, members who are themselves older adults. These individuals should not be expected to represent the attitudes and ideas of all older persons, but can speak only for themselves and perhaps for those with whom they are most closely associated.

If a volunteer job is to be a meaningful experience to an older person and also make a contribution to the agency where he is serving, some supervision by a patient, thoughtful staff member who has time to invest in giving guidance will be essential. The administration and staff of agencies using older adults as volunteers must believe in the worth and ability of older workers and must be willing to invest agency time in making them feel needed, not as free help but as co-workers. Although they volunteer time and skills, many older adults, especially those with limited incomes, will need some remuneration for carfare, lunch, and other out-of-pocket expenses incurred. In order to place the best equipped older adult into the job that will give him the greatest satisfaction, some consideration must be given to his personal preference, temperament, education, employment, and experiences. The community's volunteer bureau may be called upon by senior centers to interview those members who want to serve as volunteers and fit them into opportunities best suited to their interests and abilities.

Within the membership of most senior centers there will be many self-assured, experienced men and women who will feel no reticence in going into the community as individuals to work in unfamiliar settings. Others will be hesitant to do so but will be willing to volunteer if they can be one of a group undertaking a service project, such as preparing bulk mailings for hospitals, health agencies, or united giving appeals. After some experience in serving as one of a group, many individuals lose their timidity and are quite willing to take assignments on their own.

Individuals as members of glee clubs and drama groups enjoy entertaining in convalescent homes and hospitals for older people and children.

Even more center members are willing to volunteer in projects that can be carried on at the center as a part of the regular program. Many willing hands complete the requested layettes for the visiting nurses, the children's clothing for the needlework guild, the cancer pads for home patients, the books in Braille for the blind, or the doll's house for a nursery school for cerebral palsied children. Interest is high when lap robes and socks are needed for the geriatric ward at the hospital, lapboards for the veterans' hospital, and scrapbooks for teaching English to children recently arrived from Hong Kong. The list of projects needing the help of older adults is endless and each community will have its own special needs and ways of involving center members in them. Through their services as volunteers, older adults not only help to do essential work but also help to change community attitudes about older people. Former stereotypes of old age as a period of decline and uselessness are modified as center members volunteer to use their continuing abilities and skills in community projects.

National volunteer programs
interest some center members

A number of programs have been developed nationally to alert older adults to the community's need for their help. Through VISTA (Volunteers in Service to America), a program sponsored by the Office of Economic Opportunity, older adults as well as younger people are selected, trained, and placed as staff assistants to local public and volunteer agencies that are participants in the antipoverty program. VISTA volunteers receive room, board, and medical care and a personal expense allowance of seventy-five dollars per month. Upon completion of one year of service, the volunteer receives an award of $50 for each month served. Further information can be secured through VISTA, Office of Economic Opportunity, Washington, D.C., 20506.

The National Council of Jewish Women has inaugurated the Senior Citizens Service Corps, a program carried on in local communities under the auspices of their local branches. Through this program, opportunities for volunteer service for older adults are developed in local communities and training courses are given. Further information about this program can be secured from the National Council of Jewish Women, 1 West 47th Street, New York, New York 10036, or from local units of the National Council of Jewish Women.

SERVE (Serve and Enrich Retirement by Volunteer Experience) is a successful program on Staten Island, New York, that serves as a model for similar projects in other communities. In this program older adults are recruited for nonacademic school jobs—such as assistants in school libraries, guidance offices, nurses' offices, setting up exhibits, and developing garden projects. More information about this project can be secured through The Community Service Society, 105 East 22nd Street, New York, New York, 10010.

SCORE (Service Corps of Retired Executives), a national voluntary program for retired business executives, is associated with the Small Business Administration of the United States Department of Labor. Firms that have been approved for loans may request help from a corps of volunteer businessmen counselors, who advise on merchandising finished products, keeping books efficiently, and expanding the operation. Many retired executives find great satisfaction both in helping young businessmen develop new enterprises and in being part of the work world from which they retired.

Programs on social issues and social action
help keep older adults involved in the community

The potential power of minority groups when they vote as a bloc is becoming increasingly apparent in political circles. The aged now comprise one of the most potentially influential political subgroups in American society. Older adults themselves are becoming aware that if legislation is to be enacted that will make provisions for their legitimate needs, then they must take more responsibility to alert their communities and their elected officials to these needs.

There are many differences of opinion in the community and within boards and commissions about the roles of senior centers in controversial issues and social action. Many believe that centers should limit their efforts to providing services for their members, but others feel that services are not enough. They take the position that centers must become involved in advocacy and legislation to change some of the conditions that give rise to the deprivation and problems their members face.

Those senior centers that are sponsored by private or voluntary agencies will have more freedom in dealing with controversial issues and advocating social change than will public or tax-supported ones. Even voluntary agencies face some limitations because tax exempt status in some states is granted with the understanding that no major part of the program is formulated to influence legislation.

Not all members of a center will be interested in social issues and political action, and there will be few issues on which all will agree. The members, however, are mature adults who have functioned as responsible citizens for many years. Many retain and develop increased interest in political issues as they become older. It is important and appropriate that center programs provide opportunities for those who are interested to get facts on pending legislation and local issues that will directly affect them. Boards of directors should recognize that staff members must have freedom to express themselves as independent citizens in the community on controversial issues. The public too often identifies the staff only in their relation to the center and are critical when staff members advocate legislation that would improve adverse conditions that affect members. Maturity of judgment is needed to enable staff to know when and how to use their leadership to support legislation in which they believe, yet not to jeopardize their effectiveness in the center and in the community.

The center should never be used as a platform and its members as a captive audience to propagandize for any specific political point of view or for endorsement of any one political candidate. In order to help members know candidates and be informed on issues, however, many centers have candidate forums before elections. All those seeking public offices are invited to speak and members can query them on their positions and learn about their attitudes toward the needs of older persons. In many centers training courses are held on how to write letters to legislators and newspaper editors, how to attend hearings and give testimony, how to write petitions and recommendations, and how to visit with one's congressman and present one's point of view on legislation. Some centers arrange bus trips to the state capital to observe a legislative session and give needed support to bills in which they are vitally concerned. The testimony of older adults is effective when it is given on matters in which they have had some personal experience. These will include adequate housing at rents they can afford, property tax exemptions, reduced bus fares, increased social security payments, medical and drug costs, and frauds that victimize older people.

A forum group or social action committee on which a staff member has been the adviser can take an appropriate public position when all members are in agreement. Such action by any center subgroup should not commit the center as a whole unless so voted by all of the members. It is the staff's responsibility to maintain within the center a climate where differences in opinions and points of view are accepted and respected and where interest is not limited to matters that benefit older people exclusively. Senior citizens must also keep informed about and use their political strength in positive and constructive ways on matters that affect all age groups in the community. Some of these matters include bonds for schools, child guidance clinics, child care centers, recreational programs, peace programs, ecological projects, along with transportation and housing needs, hospital and health care services, and cultural opportunities. The role of citizen may be enhanced during the older adult years if individual older people have opportunities to be informed and use their knowledge and political strength to help effect needed social change.

Resources for Programs of Social Action

National Council of Senior Citizens,
1627 K Street, N.W.,
Washington, D.C. 20006.
> This Council is an educational and action group that supports increased medical care and social security; improved recreational, educational, and health programs; reduced costs on drugs; better housing; and other programs to aid senior citizens.
> This general education service sponsors educational workshops and leadership training; assists local groups to develop programs for the elderly; a general information service providing films, books, special reports, and other information; and encourages participation in social and political action activities.

The League of Women Voters of the United States,
1730 M Street, N.W.
Washington, D.C. 20036
> Educational materials presenting all points of view on any controversial public issues are available from local groups or from the national office.

Most older adults are highly critical of the young activists today who demonstrate, destroy, and threaten the social order. Their problems as the elderly in the society do not seem to them or to their communities to be as threatening or as urgent. To form coalitions with revolutionary youth to achieve change favorable to them would be unthinkable for most older people, but they would agree, that although the tactics of change are disturbing, the thrust of concern around human values is heartening. Their needs as well as the needs of youths, the deprived, and the disadvantaged must be considered.

*Training students is one of the ways
in which a center serves the community*

In addition to the volunteer services of its members, the center has unique opportunities for service to the community. The program and services of the center should be a resource for schools and universities preparing students for careers in working with older people. The center can serve as a living laboratory where individual students writing papers and undertaking research on aging come for observation and information. Groups of nurses and others in the health related professions and students preparing for professional careers in other direct services for older people can have firsthand experiences to supplement academic courses. Knowing something about older persons is not adequate preparation for working with them. A student needs to know individual older men and women who will exemplify the concepts and theories taught in the classroom. In one center these training opportunities were extended from the center into the homes of members who volunteered to become "special friends" of a sophomore class of nurses in a university school of nursing. Each well older adult was assigned a student nurse. The nurse visited this older person in his home, remembered him with birthday and Christmas cards, met his family and friends, and accompanied him to events at the center. Through this project, according to the instructor, "the students become acquainted with the problems and crises faced by older persons, especially in relation to the maintenance of mental health; have experience in appropriate and preventative nursing intervention; and develop their communication skills . . . nurses cannot learn how persons cope with the aging process if they see them only in the hospital setting where they come when they are ill, usually seriously ill, but they may learn something about the process of aging and how individuals cope with it by knowing older persons who are well." [1]

Before a senior center accepts the role of serving as a field work placement for students, the board, staff and members must understand the expectations and demands that will be made by the university supervisors. A policy statement should be formulated by the board indicating its willingness to allocate funds, facilities, and staff time for supervision of students. To have a student assigned to work part time at the center may seem to be an opportunity to secure needed additional professional leadership, but this expectation is not realistic because the

[1] Frances Evans, "Visiting Older People: A Learning Experience," *Nursing Outlook* 17:Vol. 3, 20-22 (March 1969).

time of a regular staff member must be diverted from the center program to the supervision of the student and for consultation with university personnel. The values of helping to train students are many and members should be helped to understand how the program will serve in the training of personnel for health and welfare agencies serving older adults. An awareness of the significant contribution they can make to the growing body of knowledge about old age motivates the cooperation of most center members. However, unless they are helped to understand what is involved in a training program they will express irritation and resentment toward the students, who will watch them while they are involved in activities, interrupt and ask them questions, have them fill out numerous research questionnaires, or ask them to leave an activity to be interviewed. When members understand the significance of the training program, most are cooperative and feel pride in being able to help young students.

The opportunity for centers to have a part in raising the quality of services available to older people by helping to provide better trained personnel is a challenging one. Many centers can meet the challenge if their existing programs are adequate in the specific field for which the training opportunity is being sought. To adapt the program or add services not yet developed to accommodate training for any specific profession would neither be wise nor expedient. The center staff and the university faculty must be careful to select students for whom the center's program can offer appropriate experiences and who can make some contribution to the continuing development of the center and to the enrichment of the lives of its members.

Services to individual members bring the resources of the community into the center

The core programs of multiservice senior centers are the group activities, and older adults join primarily to participate in them. Many members, at the time of joining, have no awareness of the individual services that are also available or any expectation that they will ever need them. They enjoy such services as the library, hot lunches, and visitors when they are ill, but do not see themselves as ever needing help from the center with personal problems. Other members, especially those who have been referred by doctors or social agencies, may be so preoccupied with personal problems that it is only after they are helped and can feel some relief from anxiety that they can enjoy participating in the activities.

Concern about the whole person and the importance of meeting as many of his needs as possible in one setting characterizes the philosophy and the objectives of multiservice senior centers. The decrease in the range of community services used by persons as they age, particularly in big cities, may result from the fact that older adults become discouraged by obstacles and difficulties that would not deter younger persons. Communities are beginning to recognize that it is not realistic to require older people to travel long distances to a number of different agencies for the help they need. A senior center where many older people gather daily is a logical place for certain social service agencies to base a member of their staff at stated times each week to support and supplement the counseling and referral services given by the center counselor and nurse. In these information and referral services, representatives from community agencies are available to counsel not only center members but also other older people living in the neighborhood. Coming to the center for a needed service often awakens the interest of a withdrawn, disinterested person in the neighborhood. Such individuals may eventually join the center as they see the activities and feel acceptance.

The following are the kinds of services that can be provided at a multiservice senior center by the staff from other community agencies.

1. Health counseling by a Public Health Nurse.
2. Information and referral for old age assistance benefits from the public welfare department.
3. Instruction on adapting to hearing loss and the use of hearing aids.
4. Counseling on social security, Medicare and Medicaid by the Social Security office.
5. Job and vocational counseling by the appropriate state department.
6. Help on legal problems and help in securing protective or guardianship services for persons unable to manage their own affairs from the neighborhood legal services office funded by the Office of Economic Opportunity.
7. Help on special diets from the Home Health Education Service.
8. Help in locating housing from the Housing Authority.
9. Glaucoma screening by the local Society for the Prevention of Blindness and chest X rays by the local tuberculosis society.
10. Casework services from a family service agency.
11. Opportunities for part-time employment from Foster Grandparents and from VISTA.
12. Escort service from the Self Help for the Elderly project of the Office of Economic Opportunity.

Not all health and welfare agencies in every community can send staff to senior centers to deliver needed services. As communities realize the potentials of the senior center as a service delivery subsystem for older adults, ways will be found to interrelate center programs with those of other health, welfare, and leisure time agencies of the community.

Guidelines for involving center members in the community, and the community in the center

1. Members of senior centers welcome the opportunity to be of service if this service can be geared to a consideration of the abilities and needs of older persons rather than only to the needs and convenience of the organization requesting the service.

2. The senior center has an opportunity to perform a volunteer function in the community by helping to upgrade personnel working with older adults. It can make this contribution by making its program and staff available for in-service training and field work experiences for professional students.

3. Action on social issues is of great interest and concern to many older persons. Programs of senior centers should provide opportunities for learning facts and receiving training for those who are interested in effective social action.

4. The community should encourage appropriate community health and welfare agencies to base workers at centers, at least for specified periods, to supplement the services that center staff can give to individual older people.

BIBLIOGRAPHY

Arthur, Julietta K. *Retire to Action: A Guide to Volunteer Service.* Nashville, Tenn.: Abingdon Press, 1970.
Carter, Howard A. "The Retired Senior Citizen as a Resource to Minimize Underachievement of Children in Public Schools." *Archives of Physical Medicine and Rehabilitation* 45 (1964): 218-23.
Freund, Janet. "Time and Knowledge to Share." *The Elementary School Journal* 65 (1965): 351-52.
Long, Fern. "Older People as Volunteers." In *Grass Roots Private Welfare,* edited by Alfred de Grazia. New York: New York University Press, 1957.
Morris, Robert; Lambert, Camille; and Guberman, Mildred. *New Roles For the Elderly.* Papers on Social Welfare, no. 10. Waltham, Mass.: Brandeis University, June 1964.
Schoenbohm, Wilke B., and Schwanke, Robert W. "Barriers to Service." *Recreation* 55 (1962): 251-52, 268.
U.S. Administration on Aging. *Designs for Action for Older Americans: A Project Report on Group Volunteer Service.* Washington, D.C.: Government Printing Office, 1969. A.O.A. publication no. 905.

16 / Programs for Older Adults With Special Needs

PROGRAMS SPECIFICALLY DESIGNED to meet the special needs of some older adults will be necessary. These will include those indviduals handicapped by limited sight and hearing, former mental hospital patients, those homebound with crippling diseases, and residents of protective home settings. Special planning will be needed also to serve older adults living in remote rural areas and in the poverty neighborhoods of large urban centers, whose lifelong patterns of deprivation have kept them apart and alienated from the rest of the community. Aging itself brings many limitations. These are greatly compounded when one is blind, hard of hearing, or poor and ill or when one lives in an isolated rural area or in an institution.

Older Adults with Visual and Hearing Handicaps

The ability to communicate with others and to move about at will are essential for the maintenance of physical and psychological health. For many elderly people these abilities are lost or become seriously restricted when blindness and deafness occur. Through his eyes and ears man receives essential information about his environment, maintains communication with his fellowmen, and makes social adjustments to others.

Individuals who have visual handicaps are often referred to as "the blind" and those with hearing losses as "the deaf." Such references suggest that the loss of these senses bring changes in the personality pattern and that all persons with such losses behave in certain set ways. Changes in visual or auditory functions do cause physiological and psychological disturbances in varying degrees and inevitably alter ways in which the individual can find satisfactions for his social and emotional needs. For many persons the adjustment to these losses is difficult

237

because they come at that period of life when other problems of aging are complicating adjustments to rapidly changing social roles and environment.

Each individual will react to the loss of his sight or hearing in ways that have characterized his adjustment to other losses and crises in his life. After the initial emotional shock, although he may need some help in establishing new patterns for his daily activities, the mature, highly motivated older person can continue to be a relatively independent person. If other health problems exist, however, both the blind and the deaf person may lack the emotional strength to accept and adjust to such handicaps. Many older people withdraw and cut themselves off from all contacts with friends and become immobilized with fear and self-pity. The emotionally dependent person sometimes becomes aggressively demanding of attention and uses his handicap to gain sympathy and to excuse his demands for unnecessary help. The sense of touch, learning to read Braille, and other aids enable a blind person to maintain communication with other people and a high degree of independence. Loss of hearing, on the other hand, is more often reflected in negative emotional reactions. Because he cannot hear what is being said, the hard-of-hearing person often becomes suspicious and imagines that others are talking about him or deliberately cutting him out of the conversation. The older person with a hearing loss can remain more self-directing and independent than the blind person, but he often becomes paranoid and makes unreasonable demands on others.

For most individuals the threat to their self-image as an adequate person and the pity that other people express toward them are more difficult to accept than the actual physical loss of sight and hearing. When older adults with these handicaps join social groups, other members become overly solicitous of their comfort and safety, speaking in loud tones, waiting on them, and guiding and steadying their every movement. Such help is not always acceptable to blind and deaf older people and they may rebuff those who are trying to help.

To be helpful to others is laudable behavior, but it has threatening connotations for the handicapped person who feels that physical help in public only calls attention to his disability, makes him an object of pity, and implies social inferiority and dependency. Before helping a handicapped older person it is best to ask if such help is needed. Visually handicapped men are often more resistant to help than women, perhaps because women are accustomed to having doors opened, chairs pulled out, and packages carried for them.

It is important that other members of the center do not view blind and deaf members as a burden. If they are expected to be available to help the handicapped member they may soon resent being deprived of the freedom to follow their own interests. Some center members may need help in accepting some of the personal appearances and behavior of blind members—their awkward groping, poor posture, grimacing, and what appear to be untidy eating habits.

The physical plant of any center serving older people with sight and hearing handicaps must be planned and operated to allow individuals to function to their maximum degree of independence without help. Well-lighted and unobstructed corridors and classrooms, hand grips on stairs, sturdy chairs and tables, and minimum distraction and noise in classrooms and program areas are essential. These, of course, are basic requirements in the physical environment for all older people.

Most blind and hard-of-hearing individuals are served in special centers

In most large cities there are long-established centers serving blind or hard-of-hearing persons of all ages exclusively. These programs and services are well developed and designed to encourage the active participation of the members. National organizations have, over the years, carried on highly effective programs of research and rehabilitation, public relations and legislation, and education on the prevention of blindness and hearing loss. Among these national organizations are the American Hearing Society, the American Speech and Hearing Association, the American Foundation for the Blind, Inc., the National Society for the Prevention of Blindness, and many services within the Veterans Administration, the Federal Office of Vocational Rehabilitation, and the National Institute of Mental Health.

Many individuals, particularly the elderly, derive comfort and security in associating with other people who are similarly handicapped and they prefer to belong to specialized centers. Other blind and deaf people feel that such segregation tends to over emphasize their handicaps and limit their social contacts with their peers. Joining senior centers becomes for them a link with normalcy and a significant step forward in their adjustment to their loss.

Multiservice senior centers that include the blind and the deaf in the membership will need to work closely with the long-established specialized centers. From them senior centers will receive referrals of older adults who can benefit from an experience within a more inclusive membership and program. Specific promotion and outreach to such handicapped older adults will be needed to interest them in joining community senior centers. Even with the best possible promotional efforts many individuals who would benefit from the programs will not be reached.

The multiservice senior center program offers opportunities for those with visual and hearing handicaps

To serve older people with visual and hearing handicaps the program and services of a center will need to include the following.

A. *Educational program.* (1) Forums and lectures on the prevention of blindness and deafness with speakers from local nonprofit organizations. (2) Demonstrations of hearing aids by an otologist. (3) Glaucoma screening days scheduled regularly at the center for all older people in the community, held in cooperation with the American Medical Association or the department of ophthalmology of a local medical school. (4) Classes in aural rehabilitation taught by students of vocational rehabilitation and speech therapy from the local or nearby college. These classes may include formal teaching of speech reading, auditory training, and speech correction. (5) Touch therapy groups, where sightless individuals are helped to develop an appreciation of art objects; sculptures in clay; handcrafted articles; flowers; herbs and foods—by touching, feeling, smelling, and tasting. Relating to one another and the leader through touch and feeling of the hands and features also is therapeutic for many blind people. (6) Film and tape programs using the fine resource materials available through public health departments and national health agencies (see the listings and addresses later in this chapter). These can be used as the basis for group discussions.

B. *Counseling program.* In all states and most local communities there are agencies to help people adjust to their handicaps. The counselor of the senior center will know about all local resources. He will also know about the income tax deductions and the provisions of the Social Security Act whereby the federal government cooperates with the states in furnishing aid to the needy blind. He will be able to help an individual receive books written in Braille from regional libraries and talking-book machines from state libraries on a free-loan basis.

Not as much help is available for the hard-of-hearing older person. The Kiwanis and Quota Clubs make hearing aids available to needy older people. Local health departments and councils of social agencies can give information on local resources for testing and using hearing aids. Membership in the American Hearing Society includes a subscription to *Hearing News,* which publishes articles that will be helpful.

C. *Activity program.* Visually handicapped older people will need more help in moving about the center but they can enjoy a broader range of activities than those with hearing handicaps. These include drama, if lines are recorded on tape or written in Braille; chorus, if there is a conductor and the songs are familiar; discussion groups, if the person can hear the discussion and his remarks are acknowledged audibly by the leader. With cards, checkers, dominoes, and bingo sets all available in Braille, table games can be enjoyed by groups of blind individuals. They also can enjoy ceramics, leather, basketry, and weaving if there is a helper for every two or three students to prevent long waits for help and minimize frustration.

Although the deaf can enjoy all crafts, service projects, silent films with captions, excursions and trips, they are unable to participate with hearing members in discussion groups, social dancing, language classes, drama, chorus, cards and bingo.

Each handicapped member will respond to his experiences at the center in his own characteristic way. Any frustration, failure, or the smallest slight may be, for sensitive older people, a devastating experience. Group leaders will need to anticipate individual failures and prevent or minimize them. The following suggestions will be helpful to leaders of groups of hard-of-hearing members.

1. Speak in a normal tone without shouting or mouthing words.

2. See that the light is shining on the speaker's face, not in the eyes of the hard-of-hearing person.

3. Face the hard-of-hearing person directly and speak on the same level with him whenever possible.

4. Remember not to talk from another room.

5. Smoking, chewing, or eating makes speech more difficult.

6. If a person has difficulty understanding some particular word or phrase, try to find a different way of saying the same thing rather than repeating the original words over and over.

7. Use a blackboard to reinforce what is being said.

8. Microphones to amplify sounds will not always be helpful. They cause distractions and distortions to people with hearing aids.

9. Hard-of-hearing people hear less well and therefore understand less when they are tired or ill.

In a brochure titled "When you Meet a Blind Person," published by the American Foundation for the Blind, the following suggestions are given for helping the blind member.

1. Let the blind person take your arm. Don't push him. The motion of your body will tell him what to do.

2. Never leave a door ajar. Keep corridors clear of clutter and tell him if furniture is moved from its accustomed place.

3. A blind person can hear as well as a sighted one and sometimes better. Always talk directly to him, not through his companion.

4. Always identify yourself when entering a room if a blind person is alone. Don't play any "guess who" games.

5. When showing a blind person to a chair, put his hand on the back. He will then be able to seat himself easily.

6. Give directions as clearly as possible, left or right according to the way he is facing.

7. If the blind person has a dog, remember that the dog is a working dog and not a pet so do not divert his attention. His master's life depends on his alertness.

8. When eating with a blind person, read the menu and prices to him. If he wants help, cut his meat, fix his coffee, and tell him the position of the food on his plate, according to position on a clock, for example meat at six, potato at seven, and so forth.

9. Treat a blind person as nearly as you can as one with sight. Do not try to find substitutes for such words as *see* and *sight*. It is embarrassing to you and to him.

Resource materials available to individuals, centers, and residential care facilities serving hearing and visually handicapped older adults

Talking book machines are supplied by the Library of Congress on a free loan basis, not only to legally blind persons but also to anyone with a physical ailment that makes holding or reading a book difficult. A statement from a doctor or any competent authority is needed in order to qualify. Application should be made through the local library to the state library. Talking books and records are sent free through the mails in special containers.

Public libraries in some large cities loan magnifiers, page turners and overhead projectors and microfilm prints of books so that handicapped and bedridden patients can enjoy reading.

The American Foundation for the Blind, under contract with the Library of Congress, publishes two pamphlets: *Braille Book Review* and *Talking Book Topics*. These are available to senior centers or any blind person who is registered with his state library.

Some thirty-five regional libraries circulate books in Braille and magnetic tapes on a wide variety of subjects. An annual catalogue and monthly bulletins of titles are available. Information is available through local libraries.

Large-type books, magazines and playing cards are available through the American Printing House for the Blind and the American League for the Visually Handicapped.

The American Foundation for the Blind administers a travel concession program for visually handicapped persons. A booklet describing travel opportunities may be secured from this organization.

Hearing News, published by the American Hearing Society, carries timely articles that have wide appeal; and a sound filmstrip, "A Change for the Better in Sight," may be rented from the Minneapolis Society for the Blind.

The following national organizations publish pamphlets and program materials of interest to older adults.

American Foundation for the Blind, Inc.
15 West 16th Street
New York, New York 10011
American Hearing Society
919 18th Street N.W.
Washington, D.C. 20006
American Printing House for the Blind, Inc.
1839 Frankfort Avenue
Louisville, Kentucky 40206
American Speech and Hearing Association
1001 Connecticut Avenue N.W.
Washington, D.C. 20006
Captioned Films for the Deaf Division,
Educational Services Bureau of Education for the Handicapped,
Office of Education
U.S. Department of Health, Education and Welfare
Washington, D.C. 20202
Knights Templar's Eye Foundation
Rhinebeck, New York 12572
Library of Congress
Division for the Blind and Physically Handicapped
Washington, D.C. 20542
National Aid to the Visually Handicapped
3201 Balboa Street
San Francisco, California 94121
National Society for Crippled Children and Adults
2023 West Ogden Avenue
Chicago, Illinois 60612

National Society for the Prevention of Blindness, Inc.
  70 Madison Avenue
  New York, New York 10016
Recording for the Blind, Inc.
  215 East 58th Street
  New York, New York 10022

The Homebound Older Adult

Although most center members will be physically well, ambulatory older adults, significant contributions can also be made to those individuals who are homebound in their own homes or in residential homes and institutions. A wide variety of homes for older people are found in most communities, and are designated by different names according to the services they provide. Convalescent and nursing homes, sometimes called extended care facilities, serve those older people needing skilled nursing and psychiatric care. The foster or boarding home provides housing as well as supervision for those who are becoming too frail or confused to live alone but who are still capable of independent action. Older people living in these homes come and go at will from the home into the community; among these are many former mental hospital patients who need the emotional support of a family-type group. Boarding homes also are known as personal care homes when they care for those individuals who can no longer move safely about in the community to shop, cook, and care for themselves. In addition to the specific physical care that these homes provide, the emotional and social needs of the residents must be an underlying concern. Even though a home may have an excellent social program, the community senior center can make a significant contribution to its residents. Its program can provide a break in the illness environment of the home and an opportunity for the residents to see new faces and surroundings, which will be a rehabilitative and therapeutic experience for them.

The multiservice senior center continues to serve members when they become homebound

One of the apparent differentials in working with older people is the great frequency with which members experience terminal illnesses and accidents that keep them permanently, or for long periods, confined to their own homes. This enforced isolation becomes especially poignant for those who have been active members of senior centers and have established meaningful peer relationships. Until ill older people are able to be brought to a homebound party at the center, get-well cards from members assure them that they have not been forgotten. Calls of inquiry from the staff also assure them and their families of the center's concern and willingness to be helpful.

After the critical days of the illness have passed, members of the Visiting Committee come to visit with the homebound member to discuss mutual center interests, give him a craft or service project to work on if he is able or interested, give him a copy of the center's newspaper, and stay to play a game or read to him. When the ill member is physically able and transportation is feasible, he is brought to a party at the center planned specifically for homebound members. If he lives in an apartment without an elevator and is dependent on a walker, wheelchair, or crutches, his transportation is almost impossible. Without buses accommodating wheelchairs and drivers who can handle handicapped persons, a homebound member probably cannot be brought to the center at all.

For those who can be transported, the monthly party at the center becomes the only time that many leave their homes. Such parties should be kept small, with no more than twenty guests and an equal number of Homebound Committee members, who act as hosts and as exclusive companions for each guest. Entertainment, group singing, and refreshments are always enjoyed. The experience of being back again in a familiar and loved spot and being remembered by old friends is a meaningful one for the homebound member. He should never automatically be dropped from the membership. The feeling of belonging often maintains the morale of the older person who is becoming progressively more frail.

Opportunities to participate in social activities to the degree that he is able, for as long as he is able, should be provided for every older person in the community. Most senior centers have limited space and staff and must limit their services for homebound persons to those individuals who have been members. Other community organizations—such as the Red Cross, churches, nursing home auxiliaries, welfare councils, and the Junior League—sponsor Friendly Visitor programs for all homebound older people in the community. Programs of some senior centers are being extended to the homebound by means of an electronic recording device that makes communication possible by means of the telephone. Announcements and news of interest, instructions for progressive games and contests, and music and inspirational talks alleviate the loneliness of the homebound person.

Older People Living in Protective Care Homes

Some older adults living in foster and boarding homes are able to relate to the center as individuals who come and go at will. However, most older people who need the protective care of a residential setting are unable to participate without being brought to the center and supervised while they are there. Whether centers can serve severely mentally and physically impaired individuals will depend on the size and skill of the staff, the available funds, and their service goals.

Some centers adopt at least one such protective care home and schedule activities at specific times for its residents. Careful planning and coordination of the responsibilities of the administrator of the home and the staff of the senior center will be essential to assure success. The home personnel is usually responsible for the transportation of the guests and for as many aides as will be needed to accompany the group to the center and to handle possible emergencies. The staff and members of the center are responsible for the program, refreshments, and hostesses who are able to relate to the guests in warm and supportive ways. Within such a group there will be individuals with all kinds of physical disabilities and all degrees of mental clarity. It will therefore be difficult to plan activities that will interest all. Moreover, the attention spans of such older people will be short and their responses minimal. The activities planned for the group will not be as important as the opportunity the program provides to break the monotony of the routines in the home and the patient's preoccupation with physical ailments and lack of hope. The experience will be more meaningful if each hostess knows a few personal facts about the guest, such as the parts of the country in which he has lived, the kinds of work he has done, his hobbies, and something about his family. This information will give him conversational leads and will enable the frail older person to feel an immediate and warm encounter with the center member. A sense of belonging to the center rather than a sense of being an outsider can be achieved by issuing each person from the home a center membership card and sending him a personal copy of the center's newspaper and a birthday greeting. Some multiservice senior centers extend their programs to the residents of other homes by sending their glee clubs, bell ringers, puppeteers, and drama groups to present programs.

In licensed nursing homes, or extended care facilities as they are now called, social programs are an integral part of the residents' total care and certain costs are reimbursed by Medicare and Medicaid. In other proprietary homes that do not qualify for such reimbursement, the costs of social programs must be passed on to the residents. In an effort to keep costs low, many homes provide a minimum program with the help of other community agencies. The staff of the multiservice senior center often helps the administrators of such homes to set up the program and train volunteers from church groups, service clubs, and teenage clubs to carry specific responsibilities. The center staff can also be called upon to hold in-service training classes for the homes' nursing aides to help them understand their relationships with the elderly, who depend on them for emotional support as well as physical care. Through adult education divisions of the public schools and community organizations, speakers and leaders for special programs can be made available. To develop a meaningful program in the small custodial proprietary home is difficult; there is, however, no other group of older people more in need of a break in the boredom and apathy that fill their days.

Older People Living in Rural Areas

The isolated rural areas and small towns and villages in which many older people live limit their opportunities for social activity. Their isolation becomes even more acute as younger family members move to larger towns and cities. In 1960, 15,600,000 older Americans lived on farms or in small towns with population 2,500 or less. At the beginning of 1970 this number had decreased to 10,454,000,[1] approximately 43 percent of the nation's total older population. The elderly make up 10 percent of the farm population and, unlike in other parts of the country, the number of elderly men exceeds the number of elderly women.

Studies of rural older people
indicate they have unique needs

A study of the social activities and life satisfactions of 1,716 men and women from sixty-five to eighty years of age living in the small towns of Missouri was recently made by the Sociology Department of the University of Missouri. The findings regarding older people in rural Missouri are considered as being typical of many other of our rural older Americans. Seventy percent of those interviewed were born and had lived all of their lives in Missouri. Half of these had always lived in the same county where they now resided. The remaining half of the group had lived twenty years or more in the community in which they

[1] Luman H. Long, ed., *The 1970 World Almanac and Book of Facts* (New York: Newspaper Enterprise Association, 1970).

were interviewed. The majority of the 1,716 respondents maintained independent households, residing with a spouse or alone. Fewer than one-fifth lived with children, relatives, or other persons. Approximately 50 percent of the men and 70 percent of the women had annual incomes of less than $2,000 and 75 percent of the men and 66 percent of the women had eight or fewer years of formal education. Almost 75 percent of both sexes belonged to no social groups and 90 percent to no civic organizations. Only six percent of the men and five percent of the women had business or professional affiliations. The largest number of the total group—83 percent of the men and 84 percent of the women—were members of religious organizations.

The findings of a study of 900 older residents of a rural agricultural county in Wisconsin were similar to those of the Missouri study. Few recreational resources or organized clubs for the aged were found and those that existed were mainly church-affiliated. Very few men were members of any groups. Approximately 69 percent of these individuals interviewed said that they had no involvement with these groups and only 1.6 percent said they were very active, attending more than once a week. The respondents said that they kept busy with the business of daily living and expressed preference for visiting with children, relatives, and friends, watching television, listening to the radio, reading the newspaper, working around the house, and going to church. The ability to keep occupied decreased with increasing age. While 73.2 percent of the sixty-five to sixty-nine age group reported having enough to do to keep busy, the percentage dropped steadily for the older age group with the result that only 39 percent of those past eighty years of age stated that they had enough to do. Keeping busy was more of a problem for men than for women, who continued traditional work roles.[2]

The social adjustments and satisfactions of the men and women in the Missouri sample were measured by the Life Satisfaction Index.[3] Those living in towns of 250 to 1,000 inhabitants received lower scores than those living in towns with populations from 1,000 to 5,000. This finding seems to indicate a direct relation between increased social contacts and life satisfactions. Other findings indicate a high correlation between life satisfaction and (1) the amount of formal education one has had and (2) the fact that one's spouse is still living.

[2] Martin Loeb, A. Pincus, and J. Mueller, *Growing Old in Rural Wisconsin* (Madison: University of Wisconsin School of Social Work, 1963).

[3] Bernice L. Neugarten, Robert J. Havighurst, and Sheldon S. Tobin, "The Measurement of Life Satisfaction," *Journal of Gerontology* 16:134-143. (April 1961).

All older Americans living in rural areas
were contacted by the Medicare Alert program

The first concerted and effective effort to contact older people living in rural areas was made in 1966 as part of the federal Medicare Alert program. Workers went into all the remote areas across the country to find all citizens sixty-five years of age and older to register them for Medicare and to assess their social and economic needs. Continuing efforts to inform isolated older persons of governmental programs and services available to them have been made by project FIND (Friendless, Isolated, Needy and Disabled) developed as a part of the Office of Economic Opportunity program. Interviewers found many rural older people to be suspicious of anything that is government-sponsored and resistant to giving personal information. Others welcome any interruption of their isolation and the promise of help. The post office, telephone exchange, grain store, and social security offices are in touch with most older people in any community and can channel information about programs and services to them.

The structure and program of the urban
senior center may not be adaptable to
the needs of the rural aged

The organizational structure and program of the multiservice senior center, as well as other social institutions developed to serve elderly people in urban settings, may not be feasible ways to meet the social needs and interests of older people who live in the open country, miles away from their nearest neighbors. Some county-wide centers have been set up in communities that are the seats of county governments. These communities house other county services that should become involved in the development of such centers—welfare departments, university extension services, representatives of the United States Department of Agriculture, county medical societies, school departments, and ministerial associations. A network of small satellite groups meeting in homes of members in the neighboring towns is an integral part of a central center located in the larger community, which is the county seat. This center serves as a lounge where older people who come to town to shop and transact business drop in, rest, and meet friends. Here, also, training sessions are held for leaders of neighborhood social groups, and information of interest to all older people in the county is available.[4] In some counties the center is housed in the courthouse, firehouse, or grange hall. In other counties the merchants have joined together to rent a store front building to house the center and have provided a minibus for transportation to the center and for shopping.

Because the studies of the older people both of Missouri and of Wisconsin found that more elderly rural people belong to religious groups than to any other groups, churches would be logical sponsors of the project. A subsequent study at the University of Missouri showed that only a small proportion of the rural churches in that state had any specific programs for older people.[5]

The urban senior center can contribute to the development of rural projects

The nearest urban multiservice senior center can be helpful in the development of rural projects. The city center serves as the home away from home when groups from outlying areas come to the city for sightseeing, or attending the theatre, concerts, and other civic events. The staff of the urban center can help in interpreting to county officials and leaders the social needs of older residents and in enlisting support for proposed programs. Members of rural clubs can be invited to workshops for training group leaders and can be included in conferences on current state and national legislation and on trips and excursions initiated by the urban multiservice center. In these ways older people living in rural America can be kept informed and can participate in mutually helpful ways with their peers who live in the big cities.

The lack of transportation increases the isolation of the rural aged

The isolation of rural elderly people is increased by the lack of transportation. Few have automobiles or sufficient income for their maintenance. Where the members of a group live relatively near one another, their adult children often take turns running car pools. In some rural counties, school buses are used during free hours to bring older people

---

[4] The development of the Harrison County Senior Citizens Center in Clarksburg, West Virginia, is an example of this pattern.

[5] *Restudy of the Rural Church in Missouri,* a (mimeographed) study made in 1968 by John S. Holek and E. W. Hassinger of the University of Missouri; based upon an original study the same year by Rosencrans, Pihlblad and McNevin, entitled "Social Participation of Older People in a Small Town."

to the centers. Other projects that help break the isolation of many rural elderly are the mobile units of the county libraries and the telephone reassurance plans whereby individuals living alone in remote areas receive a call each day from a member of a County Telephone Reassurance Committee. Agreements are made with the sheriff's office to investigate if a telephone call at the appointed time goes unanswered.

Rural Americans will be less isolated in the future

In the future the older people who live in rural areas may no longer experience the isolation that characterizes their life-style today. In many sections of the country there is a trend for families to relocate in rural areas to escape the crowded conditions, the violence, and the smog of the cities. As a result, many older people will have more neighbors living nearby, some of whom have had experience in urban organizations. These may be potential volunteers to help develop more social services in the rural areas and small towns across America.

As intercommunication systems, teaching machines, and closed circuit television systems become more available, old people in rural areas, as well as residents in institutions and individuals who are ill and homebound, may all be linked to the programs in large multiservice senior centers. Thus, even the most isolated older person may keep in touch, if he wishes, with the developments in his fast moving world.

The services of many national organizations have been designed specifically for older adults living in rural areas and small towns

The following national organizations are a source of information and materials for meeting the need of the rural aged.

> Cooperative Extension Services,
> U.S. Department of Agriculture,
> Washington, D.C. 20250,
> or Cooperative Extension Service office located in most county seats.
> Health Services and Facilities for American Indians,
> Division of Indian Health,
> Public Health Service,
> U.S. Department of Health, Education and Welfare
> Washington, D.C. 20201.

Home Management Education for Aged Welfare Recipients,
County Extension Agent, or Director of Extension at nearest
State Land-Grant University.

The Financially Disadvantaged Aged

In 1964, Congress enacted legislation establishing an Office of Economic
Opportunity within the executive office of the president of the United
States. Through it money was made available to local communities for
projects to meet the needs of Americans living below minimum standards of health, safety, and decency. Local Community Action Councils
were formed and were charged with the responsibility of involving the
poor themselves in projects designed to break their lifelong poverty patterns. Many Americans, as they grow older, must live on annual incomes
much less than those of their working years. For such older people
poverty may be said to be age-related. But there are other older persons
whose lifelong pattern has been one of extreme deprivation and marginal
living. The added years have emphasized patterns of individual and
family pathology. These are the elderly who today are living in the dark
back rooms of dilapidated apartments, in ghettos crowded with children
and grandchildren, in walk-up, cold water tenements, and third-class
hotels. They are hardly visible to the community at large. They live in
seclusion, apathy, suspicion, and despair. Many are not even known to
community welfare agencies, whose philosophy may be that a citizen who
needs help must come and ask for it—an unrealistic expectation for the
aged poor. Welfare systems have become too complicated and imper-
sonal and their offices too far distant from the slums where such old
people live; these citizens will not leave their familiar neighborhoods and
travel long distances to get help with their problems. New patterns of
delivering existing services to the people who need them must be developed. In many communities eligibility workers from the Public Social
Services Department, Public Health Nurses, and representatives from
Medicare and the Legal Aid Society are assigned for specific times to
visit the centers where poor older persons meet. Here their clients can
find them and receive help.

In many communities aged poor people do not know where to get the
help they need or even that it exists. In 1963 the Sociology Department
of Pennsylvania State University studied the aged persons living within
the low-income areas of Philadelphia. It was found that in a sample of
1,039 persons over sixty-five years of age only 14 had been to an agency
in the past year for help with a family problem; 37 others knew of an
agency that would provide help if a problem arose. Only 21 respondents
had used the Visiting Nurse service; 353 others knew of the service.

Only 4 respondents had used a homemaker service and only 119 had heard of it.[6]

The intent of the Community Action Agencies of O.E.O is to see that the older poor person receives equal quality and amount of services. Through innovative programs they aggressively search for and find those who need help in order to make their remaining years more comfortable and satisfying. Those who are physically and mentally able and want to work are employed in projects known as Self Help for the Elderly. They work as friendly visitors and case finders and serve as escorts to accompany frail individuals to shop, visit the doctor, and go to the clinic and the senior center. Others serve as aides in the center programs.

Few of the aged poor are members of senior centers

Few low-income urban aged people have participated in community-sponsored clubs and centers, partly because of the fact that these groups meet in areas of the city that are inaccessible to the aged poor who are without automobiles, money for public transportation, or friends who can give them transportation. Programs have also been irrelevant to the needs and interests of poor older adults who often harbor deep feelings of inadequacy and resentment. In the Pennsylvania State University study it was found that only 20 percent of the sample of 1,039 individuals had at least one affiliation with any formal association. Only 5 percent of these memberships were with senior citizens' groups, and 14 percent were with general social or recreational groups. Forty-three percent were with church or religious groups, and 11 percent were with racial or ethnic unions and political groups. It was found that larger numbers of low-income black people than low-income white people belong to voluntary associations. The study explains this finding on the basis of the greater rate of religious activity among black respondents.

"In Detroit [Mich.] a group of 100 aged persons was asked 'What single opportunity or service not now available to you would be most important in your daily life?' Only 4.9% of the respondents expressed an interest in the kinds of services and programs which could be provided by a club or center. The others named functional concerns, such as money, employment, improved transportation, housing, health, companionship in the home and improved general social conditions." [7]

[6] Carl Hirsch, Donald Kent, and Susanne Silverman, *Homogeneity and Heterogeneity Among Low-Income Negro and White Aged* (University Park: Pennsylvania State University, 1968).

[7] George Henderson, "The Negro Recipient of Old-Age Assistance: The Results of Discrimination." *Social Casework,* 46:208-14 (April 1965).

The typical multiservice senior center program—with its emphasis on self-improvement, recreation, travel, education, and service to others—has little meaning for poor older persons. Their one compelling concern has been to get enough money on which to exist. A Fix-it Shop where men can do small carpentry and electrical repair jobs for members and a workshop program and outlet shop where articles can be made and sold for profit are appropriate programs for these older poor persons. A Next-to-New Clothes Closet, where donated articles can be bought at minimum cost, and hot lunch and carry-home suppers will be more meaningful and relevant programs for the aged poor than the present programs of many multiservice centers.

The senior center can be helpful in developing programs for the aged poor

The kinds of help needed by the elderly in any community are many and varied, and it should be the goal of community-sponsored multiservice centers to deliver as many services as possible to these older people who need them. Special centers, at least initially, can effectively highlight the needs and provide specific help to the aged poor of the community. Members of the senior center board and staff should serve on the advisory committees developing these projects in order to become better informed about the needs of this group of older people and more effective in advocating welfare rights programs. These senior center leaders can then be interpreters to the community and promoters of legislation needed for changes in welfare programs.

In the intense competition in today's society for the tax and voluntary dollar, it is apparent that the needs of older people are too often relatively low among local and national priorities. Organizations and programs to serve them cannot proliferate unnecessarily. The leadership of community-sponsored multiservice senior centers and their satellite groups will need to create new and as yet untried ways to make their facilities and programs available and responsive to the needs of all older people of the community.

BIBLIOGRAPHY

Boninger, Walter B. "Aging and Blindness." *New Outlook for the Blind.* 63 (1969): 178-84.

Booth, F. Estelle. *Reaching Out to the Hard-to-Reach Older Person.* San Francisco: San Francisco Senior Center, 1968.

Boyd, Rosamonde, and Oaks, Charles. *Foundations of Practical Gerontology.* Columbia: University of South Carolina Press, 1970.

Brody, S. J.; Finkle, H.; and Hirsch, C. "The Origin and Development of a Model for the Delivery of Services to Low Income Elderly." Paper presented at the Eight International Congress of Gerontology, 26 August 1969, Washington, D.C., p. 4.

Canfield, Norton. *You and Your Hearing.* Public Affairs Pamphlet, no. 315. New York: Public Affairs Committee, 1967.

Case, Maurice. *Recreation for Blind Adults: Organized Programs in Special Settings.* Springfield, Ill.: Charles C. Thomas, 1965.

Chandler, Suzannah. *A Comprehensive Program for the Elderly in Rural Areas.* Washington, D.C.: National Council on the Aging, 1968.

Glascock, Martha McClain, and Scholer, E. A. "Two Experts View Camping for Older Adults." *Camping Magazine,* 41 (March 1969).

Josephson, Eric. *The Social Life of Blind People.* Research Series, no. 19. New York: American Foundation for the Blind, 1968.

Lieberman, Morton A. "Institutionalization of the Aged: Effects on Behavior." *Journal of Gerontology* 24 (1969): 330-40.

National Council on Aging. *A Comprehensive Service for the Elderly in Rural Areas.* Prepared for the Community Action Program of the Office of Economic Opportunity, Washington, D.C. 1967.

National Recreation Association. *Meeting Some Social-Psychological Needs of Homebound Persons Through Recreation Experience.* New York: National Recreation Association, 1962.

Parker, Elaine N., and Tine, Sebastian. *A Basic Skills Program for Older Blind Persons in a Senior Center Setting.* Presented at Annual Meeting of the Gerontological Society, 1968, at Denver, Colorado.

Pihlblad, C. T., and Rosencranz, H. A. *Social Adjustment of Older People in the Small Town.* Columbia: University of Missouri, 1969.

Poe, William D. *The Old Person in your Home.* New York: Charles Scribner's Sons, 1969.

Rachlis, David. *Mini Cost Programs and Services for the Aging Poor.* Washington, D.C.: National Council on the Aging, March 1969.

Rosencranz, H. A., Pihlblad, C. T., and McNevin, T. E. *Social Participation of Older People in the Small Town.* Columbia: University of Missouri, 1968.

Scott, Robert A. *The Making of Blind Men: A Study of Adult Socialization.* New York: Russell Sage Foundation, 1969.

Stern, Mildred. "Activity or Idleness: Restoration of Social Contacts Among the Elderly Blind." *New Outlook for the Blind.* 63 (1969): 185-189.

Thompson, Morton. "Social Rehabilitation of the Homebound." *Recreation.* 54 (1961): 302.

Tirocchi, Selma L. "Social Aspects of Eye Problems in the Aging." *The Sight-Saving Review*. 31 (1961): 23-24.

U.S. Administration on Aging. *Designs for Action for Older Americans: A Project Report on County-wide Information and Referral*. A.O.A. Publication, no. 907. Washington, D.C.: Government Printing Office, 1969.

Wood, Maxine. *Blindness: Ability, not Disability*. Public Affairs Pamphlet, no. 295 A. New York: Public Affairs Committee, 1968.

Wright, Beatrice A. *Physical Disability: A Psychological Approach*. New York: Harper & Brothers, 1960.

Youmans, E. G. *Older Rural Americans: A Sociological Perspective*. Lexington: University of Kentucky Press, 1967.

17 / Administrative Procedures and Practices

THE MAINTENANCE OF AN EFFECTIVE ORGANIZATION that permits growth and development of the center program and harmonious, cooperative relationships among board, staff, and members is the responsibility of the executive director.

The structure of the center establishes a framework to facilitate cooperative relationships and communication among individuals and groups involved in the management of the program. The structure will differ, depending on the size and diversity of the program and whether the center is a unit within a larger sponsoring organization, an independent and private agency, or a program within a large, municipal recreation and parks department. In a small center, where most relationships are face-to-face, a simple structure will be adequate. In a large multiservice center, where staff, board, and member relationships are more indirect, a more complex organizational pattern will be needed. The administrative structure of a center must be continually evaluated and revised to allow for growth and changing conditions. Charts 5 and 6 show the organizational structure of a typical multiservice center and that of a center which is part of a large, municipal recreation and parks department.

The executive director of a multiservice senior center has specific management tasks that include (1) working with a board or commission and its committees, (2) selecting, organizing, and developing staff, (3) keeping the operation effective through evaluation and planning, (4) managing the budget, (5) supervising the building and equipment maintenance, and (6) keeping the center related to other community agencies.

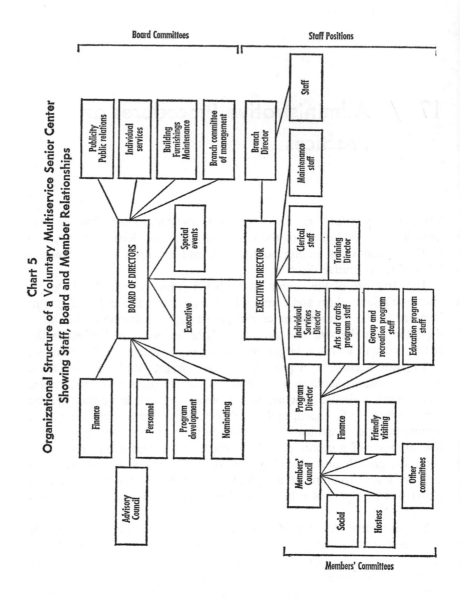

Chart 5

Organizational Structure of a Voluntary Multiservice Senior Center
Showing Staff, Board and Member Relationships

Working With a Board of Directors or
Commission and its Committees

In a center sponsored by any public department, the authority is invested in a committee or commission appointed by the city council with duties and responsibilities established by ordinance. In a voluntary, nonprofit center, authority is invested in a board of directors whose duties and responsibilities are established in a constitution and bylaws. Such centers are usually legally incorporated as nonprofit organizations. Their articles of incorporation grant the board legal authority to hold title to tax-free property and to receive gifts that are tax deductible to the donor. They guarantee that individual members of the board are protected from personal liability in any legal suit against the center. The constitution and bylaws establish the structure of the center management and describe responsibilities of various officers and board committees.

The members of the board should reflect a wide diversity of groups within the community. Affluent and poor individuals, people of various age groups, and members of differing ethnic, religious, and political power groups should all be represented. In addition, professionals from such fields as medicine, law, education, and social work, as well as members of service clubs and of the center itself, should be named to the board of directors. To assure a broadly representative group and adequate leadership to carry out the work of the committees, a board should have at least twenty working members. Large centers will need boards of thirty to forty members. The board of directors or the commission formulates policies for the center's operation and delegates to the executive director the responsibility of operating the center according to these policies. Sometimes board members who have program skills serve as teachers or group leaders within the program. In this role they function not as board members but as staff, and they are responsible not to the executive director, but to the staff member who is supervisor of the activity group.

How board members are chosen and function

Individuals are proposed for board membership by a nominating committee, a standing committee of the board. They are then elected by the board to become its new members. The staff can be instrumental in helping to build a strong board by recommending to the nominating committee individuals known to be interested in and to have a contri-

Chart 6
Organizational Chart Showing Lines of Staff
Authority and Supervision of a Municipal
Recreation and Park Department Senior Center

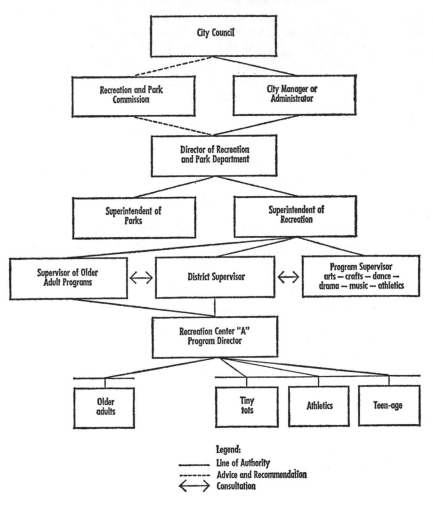

Legend:
——— Line of Authority
------- Advice and Recommendation
⟷ Consultation

bution to make to the center's development. The bylaws of most centers limit the number of terms a member can serve on the board. This arrangement provides for a continuous flow of new leadership into the center and eliminates the possibility of any individual or clique of members remaining too long in control. The acceptance of the center in the community will be closely related to the status of the members of its board in the community and how much confidence the general public places in them. In order to retain the interest of retiring board members who have given outstanding service and to utilize their experience and expertise, some centers organize advisory councils, honorary groups named by the nominating committees. The advisory council is invited to attend the annual meeting and special events of the center. It holds at least one meeting during the year and undertakes special fund-raising projects to benefit the center.

The officers of the board, who may also be selected by the nominating committee or elected by the board itself, usually include the president, two or more vice presidents who serve as chairmen of the finance and personnel committees respectively, a secretary, and a treasurer. These officers form the executive committee. The board works through committees established to carry out specific assignments such as nominating, finance, personnel, publicity and promotion, and individual services. Ad hoc committees are sometimes needed to carry short-term assignments, but no committee should be appointed routinely unless there is a job to be done. A committee of five to seven members makes possible a stimulating interchange of ideas and attitudes. With fewer members committee deliberations are less fruitful; when they are too large they become unwieldy and only the most articulate members become involved. Some centers include individuals other than board members on their board committees. This plan makes it possible to benefit from the expertise of professionals who are unable to give time to serve as members of the board but can give time to a specific committee. It also makes possible the use of the continuing help of former board members and gives some initial experience to individuals who are potential board members. The executive director serves as consultant to the president of the board as he names the chairmen and the members of the various committees. With members of the staff whom he delegates, he serves to help these committees as they work on their assignments.

A board manual is a helpful tool for
on-the-job education of board members

When individuals are elected to the board it is important that they be oriented as quickly as possible to the center and its program in order to be knowledgeable and effective in carrying their assignments. A board manual should include (1) a copy of the center constitution and by-laws; (2) a list of board members, their addresses, and telephone numbers; (3) a history of the center and a statement of goals for future development; (4) a statement on the numbers and needs of the aged in the community, the kinds of programs and services provided for them, and the specific role of the center in this spectrum of services; (5) a list of national, state, and local organizations with which the center is affiliated; (6) a statement of current concerns of the board and a projection of directions for the future development of the center.

Selecting, Organizing, and Developing the Staff

With the recommendation of the personnel committee, the executive director is selected and employed by the board of directors to which he will be responsible as he carries on his administrative tasks. Other staff members are selected by the executive director, and—on his and the personnel committee's recommendations—they are then employed by the board. In a multiservice center operated by a municipal department, the staff members may be civil service employees and are appointed after competitive examinations or according to promotional and seniority policies.

Professional staff are attracted to those community agencies that have good personnel policies and pay salaries comparable to those of similar agencies. During the developmental years, senior centers have had to compete with well-established agencies for experienced and trained staff. Many centers, as affiliates of national organizations, have had excellent personnel policies, good salary standards, and promising opportunities for professional advancement. As senior centers have achieved status and recognition from other community agencies and more adequate financing, they have been able to attract better qualified workers.

Working with older adults is attractive to certain professional workers. Among these are individuals who have worked in youth-serving agencies for a number of years. As they grow into their middle-adult years, they feel more compatible with the needs and interests of older adults. Some women with training in one of the helping professions, who left their positions when they married, seek reemployment after their children have grown and prefer working with adults rather than youth. Mature volunteers may find such satisfaction in working with older adults that they become interested in returning to universities to take professional degrees. They then look to senior centers for employment. The graduate student who has had his field work placement in an agency serving older adults may have had such a meaningful experience that he applies for full-time work in the center when he graduates. As senior centers become able to meet the salary scales of other community agencies and have commensurate personnel policies and practices, they will be able to attract more experienced and mature staff members.

The executive director interviews applicants and selects the staff

The executive director interviews and selects the most qualified applicants for staff positions. If another staff member will be the applicant's supervisor, he also has an opportunity to interview him. Facts about the applicant's training, experience, and present employment are usually stated in his letter of application. Of equal importance is the warmth of feeling and interest in older people shown by the applicant during his visits to the center to observe the program in action. The ease with which he encounters the members, the ways he relates to them, the interest he shows, and the questions he asks will reveal how effective he may be as a leader with older adults.

When the executive director has selected a staff member, he discusses his decision with the personnel committee and, if it seems desirable, the applicant meets the personnel committee. The personnel committee recommends to the board that the applicant be employed. The executive then writes the prospective staff member stating information previously discussed, including the initial salary and when the employee may expect an increase. He also includes a copy of the personnel policies and a description of the job and the specific duties and responsibilities the applicant will be expected to carry. A personnel record folder is established in the office of the executive director for each worker as he joins the staff. The information received in his initial interview, letters of recommendation, reports on his preemployment health examination, and copies of his annual evaluations or service ratings are accumulated in this folder. These records are confidential and should be used only by the executive or anyone who has his permission to see them.

*Good personnel policies help raise
the quality of job applicants*

Personnel policies serve as an official statement to the employee of the conditions of his employment and what he can expect from the employing agency. Personnel policies give staff members a sense of security, help maintain staff morale, build loyalty, and reduce staff turnover. The policy statement plan for staff evaluations and the salary ranges for each position make up the center's personnel manual. Personnel policies should cover the following related subjects: (1) work schedules, defining the number of hours of work, compensation provisions for evening and weekend work, vacations, legal holidays, and other leaves; (2) statements of salaries and other compensations, defining salary ranges for each position, retirement benefits, health and workmen's compensation insurance, and other reimbursable items; (3) evaluation and termination procedures, stating the length of the probationary period, the agency's responsibility to help employees grow in professional competency and steps to be taken when either the employee or the center wishes to terminate employment.[1]

The following is a description of the typical functions of a personnel committee and suggested policies governing the employment and working arrangements with the staff.[2]

THE PERSONNEL COMMITTEE
    a. The Personnel Committee shall consist of at least five members of the board appointed by the president for a term of one year. It shall meet at least three times a year. There shall be such sub-committees as may be necessary from time to time. This committee shall be delegated the responsibility to establish, maintain, revise and/or change personnel standards and employment practices and policies. Staff may suggest changes or revisions in these policies for the consideration of the committee. The president of the board and the executive director shall serve as ex officio members of this committee.
    b. The committee may also receive requests from employees for adjustment of all unsolved personnel problems, provided in each situation such problems have been previously discussed by employees with the executive director. This committee has the right

---

[1] "A Guide for Developing Standards for Professional Personnel Policies and Practices in Senior Centers" has recently been drawn up by an Advisory Committee on Senior Centers and may be ordered from The National Council on Aging, Washington, D.C.

[2] From *Personnel Manual,* San Francisco Senior Center, San Francisco, California.

to refer such problems to the executive committee of the board of directors.

TERMS OF EMPLOYMENT

a. There shall be an executive director and such employed staff members as are necessary to carry on the work of the agency. The executive director shall be employed and may be dismissed by the board of directors.

b. The executive director shall, under the direction of the board of directors, be general executive officer of the senior center. He shall select and supervise the employed staff and volunteers and have such other duties as may be delegated by the board of directors.

c. At the time of first employment, there shall be a probationary period of six months for professional employees. Evaluation of the work of the probationer by the executive director shall be the basis (a) for dismissal at any time, upon notice of two weeks, during probationary period or (b) for retention in regular status at the end of six months. At the time of first employment by the agency, the probationer shall be given in writing a job analysis and a copy of those employment practices which, with a letter of acceptance from the worker, shall constitute the employment agreement. At the time of regular employment the probationary period of six months shall be applied toward the time of earned vacation. If the worker is dismissed before or at the end of six months, he shall not be entitled to vacation.

EVALUATION PROCEDURES

There shall be an annual evaluation of the work of each regular employee made with the executive director. An evaluation of the executive director is made by the executive and/or personnel committees of the board. The executive or the board can initiate the request for such an evaluation conference. Evaluations are used as the basis (a) to take personal action such as determining status, promotion and dismissal, (b) to assist the worker in his professional development, (c) to assist the agency in strengthening its program of serving.

TERMINATION OF EMPLOYMENT

a. Executive director: Notice of dismissal or of resignation is required to be given in writing one month in advance.

b. Other employees shall advise the executive director in writing at least two weeks in advance of leaving the job.

c. If a full time regular employee is dismissed, he must be advised by the executive director at least one month in advance (except in case of emergency, such as gross negligence or misuse of information). If he prefers, the employee may have the reasons for his dismissal given to him in writing. He shall be entitled to appeal through the president of the board for review of his case by the executive committee and subsequently by the board if he so desires. The decision of the board is final. The employee shall be entitled to all salary due. There shall be an adjustment of the employee's salary if, at the time of termination of employment, vacation taken exceeds amount earned. It shall be the duty of the employee to bring up-to-date all assigned work before he leaves his job.

HOURS OF EMPLOYMENT, VACATIONS, SICK LEAVE,
LEAVES OF ABSENCE, LEGAL HOLIDAYS

a. The length of the working week shall be 37½ hours for all full time employees, with the understanding that time spent on occasional conferences with consultants outside of schedule will not be considered as over-time. Over-time work will be subject to the approval of the executive director. Approved over-time work shall be recompensed by corresponding time off, to be arranged by the executive director, if possible, within the month immediately following.

b. Sick leave: Fifteen working days per year as sick leave without reduction of salary shall be allowed all workers with permanent status. This is cumulative over a three year period to forty-five working days. If an employee is absent more than ten consecutive working days, a doctor's statement shall be submitted by the employee estimating the duration of illness and probable absence. Longer absences without salary reduction shall be permitted only upon approval of the board of directors.

c. Time off for death or illness or personal emergencies: Three days with full pay may be allowed at the time of death or serious illness in the employee's immediate family, or for personal emergencies. The executive director may extend this time upon approval of the board of directors.

d. Maternity leave: Maternity leave without pay may be granted for staff members who have been employed at least two years.

e. Vacations on salary: For the professional staff, an annual vacation of twenty-two working days during the summer months if possible. Vacations should be taken in as long a period as can be worked out between the employee and the agency, both in order to give more adequate refreshment to the employee and to avoid too frequent interruptions in the agency work. Vacation period for more than six months but less than one year of employment shall be arranged on the basis of five and one-half days of vacation for every three months of employment. A vacation of four working days shall be arranged at Christmas time. No vacations are cumulative.

f. Leaves of absence: For the professional staff, with or without salary for study (or for any other purpose) shall be subject to the recommendation and approval of the personnel committee. The final decision is made by the board of directors, each case to be decided upon its own merits.

Time to attend institutes and conferences may be allowed by the executive director. Conference expense may be paid in whole or in part at the discretion of the board of directors.

After five years of service, a leave of absence of three months with full pay (in addition to the annual vacation of one month) shall be granted for education purposes if there are sufficient funds to employ substitute workers. When several members of the staff are eligible in one year, not more than one may take his leave during any six months period, those of greater seniority having the choice of time. If any eligible staff member cannot take his leave when it is due, he must waive his rights in the interest of the next person in line.

g. The center shall be closed on the following legal holidays and at any other time upon the approval of the board of directors:

New Year's Day	January 1
* Washington's Birthday	February 22
Memorial Day	May 30
Independence Day	July 4
Labor Day	First Monday in September
Thanksgiving Day	as proclaimed
Christmas Day	December 25

* If these dates fall on days when the center's program is in operation the time off is staggered among the staff so that the program itself is not curtailed.

h. Staff members who are called for jury duty may serve without loss of pay. Compensation as a juror shall be turned in to the center.

SALARIES AND OTHER COMPENSATION

a. Salary increases shall be made annually for satisfactory performance, provided that such increases are consistent with salary ranges established by the personnel committee for specific positions.

b. In addition to the salary and social security payments, the center also finances certain fringe benefits. These include workmen's compensation insurance, its proportionate share of employees' retirement payments to National Health and Welfare Association or other pension plans, group hospitalization and health insurance. The center will also reimburse the staff member for the use of his personal automobile for authorized trips at an established rate. It will pay 50 percent of the cost of luncheons and dinners that the staff member is authorized to attend as a part of his job.

Annual evaluations help staff and executive director improve their professional practice

Although the evaluation of staff goes on continuously in informal ways, the executive director has annual conferences with workers, especially if they are new, to review with them their job performance. For an experienced worker an annual evaluation may not be necessary, although it should be given if he requests one or if there is any question about his work. Such conferences are less threatening to the staff if they are structured to allow the employee to take the initiative and evaluate his own successes and failures and satisfactions and disappointments on the job. Such questions as the following given him before the conference will help to keep the evaluation focused and helpful. (1) Considering your committees and areas of responsibility what progress have you made this year in helping to achieve their objectives? What problems have you had in doing this? (2) Should all groups for which you have been responsible be continued next year? What are your goals for them? (3) What new program should be added? Why? (4) What has made your job difficult? (5) What suggestions do you have to help the staff work together more effectively and for the center to be more responsive to the needs and interests of its members? (6) What have been your greatest disappointments this year? Your greatest satisfactions?

In the guided interview the executive director or the supervisor can interject any concerns he has had about the staff member's performance and help him to discuss them objectively. After the conference the executive director or supervisor writes a summary of the points made and submits it to the staff member for his concurrence and signature. If the staff member is not in agreement with the evaluation he will discuss his objections with the executive director and together they can make changes by agreement. If there are still differences, the employee may submit his own statement noting his objections. These evaluation statements become a part of the employee's personnel record file and are used by the executive director as the basis for recommending salary increases and for letters of recommendations when the worker changes jobs. The evaluation records of municipal employees in senior centers follow local department practices for evaluation.

After the initial probationary period, when a staff member's skills and ability to work well with older adults have been demonstrated, he should be able to feel secure and assured that he will not be dismissed or demoted unless the center's income is seriously curtailed and his job is eliminated.

In-service training increases
the effectiveness of staff leaders

Although many applicants for positions in senior centers have basic professional training, they may have had no experience working with older adults. This skill can be acquired on the job through in-service training opportunities that include the following:

1. *A series of orientation conferences.* In the first session, the executive director describes the history and philosophy of the center and discusses the board's organization and structure, sources of financial support, and the strengths, weaknesses, and future goals of the center. In subsequent sessions, a member of the office staff discusses records, reports, and all office and business procedures in which program staff is involved; the program director describes the program and the specific groups for which new staff members will be responsible. It is also most helpful to invite staff members of other agencies with whom the new staff member will be working to describe their services and how the agencies work together. This orientation should extend over a period of time so that staff members will not be confused with too many details before they have begun to feel acquainted.

2. *Supervisory conferences.* These are scheduled regularly by the executive director or the supervisor of the program staff. Most senior centers are not so large that special supervisory visits must be made to observe specific groups. The executive director or supervisor is involved in many of the programs and sees the worker in action daily in informal and casual ways. In the supervisory conference the executive director or supervisor can help the staff member gain perspective on problems he may be having with individuals or in the functioning of his groups. Casual conversations over a cup of coffee are sometimes productive in providing help and guidance.

3. *Staff meetings.* Meetings for the professional staff are held regularly; the clerical and maintenance staffs are included when items on the agenda involve them. Staff meetings fulfill a variety of functions, such as clearance for dates and the use of rooms and equipment, reviews of social histories of new applicants for membership, joint planning for all-center events, brainstorming sessions, discussions of special problems, and opportunities to hear from representatives of other agencies about

their services. Reviews of recent books and articles and reports from conferences are important for meetings of the program staff. In some centers the agenda is planned by a staff committee; in others the executive director carries this responsibility. Regular well-planned staff meetings help to develop morale and a sense of cohesion within the staff and reduce that anxiety that may develop around false information or the lack of information on subjects of critical interest to the staff.

4. *Opportunities to attend conferences and meetings.* Too often only the executive director attends important conferences, but those that stimulate thinking and widen perspective are essential for the staff. Staff time at conferences and meetings should be accepted as work time, and the cost of such attendance should be jointly shared by the center and the staff member.

5. *Books and professional journals help the staff in their professional development.* A center member who has been a librarian or a community volunteer with this skill can be enlisted to catalogue materials and set up a library for the use of center leadership. Some publications that should be included are the following.

> *Newsletter* of the National Institute of Senior Centers, published by the National Council on Aging, 1828 "L" Street N.W., Suite 504, Washington, D.C. 20036.
>
> *Gerontologist Magazine,* a publication of the Gerontological Society, Inc., 660 South Euclid Avenue, St. Louis, Missouri 63110
>
> *Aging,* a monthly news magazine published by the Administration on Aging, Department of Health, Education and Welfare, Washington, D.C. 20201
>
> Professional journals, such as *Social Work,* the journal of the National Association of Social Workers, 2 Park Avenue, New York, 10016; *Park and Recreation,* magazine of the National Parks and Recreation Association, 1700 Pennsylvania Avenue, Washington, D.C. 20006
>
> Reprints from journals and copies of papers on various subjects related to programs of senior centers may be borrowed from the library of the National Council on Aging, 1828 "L" Street, N.W., Washington, D.C. 20036
>
> *Aging and Human Development,* an international journal of psychosocial gerontology, Robert Kastenbaum, Wayne University, Detroit, Michigan 11699.

6. *Leaves for study.* Personnel policies should provide opportunities for staff members to have extended leaves and sabbaticals to participate in short-term courses and advanced professional educational courses in social gerontology now offered by many colleges and universities.

7. *Increasing professional growth and competence.* Staff members

should be encouraged to join and participate in national, state and local chapters of professional organizations, the National Institute of Senior Centers, and the Gerontological Society.

Increasing one's skills as a worker with older people is a continuous process for all leaders. It can only be achieved if the total staff is able to communicate openly with one another with mutual respect and confidence in an atmosphere that permits an easy interchange and acceptance of ideas. The most effective administrator is one who permits competent professional staff members to carry their responsibilities with minimum regulations and direction. He remains aware of the actions and interactions within the center but he does not feel that he must be involved in the details of work assigned to others. He is sensitive to the tensions and eliminates their causes. He strives to remain impartial in his relations with each staff member and takes no privileges for himself that he does not grant to others.

Keeping Operation Effective Through Evaluation and Planning

Evaluation is the process for measuring what progress is being made in achieving a center's stated goals. The process is a continuous one, sometimes scheduled and structured, often casual or informal. All persons who carry leadership responsibility—board, directors, staff, and members—must be involved. Each has his own area of responsibility and goals to achieve.

The board of directors carries the ultimate responsibility for how well the center fulfills its function in the community. Its members must ask and answer the following questions. Is the center reaching the older people who need its services? Do center statistics indicate that more members are being served each year? Do the financial reports show that the budget is in balance and that financial assets are increasing? Does the executive director's annual report indicate that new and innovative programs are being developed? How can the center's program be improved?

The executive director guides the total evaluation process. He must continually be aware of how effective he is in keeping the organization strong, its services helpful, and its relations to other community organizations productive. He must keep informed about how well staff members are carrying the responsibilities assigned to their positions, how they are growing in their professional skills, and how he, as the supervisor of staff, can help them become more competent. In addition, each program leader must look critically at how well each group he supervises provides a meaningful experience for its members, how successful they are in becoming less dependent on him, and how well they work together. Center members who plan special events evaluate by asking, "How do you think it went? It took lots of time; was it worth it and should we do it again? How could we do it better another time?" The evaluative judgments made by board, staff, and members are all important in and of themselves, but they are primarily important because they indicate how well the total center is achieving its goal of providing opportunities for the members to grow as persons.

Program evaluation based on subjective judgments is difficult

Personality growth and behavioral and attitudinal changes are extremely difficult to measure by objective methods. Changes in feelings of alienation, loneliness, and despair are not readily quantifiable; only the differences in behavior that result from such changes and growth can be measured. Staff members often comment, "We can see people actually change when they become active in the center." The depressed and discouraged become more friendly and outgoing; apathetic members take new interest in life; complaining and ego-centered individuals find other interests than themselves to discuss; the hostile become more cooperative and the aggressive more considerate. These judgments of the staff are all subjective and do not lend themselves to objective measurements.

In order to validate personality changes, a psychological or psychiatric evaluation at the time the individual becomes a member and a follow-up testing after he has participated for a period of time would be needed. Only then could one know what actual changes, if any, had taken place in the member's self-image and social functioning. Even these, however, would not be conclusive evidence of the center's influence in the change because many variables operate in the life of every individual. One could never be sure whether it was the member's experience at the center or outside factors that brought about the improvement—his doctor's informing him that his blood pressure was now normal; a letter from a son who had not written for a long time inviting him to visit; his finding more desirable living arrangements.

It is unrealistic to expect that every older person who joins senior centers will become a happier, better adjusted individual. Center programs can offer opportunities for change, but how well the individual uses them is dependent on many individual factors.

Quantitative assessments of progress are relatively easy to make. They are not ends in themselves but are important criteria and form the basis from which objective evaluations can be made. When the center administration determines what information is needed, concise record forms can be designed that will gather and keep current the information that will be a basis for evaluation.

There are regular forms for keeping records to be used in evaluation.

1. *The individual member's Personal Data card* (see chapter 11). On the back of this form the counselor records all contacts with the member or with others on his behalf concerning personal problems. This card becomes the member's personal history and is closed only at his request or when he is deceased.

2. *Total daily attendance records.* These indicate the volume of service given; whether the number of members attending the center is increasing or decreasing; whether some days of the week are better than others for the program; whether seasonal changes affect attendance; the basic cost of each unit of service.

3. *Individual attendance records.* These records, indicating when and how often each member attends, give some indication of how meaningful the activities are for him. Unless a member comes to the center, the program can hold no potential benefit for him.

4. *Individual finance records.* These are an orderly way of receiving the member's contributions for the operation of the center and give an accurate picture of each member's support.

5. *Group attendance records.* These are kept by the leader or secretary of each class, club, and interest group. They indicate the most popular activities, those that sustain member interest, and those that do not generate enough interest to justify continuance.

The information received through these statistical forms is compiled on a *Master Statistical Record* by a member of the clerical staff (see Form 3). Although narrative group records must be minimal in many centers because of staff time limitations, it is important that some descriptive records be kept. Group records describe the content of each meeting and indicate the general level of member involvement, the participation and growth of each individual, and future goals. Group records should be kept on new and experimental groups and on any that are having problems. They are most useful for staff and supervisory conferences.

FORM 3. MASTER STATISTICAL RECORD

I *Group Services*

	Month						
	Staff						
	No. enrolled	No. of sessions	1st week	2nd week	3rd week	4th week	5th week	Total monthly attendance

Groups and classes with definite enrollment							
Large group activities without definite enroll-ment							
Special events							
Committee meetings							
Volunteers							
GRAND TOTALS							

II *Individual Service to or on Behalf of Older Persons*

	Total	Report of Case-Worker(s)	Report of other professional & technical staff
A. No. of persons counselled	———	———	———
1. Members	———	———	———
2. Non-member	———	———	———
B. Total no. of interviews	———	———	———
1. Intake	———	———	———
2. On activity or program problem	———	———	———
3. On personal problems	———	———	———
a. With individual	———	———	———
b. With collateral to secure information, locate resource, etc.	———	———	———

	Number of units of service	
C. Other personal services to members	Staff	Volunteers
1. Friendly visiting	———	———
2. Transporting or arranging for transport ..	———	———
3. Other (specify)	———	———

III *Responsibilities Carried in the Community*

	Number
A. Interpretation of services for and needs of aged, total	———
1. Appearances on radio and TV, of staff or volunteers	———
2. Interviews with press	———
3. Publication of articles, reports, brochures, etc.	———
4. Oral presentations before groups	———
a. Lay groups	———
b. Professional groups	———
5. Conducting group tours of facility ... ,,,...........	———
6. Other (specify) .... ,,,,,,	———
B. Participation in planning for needs of aged, total	———
1. Advising with other agencies in developing programs	———
2. Attendance at committee and council meetings	———
3. Participation in conferences and workshops	———

Indirect methods can be used for evaluating the center's program

The staffs of many centers find day-long conferences scheduled at the end of the program year to be helpful for program evaluation. These conferences are often held away from the center, and staff can talk in leisure about the achievements and difficulties of the year and project plans for the future.

The annual report of the center serves as an evaluative tool. In it the year's achievements are reviewed, trends are noted, and directions for future developments are forecast. The quality and content of brochures in which the center describes itself help the community appraise the operation and program. Although the community is not directly related to the evaluative process of the center, it has several ways of indicating its appraisal of the program—by increasing or decreasing allocations from funding agencies, by its coverage of the center in the mass media, and by the volume of memorial gifts and legacies that are given to the center.

Records often indicate areas for research

Records reveal problems that need to be looked at more critically and often become the basis for further study, research, and new programs. The director of one center became concerned about the persons who applied for membership, visited one or two times, and then dropped out. In reviewing all applications for the previous year it was found that the counselor had interviewed 203 individuals who had applied for membership; 80 had not returned to become members. The fact that a large number of the applicants who did not come back had been referred by social agencies was disturbing; they were persons known to be lonely and in need of new relationships and interests in life. The executive director considered whether giving these hard-to-reach persons more individual attention would involve them in the program and enable them to form sufficiently satisfying relationships to prevent further withdrawal. To test this hypothesis a proposal was designed to find ways to involve unmotivated older persons who needed social activities. Funds were secured from the government and private foundations to employ a trained and experienced caseworker and to rent a small space for operation. The project was located in a store-front building with easy access to the sidewalk, whose large front windows made it easy for individuals to look in and see what was happening before entering the room. For the first six months of the project the caseworker spent all of his time visiting the hard-to-reach older persons in their apartments and hotel rooms, encouraging them to visit the store-front center. A group worker was on duty at the center and related on a one-to-one basis as the referred individuals eventually came in. Gradually groups formed as these desolate individuals began to know and trust one another. After a demonstration period the evidence was conclusive that many older adults, if given enough initial supportive help, would join and benefit greatly from a center program. Permanent funding was secured and the demonstration project, serving hard-to-reach older adults, became an established branch of a multiservice senior center.[3]

Funds for research and demonstration projects are becoming increasingly available to senior centers and other nonprofit organizations serving older adults. Through the Older Americans' Act, grants are made by the federal Office on Aging to state councils on aging, which, in turn, allocate funds at their discretion to promising demonstration and research projects in local communities. Securing such funds calls for new administrative skills frequently referred to as "grantsmanship." Imaginative proposals with adequate community backing must be written; designated channels for submitting the proposals must be followed up patiently and persistently; and exacting accounting records and reporting must be kept.

The Department of Health, Education and Welfare's annual publication *Grants-in-Aid and other Financial Assistance Programs,* describes the many grant programs available to senior centers and other eligible organizations. The staffs of community health and welfare planning bodies and united funds should be asked about possibilities of grants from local foundations. The regional offices of the Administration on Aging and of the National Council on the Aging are also excellent sources for information on funds and help in writing proposals.[4]

The operations of future senior centers cannot be by trial and error methods, but will be meaningful and effective only as they are geared to the new knowledge that comes from demonstrations and research. Senior centers have a unique and important role to play in producing this research. Board and staff members must begin to ask and find answers to these questions: What do we need to know? How can we

[3] This demonstration project, funded by the California Commission on Aging, became the Downtown Branch of the San Francisco Senior Center, San Francisco, California.
[4] David Rachles, *How to Obtain Grants for Programs for the Aging Poor* (Washington, D.C.: National Council on Aging, 1968).

finance needed research? How can we interest research workers in securing the knowledge we need to assure a quality program?

Managing the Budget

All programs, whether of small social clubs or large multiservice centers, need to be adequately financed. A group that meets monthly or even weekly with volunteer leadership or staff provided by the sponsoring agency in a room provided rent free will need only a small budget. In most instances such a project can operate with members' contributions and the funds earned from money-making projects. Multiservice senior centers, however, will require larger budgets to finance larger facilities, staff salaries, and extensive programs and services. When the center is a part of the total program of a municipal recreation, education, or health department, tax funds provide the facilities and their maintenance, equipment, and furnishings, staff salaries, and many program costs. If the center is sponsored by a nonprofit agency or is an autonomous organization with a voluntary board of directors, then private and perhaps tax funds are needed for its support. Communities have long recognized their corporate responsibility to provide schools and playgrounds for the welfare of their children and youth. A similar responsibility to provide opportunities for the well-being of their older citizens is accepted by most cities today.

The budgetary needs of a center grow out of the program evaluation process. When staff members become aware that additional funds will be needed for some aspects of the program, they channel requests to the executive director. His responsibility is the interpretation of these needs to the board finance committee when it prepares a budget for the coming year. In its final form the budget is submitted to the board for approval. In a public agency the center's financial needs are submitted to the head of the sponsoring department and then incorporated into the total department budget, which, in turn, is submitted to the city manager and city council. Those senior centers that are financed through funds allocated to them by united fund-raising agencies operate under their general financial policies and budgeting processes. Participating in united community funding assures the center of a continuity of income, but it often limits the center's freedom to solicit additional funds from the community for special needs, capital improvements, or expansion of services.

Sound financial administration is the ultimate responsibility of an executive director acting in behalf of and under the direction of a board of directors. Accounting practices must provide contributors and funding agencies understandable information and reflect management integrity. Budget interpretations should make clear the significance of the relationship between total members served and the financial needs of a multiservice center that provides individualized services rather than mass activities limited to recreational events.

The many variables in size and methods of operation and the type and range of services make it impossible to describe specific budget formulations or percentages of the total income needed for each category of expenditures. Staff salaries and wages are usually the largest budget item. In centers that operate buildings, the expenditures for salaries, wages, social security, pensions, and health benefits are approximately 50 percent of the total budget. In those centers where facilities and maintenance are provided without charge, the expenditure for salaries is often as high as 75 percent of the total budget. Other operating expenses include printing, postage, office supplies, telephone, insurance, mileage for staff cars, and repairs and replacements for furnishings and equipment. Publicity and education expenses include publicity projects, conferences, and meetings, and publications and subscriptions. There are also expenses for program and household supplies, including food, craft supplies purchased for resale, and supplies for all classes, parties, and programs.

In a 1969 study of the 1,242 senior centers in all parts of the United States that are open three or more days a week and have nonvolunteer staff, it was found that the average center operates on an annual budget of approximately $27,000, but this median figure is inflated by 76 centers that have budgets over $50,000. Half of the centers studied have budgets of less than $15,000, and 166 operate on less than $3,000 a year. Only 432 centers reported full-time (at least forty hours a week) directors. The average pay of full-time directors is $5,000 to $8,000; approximately fifty-four earn $10,000 or more; ninety-four are paid under $5,000 a year. Aproximately 400 centers were receiving Older American Act, Title 14 support and they generally showed "slightly more accomplishment of the national senior center goals which were measured." [5]

Policies concerning the control of funds contributed or raised by active members of a center are made by the members' council in consultation with the staff. In many centers, a member who has been elected as the treasurer works with a finance committee to collect funds and make

[5] Nancy N. Anderson, *Senior Centers: Information from a National Survey* (Minneapolis, Minn.: American Rehabilitation Foundation, 1969).

certain expenditures in areas designated as their responsibility. The treasurer and the committee are accountable to the general membership. This plan can work only if they are responsible, capable men and women and when mutual trust, communication, and cooperation are maintained with the executive director and all the members. In other centers, a members' finance committee receives all contributions from members, accounts for the sums collected, and turns them over to the staff book-keeper. All bills are paid by check and monthly and annual accountings are made to the members. To avoid conflict and misunderstanding, it is important that members understand how the center is financed and their responsibilities for its support.

It is important for individual members to make regular contributions to the center's support

The question of how much responsibility the older people themselves should carry for financing their groups is one on which there is wide divergence both in philosophy and in practice. Many groups expect no financial contribution from the members but believe that older people should be the recipients of services provided for them by the community. Other projects operate on the premise that free services patronize and demean older people and that the users of services should carry some responsibility for meeting their costs. Some understanding of the meaning of money to people, and especially to older people, will help centers to decide the best practice for the group. Money is a symbol of security, independence, and self-determination. Old age brings with it many experiences of increasing dependency to which older people react in a variety of ways. Some react with resentment and hostility; others, with apathy. Pride becomes a strong ego defense in the later years, and many older persons refuse to identify themselves with a group in which they are made to feel dependent on someone's charity. On the other hand, some individuals will express unconscious hostility at being made dependent by becoming increasingly grasping and unreasonable in their demands and expectations of the sponsoring group. It is both unwise and unsound to operate on the premise that because people are old they must be given everything free. Payment for services represents an opportunity to maintain the normal patterns of responsible adults.

Some clubs establish a specified amount as a membership fee. Too often these fees are set without thought of the older person who has limited financial means and, as a result, is excluded. The amount that many older people can contribute for the support of their group will be limited, and it must be made flexible to accommodate the differences in economic status. It is important, however, that there be some expectation that elderly individuals will help support the groups they join. Older persons may support their clubs in a variety of ways.

1. Members may be asked to drop contributions into a donation box each time they attend the group. Small and informal groups often find this a satisfactory procedure, although sometimes it leads to dissension and conflict within the club when some individuals fail to contribute and others complain. To substitute voluntary donations for a regular individual contribution is a rationalization. Although the older person's ability to contribute is recognized, he is denied the opportunity to commit himself to a specified amount that he decides he can pay to the organization he has chosen to join. Even though the members are individuals with incomes below the poverty level, some membership contribution—even a minimal one—should be expected. Paying even a nominal fee gives the older adult a feeling of belonging and carrying his responsibility for the support of the club.

2. Members may be asked to give a regular monthly contribution, the amount voluntary, depending on what the individual himself thinks he can afford. The exact sum is confidential and is determined by the individual with the nongroup-member leader when he joins the group. The receipt and the accounting for these payments become the responsibility of the treasurer or of a finance committee of the members. The members' payments to the group are kept on individual finance cards (see Form 4).

Form 4. (Face of Card)

FINANCE CARD

Name .... No. ....

Address .... Tel. ....

Name of Club

Address

As an expression of my participation and interest in the .... Club and my desire to help promote its program, I pledge the following monthly contribution for its support:

Amount per month: $...........

From January 1, 19.... to December 31, 19....

(Back of card)

Bal.			PAYMENTS			
	Date	Rec'd	Amount	Date	Rec'd	Amount
Bal.			Bal.			
Jan.			July			
Feb.			Aug.			
Mar.			Sept.			
Apr.			Oct.			
May			Nov.			
June			Dec.			

The advantages of this procedure are as follows. (a) The individual has a sense of carrying his share along with others for the support of the group, and he therefore becomes more involved and identified with the success of the group. Such a plan formalizes and dignifies the members' responsibility for support. (b) The amount of income from the membership can be estimated and a yearly budget established.

3. Another method of member support is participation in fund-raising events, such as bazaars, play productions, and concerts. Projects undertaken by the members for the purpose of meeting expenses are important also as meaningful program experiences. Projects and money-making activities involve many individuals in preparing for the event, and thus bring the group and the potentials of all older people to the attention of the community in positive ways.

In addition to all of the bookkeeping records that are essential for efficient accounting and controlling of receipts and expenditures, the following records should also be kept to provide fiscal and program accountability to the board and the community: (1) an annual audit by a firm of public accountants; (2) petty cash requisitions and expenditures; (3) purchase orders for large expenditures; (4) insurance carried, the amounts of the premiums and when due; (5) security bonds for all employees who are responsible for handling cash and signing checks (these provide protection for organizations against theft or fraud); (6) Inventories of furnishings and equipment, their cost, when and from whom purchased, and any expense for repairs; (7) Personnel records of staff, their social security numbers, the dates of their employment, beginning salaries, dates and amounts of raises, and dates of sick leave and vacations; (8) Accident report forms.

In order to provide a secure base for its operation many centers set up a capital fund account. Capital funds are kept in reserve to provide for capital improvements and as a backlog in the event of an emergency curtailment of operating funds. Some senior centers establish endowment funds, the income from which can be allocated to program experimentation and development. Gifts from foundations, legacies from individuals, memory funds and income from special projects help to build up essential resources. Members of the board enlist the interest of lawyers and trust officers of banks who draw up and administer wills, legacies, and endowments. They contact these representatives regularly and enclose information about the center so that they can suggest the center as a beneficiary if it seems appropriate. The boards of some centers create investment committees that advise and guide the boards in their investment program.

Today there are many new and critical social needs in communities, and there is much competition for the tax and voluntary dollar. Services for older adults often seem to have low priority for community interest and support, and those who are responsible for their funding face a serious dilemma. The public responds most readily to appeals on behalf of individuals, especially children, who are in distress and who readily elicit their sympathy and compassion. Societal attitudes, however, can no longer cast the aged as objects of pity and play up all the possible negative aspects of aging. To do so belies the facts about old age, and does a great disservice to the older person's integrity, dignity, and pride. Maintaining old stereotypes about the inadequacies of elderly people and about illness and poverty as characteristic of all older adults is no longer true or acceptable. Yet when programs call the positive aspects of old age to the public's attention, questions are raised as to why the community's support is needed for programs for the aged. One of the crucial challenges facing centers is an adequate interpretation of their role and contribution in the community. All communication media must be used in new and creative ways if the public is to have a true picture of old age and its potentials.

Supervising the Building and Equipment Maintenance

Maintaining the physical facilities of a center is another responsibility of the executive director. He will not carry the details of this task but will delegate them to dependable and capable maintenance and house-keeping personnel. The harmony, efficiency, and comfort in which the program staff works and the groups meet will be greatly influenced by the cleanliness, order, comfort, and safety of the building.

Senior centers operate in various kinds of physical facilities. During the last decade a number of multiservice senior centers in large cities have moved into new buildings especially designed for their programs. These have been financed through local bond issues by municipal departments in conjunction with public housing projects and with funds from the Department of Housing and Urban Development. Many more centers are utilizing existing buildings that have been remodeled for their use. Some have the exclusive use of such facilities, and some share them with other groups. Social rooms of churches and libraries, old residences, store fronts, grange halls, and firehouses have all been adapted for use as senior centers. In some communities a city-owned building that has become surplus is made available for a token rent to a nonprofit sponsoring group, enabling the sponsors to use their limited funds to employ experienced professional staff. Few privately sponsored centers have been financially able to build new buildings and also employ adequately trained staff.

If the center is sharing facilities with other groups, certain arrangements must be mutually agreed on to assure the stability of the center and the comfort of its members. These include the following.

1. The rooms must be available to the center regularly at the time agreed upon on a continuing basis and without interruption. There are some advantages in the center's meeting in a building in which classes and activities are scheduled for other age groups but are open also to older adults. Center members should not, however, be placed in competition with younger groups for the use of rooms and should not be made to feel as if they are intruders.

2. All arrangements about janitorial service, heat, light, garbage disposal, and payment for the use of the rooms must be clearly defined with the organization that owns or controls the building.

3. Storage areas for the exclusive use of the senior center are essential. Older people have little patience if others borrow or use their supplies and equipment without permission.

4. Minimum standards of health and safety must be maintained. These are the same for older people as for any other group.

Older adults respond to beauty and order. They also appreciate the thought that they are worthy of attractively furnished quarters, which often contrast greatly with the crowded and dark rooms in which they live. Furniture designed for the comfort of older people, sturdy card tables, and chairs that can be easily moved are important. Centers that must use cramped quarters or basement rooms furnished with worn rugs and unmatched, cast-off furniture do little to lift the spirits and morale of the members. Many older adults who have a sense of pride and self-worth will not join centers whose physical appearance seems to depreciate their members and lower their social status in the community. Center directors must learn to decline graciously gifts of used furniture, pianos, and television equipment that are unsuitable for center use. Some excellent programs are carried out in very poor facilities, but a well-planned, attractively furnished, and adequately equipped building is a definite asset to those responsible for the development of a center. Adequate facilities and equipment *do* result in programs of better quality.

The following guidelines suggest criteria to be considered in selecting facilities for a center program.

1. The building should be centrally located in relation to concentrations of older people and on direct bus lines easily reached by those who come from other neighborhoods in large cities. Although there may be one or more large multiservice centers in the downtown areas, smaller ones should be provided in neighborhoods for those older people who cannot participate in groups too far from their homes, either because of unavailable transportation, lack of funds to use transportation, or limited physical strength. In rural communities, because of the distance and lack of transportation, centralized clubs exclusively for older people may not be the best pattern. Increased visiting by ministerial groups, more public health nurses, and grange and church social events planned for family groups will be more practical.

2. The facility should be easily accessible from the street and confined to one floor if possible. If two or more floors are used, the upper floors should be reached by an elevator or by well-lighted stairs that are not too steep and along which there are handrails. Activities on more than one floor, where there is no elevator, limit the participation of some persons who are physically unable to walk up and down stairs. Other factors that make it desirable to have all activities on one level are related to ease of supervision by staff and the greater possibility of exposing individuals to new activities and motivating them to participate.

3. The facility should provide a number of rooms for classes, interest groups, and committee meetings, as well as a large social hall for general meetings and social activities.

4. There should be adequate office and desk space to assure the staff

of privacy and quiet for working and talking confidentially with members and volunteers.

5. The rooms should be well lighted and heated, with good ventilation that does not produce drafts. Older people are more conscious of physical conditions that affect their comfort than are younger people. A wider variance in temperatures and ventilation is required for comfort.

6. Rest rooms for men and women should be conveniently located. At least one toilet in each should be equipped with a grip rail.

7. A small quiet area that can be made private, equipped with a cot, should be set aside for use when a member has had an accident or is temporarily ill.

8. A well-equipped kitchen for limited food service and for preparing refreshments is essential.

9. Minimum equipment includes tables, chairs, dishes, a piano, storage cabinets for games, crafts, first-aid supplies, and program supplies. There should also be locked storage areas for group-owned equipment, such as looms, kilns, record players, movie projectors, tape recorders, sewing machines, mimeograph machines, and typewriters. As the program develops, additional equipment will be needed and may be furnished by service clubs or interested individuals if the budget cannot provide it. Racks for coats and packages should be placed in a well-lighted area and in full view for easy supervision so that individuals with poor eyesight will not take the wrong coat by mistake.

10. Some senior centers own and operate buses to bring individuals to the program if they are physically unable to take public transportation or live in neighborhoods where public transporation is not available. The passengers pay a fare, but most of the driver's salary and the insurance and operating costs must be a part of the center's budget. The need to manage schedules and the fact that the number of passengers who use the bus each day is uncertain make this a difficult and expensive service that few centers can offer. The lack of transportation for many individuals who need the center and would benefit from its program remains an almost unsolvable problem.

The kinds of facilities needed are determined by the goals of the program

The executive director is responsible for developing and maintaining the facilities as an attractive, comfortable and safe setting for the center's members. The pride and morale of the members and the *esprit de corps* of the staff will be directly related to their adequacy. The board and executive director will need to make constant and wise decisions about the portion of the center's limited income that is allocated to the maintenance of the building and the purchase of new equipment and what portion should be used for the employment of staff. These decisions will be directly related to the goals that the board and the administrator have for the center's program and to the welfare of each individual member who comes into the building.

Relating the Center to Other Agencies

A multiservice center operates not unilaterally and independently, but in cooperation and coordination with a network of other community organizations that also serve the elderly. Establishing these relationships and working effectively within them are important administrative tasks. Staff and board members are involved in community councils and planning committees, but it is the specific responsibility of the executive director to keep the center a part of the broad constellation of community programs and to work with other groups to create new programs when gaps in services exist.

Government is recognized as the instrument for meeting those needs of citizens that they themselves, by individual or group effort, are unable to meet. Public policy and legislation are the methods used. The needs of older adults for adequate income security, health care, and good housing at rents they can afford are beginning to be met by such government programs as social security, Medicare, Medicaid, and government-funded housing projects. Other needs of older adults have become the concern and responsibility of groups of citizens joining together to initiate programs and services that they believe are necessary. Centers have often been developed within communities without consultation or clearance with other agencies and with little knowledge or thought as to whether another center was the most pressing need or if some other service should have priority.

As senior centers and other services for older adults were initiated, numerous umbrella-type agencies were needed to coordinate the planning. Typical planning groups that were involved were committees on aging in community welfare councils, councils of social agencies, mayors' committees, interdepartmental committees on aging in city government, economic opportunity councils for the elderly poor, and committees of councils of churches. State commissions on aging and federal grant programs have indirectly participated in local community planning through the grants they make for demonstration and research projects.

In rural areas the coordinating function is often carried by the county welfare worker, the consolidated school district, or the public health nurse. The center itself in some communities dramatizes all the needs of older adults to other agencies and becomes the catalyst to stimulate them to extend their services to the aged.

Until the late 1950s most planning on a community-wide basis was done by committees within health and welfare councils. Representatives from all the public and private agencies serving older adults participated in these councils; through education, manipulation, and coordination they planned and created needed new services. Older persons served on some of these committees. These planners were legally and structurally tied to the agencies and organizations they represented. They were able to speak authoritatively with city officials, were knowledgeable about regulations and laws, and were able to handle figures and budgets. They and their agencies in the vernacular of the late 1960s made up "the establishment."

In the early 1960s, with the initiation of the war on poverty, the civil rights movement, and new programs in housing, redevelopment, and urban renewal, many centers found themselves identified as part of the establishment. New community planning bodies, using strange new terminology and unfamiliar techniques, became active. These groups no longer talk about social planning and coordination but about change through mobilizing older people who are directly affected by the lack of services and directing and enabling them to take social action to bring about change. Community developers who work in the field of aging are not necessarily recreation or social workers but individuals who can identify with those older people who feel themselves deprived. The worker must be acceptable to them and trusted by them. Today social conflict has become an important tool in social planning, and protests and demonstrations are acceptable methods for achieving desirable ends.

The proliferation of planning groups and their new ways of operation become confusing and often disturbing to the community at large. The executive director of an established senior center, who must involve himself and the center in many planning meetings called by various coordinating bodies, finds a large portion of his time involved in meetings and conferences that lead only to frustration when real coordinated action cannot be taken. Many diverse and conflicting opinions arise in the community as to which planning group can most quickly and effectively mobilize all resources and bring about needed development of programs and services. Whatever community planning structures are used, they must be in tune with changing community needs and responsive to all groups and factions working in the interest of older people. Coordination of resources and services of individual agencies can take place only if there is a voluntary desire on the part of all to cooperate. Each agency, as an autonomous organization, has accepted a special function in the community and has built its public image and prestige on its success in carrying out this function. This fact must be recognized and each agency must have the freedom to act in ways that are consistent with its accepted roles as they relate to community needs.

Staff members and boards of directors sometimes become too protective of their agencies and jealous of their status in the community. They become absorbed in needs for agency prestige more than in the needs and interests of the older people they are committed to serve. Communities should experiment with various models of activity centers and systems of delivering services which may be evolved through planning groups. Research components must be a part of new approaches and demonstration projects in order to evaluate the comparative effectiveness of various models. Planning and coordinating center programs and services with those of other agencies is often not an easy task. It requires patience, understanding, forbearance, and vision on the part of all involved. Without such cooperative relationships tensions and jealousies arise, duplication of services results, competition for limited community and government grants is inevitable, and older people are deprived of services they need.

Centers work within a network of agencies

In most communities there will be an extensive network of agencies with which the center will have reciprocal relations. Some agencies will also serve other age groups; some will serve older adults exclusively. These agencies will include the department of employment, the social security administration, the department of public social services, the family service association, the school department, the department of parks and recreation, the health department, community mental health services, economic development councils, self-help for the elderly, friendly visitors, escort services, meals-on-wheels, the medical society, the hearing society, the society for the prevention of blindness, heart, arthritis, cancer, and tuberculosis associations, the volunteer bureau, the Red Cross, the public housing authority, hospitals, nursing homes, vocational rehabilitation agencies, residential institutions, legal aid, the court, and the public defender. A team of consultants consisting of an educator, lawyer, physician, social worker, and psychologist will be of inestimable aid to a planning group in enabling it to maintain perspective on its task and to cut through bureaucratic red tape to facilitate action on behalf of older adults.

GUIDELINES FOR MANAGEMENT TASKS IN SENIOR CENTERS

1. The strength and effectiveness of a senior center will depend on how its operational structure has been conceived and its administrative procedures carried out by staff, board, and active members.

2. The quality of a center's program will be dependent on the skill and experience of the staff, the board, and other leaders. It is the responsibility of the center to provide in-service training opportunities to all leaders to enable them to increase their skills and competency.

3. The acceptance and support of the center by the total community will be dependent to a great extent on a representative board with members who are respected by the community.

4. Older adults, within the limits of their ability, should be given the opportunity to help meet the program costs of the groups of which they are members.

5. Continuous and comprehensive evaluation of staff, program, and administrative procedures is essential to measure progress in achieving the center's stated goals.

6. The building in which the program is housed will determine its diversity and the comfort and morale of members and staff. If physical facilities are shared with other groups, specific and firm arangements must be made to assure the continuity of its use by center members without interruptions by other groups.

7. Planning for older adults should not be limited to the national or local experts, but should involve older adults themselves.

8. Planning should be problem-centered and the planning group must involve leaders identified with and accepted by major subgroups in the community.

9. Those who plan programs must be creative and imaginative and able to develop programs based on current knowledge about the aging. New programs should be structured with a research component in order to supply new knowledge to the field and provide for objective evaluation.

10. Sound community planning does not emphasize the needs of older people to the neglect of the needs of other groups in the community. However, until such time as services for older adults are more nearly

commensurate with those of other more active and vocal groups, special planning for the aged will be necessary.

BIBLIOGRAPHY

Allen, Yorke. "How Foundations Evaluate Requests." In *Foundations: 20 Viewpoints.* New York: Russell Sage Foundation, 1965.

Beattie, Jr., Walter M. "Matching Services to Individual Needs of the Aging." *Selected Readings in Aging.* Curriculum Project in Applied Gerontology. Washington, D.C.: Gerontological Society, 1965.

Binstock, Robert H. "What Sets the Goals of Community Planning for the Aging." *The Gerontologist* 7 (1967): 44-46.

Blumenthal, Louis. *How to Work with Your Board and Committees.* New York: Association Press, 1954.

Brodsky, Irving. *Manual for Board Members.* New York: National Jewish Welfare Board, 1965.

Culborn, Fern. *Buildings of Tomorrow: Guide for Planning Settlements and Community Buildings.* New York: William Morrow and Company, 1955.

Dahl, Robert A. "The Analysis of Influence in Local Communities." In *Urban Planning and Social Policy,* edited by Bernard Frieden and Robert Morris. New York: Basic Books, 1968.

Goldstein, Harris K. "Guidelines for Obtaining Funds for Training, Services, and Research." *Social Casework* 49 (1968): 22-27.

Guide Specifications for Positions in Aging at State and Local Levels. U.S. Department of Health, Education and Welfare. A.O.A., October 1965.

Hall, Selma. *Self-Evaluation Check-list for Older Adult Programs in the Jewish Community Center.* New York: National Jewish Welfare Board. 1959.

Housing Research Center. *Housing Requirements of the Aged: A Study of Design Criteria.* Ithaca, N.Y.: Cornell University. November 1958.

Johns, Ray. *Executive Responsibility.* New York: Association Press, 1954.

Kahn, Alfred J. *Theory and Practice of Social Planning.* New York: Russell Sage Foundation, 1969.

Kaplan, Jerome. "Evaluation Techniques for Older Groups." *American Journal of Occupational Therapy* 13 (1959): 222-25, 245.

Knowles, Malcolm S., and Knowles, Hulda. *Introduction to Group Dynamics.* New York: Association Press, 1959.

Kurtz, Russell. *Community Organization: A Social Work Method.* New York: National Association of Social Workers, 1958.

Lawton, Powell. "Planning Environments for Older People." *Journal of American Institute of Planners* 36 (1970): 124-29.

Maves, Paul B. "The Church in Community Planning for the Aged." *Geriatrics* 5 (1950): 339-42.

Maxwell, Jean M. *Centers for Older People: Guide for Programs and Facilities*. New York: National Council on Aging, 1962.

Meyer, Harold D., and Brightbill, Charles K. *Recreation Administration*. Englewood Cliffs, N.J.: Prentice-Hall, 1956.

Moore, Elon H. "Community Organization for Older Persons." *Geriatrics* 3 (1948): 306-13.

Morris, R., and Randall, Ollie A. "Planning and Organization of Community Services for the Elderly." *Social Work* 10 (1965): 95-102.

National Association of Social Workers. *Defining Community Organization Practice*. New York: National Association of Social Workers, December 1962.

National Council on the Aging. *Resources for the Aging: An Action Handbook*. Prepared by National Council on the Aging for the Community Action Program of the Office of Economic Opportunity, 1969.

New York City Housing Authority. *Memo to Architects, Design of Centers*. New York: New York City Housing Authority, February 1952 (revised 1959).

Nigro, Felix A. *Modern Public Administration*. New York: Harper & Row, 1965.

Ogg, Elizabeth. *Tell Me Where to Turn; The Growth of Information and Referral Services*. Public Affairs Pamphlet no. 428. New York: Public Affairs Committee, 1969.

Patills, Manning M. "Preparing the Foundation Proposal." In *Foundations: 20 Viewpoints*. New York: Russell Sage Foundation, 1967.

Rachles, David. *How to Obtain Grants for Programs for the Aging Poor*. National Council on the Aging, January 1968.

Ross, M. *Community Organization, Theory and Principles*. New York: Harper and Brothers, 1955.

Stern, Max. "Community Organization Process in Planning for the Aged Across Social Agency Lines." *Journal of Jewish Communal Service* 40 (1964): 407-17.

Tibbetts, Clark. "Social Gerontology in Education for the Professionals." In *Graduate Education in Aging Within the Social Sciences*, edited by Rose E. Kushner and Marian E. Bunch. Ann Arbor: University of Michigan, Division of Gerontology, 1967.

Trecker, Harleigh B. *Citizen Boards at Work: New Challenges to Effective Action*. New York: Association Press, 1970.

U.S. Department of Health, Education and Welfare. *Demand for Personnel and Training in the Field of Aging*. A.O.A. Publication, no. 270. Washington, D.C., 1969.

U.S. Department of Health, Education and Welfare. Public Health Service. *General Information and Instructions: Application for Research Grant*. Washington, D.C., 1962.

18 / Social Programs in Residential Settings

ALTHOUGH THE CONTENT OF THE PRECEDING CHAPTERS has focused primarily on programs and services for aged individuals living independently in the community, many older adults today live in congregate residential settings with age mates. As clubs and centers have been organized to meet social and emotional needs of older adults, so a wide variety of housing facilities have been designed to meet a broad spectrum of shelter and physical care needs of this group. At the beginning of the century, when it became necessary for an aged person to give up his home and seek protective care, he had little choice of where he could go. If he had children, it was expected that he would become a member of one of their households or be rotated to live for a period of time with each child. If he had no children or close relatives, he applied for admission to an institution for the old sponsored by a church, lodge, or other benevolent organization. If he was not financially able to pay the entrance fee to those institutions, his only remaining choice was the county farm or poorhouse.

New housing patterns meet
differing individuals needs

If an older adult today decides to move into congregate age-segregated housing, he may choose from a wide variety of settings, sizes, sites, services, and sponsorships. He may prefer to live with other retirees in a high-rise apartment or hotel in the center of a large city or in a mobile home in a trailer park in a rural setting. His new home may be one of hundreds of similar dwellings in a nonlicensed, self-contained, country club type community built by private capital, or he may settle in one small room in a licensed church-sponsored institution for only thirty other residents. If he has limited savings and his monthly income is small, he may be able to rent a well-designed, attractive apartment in a public housing project. If he has capital to invest and sufficient income to meet monthly charges, he may buy a condominium apartment or manor house in a community where residents are restricted to retired persons. A new kind of old age institution, often designated as a retirement home and designed to meet the changing physical needs of its residents, is being built in many communities with federal funds loaned to nonprofit organizations at very low interest rates. These retirement homes offer various levels of care: (1) residential care, which includes basic housing and activity programs for the well, ambulatory resident; (2) intermediate or personal care with supervision of dressing, daily cleanliness, taking of medications, and eating when waning physical and mental health make some protective care essential; (3) extended care for short-term posthospital convalescence and rehabilitation; (4) long-term care for the chronically and acutely ill. Retirement homes provide continuing care for their residents as they move from self-sufficiency to possible total dependency, and many older adults today seek the security of such arrangements.

Providing housing and meeting the needs of older adults for various levels of care is a fast-growing enterprise in which both benevolent nonprofit organizations and proprietary interests and private capital are involved. The terminology used to designate the different kinds of residential settings, the services provided, and the licensing agents differ in various regions. The institutions described in the following paragraphs may be called by different names in different states but their general characteristics and services provided will be essentially the same.

Older adults become members of age-segregated housing for many reasons

There are many reasons why older adults or those responsible for them decide, either by preference or necessity, to give up former housing arrangements and independent living in the community. Some people, as they grow older, want to get away from changing neighborhoods and the smog and congestion of the inner city. For others who have lost their husbands or wives, congregate living offers physical and emotional security and a defense against isolation and loneliness. Many retired couples want to live near their children, but do not want to become dependent on them for care. A residential institution in which they can be assured of care and in which they can be near enough to their children for frequent visits is the best answer to their need. Other older adults choose to live in retirement housing because it provides them freedom to travel. They feel secure and know that their apartments and possessions will be safe while they are away over long periods of time.

When an older person is faced with a crisis that necessitates immediate protective care, adult children often make arbitrary decisions for immediate placement in institutions. When an older parent has no part in making the decision, the experience is traumatic and the adjustment to the new situation is long and often unhappy. Studies of adjustments in moving into institutions under stressful and anxiety-ridden conditions indicate that higher mortality rates than would normally be expected result in the first year of placement.

New living patterns demand
difficult individual adjustments

With the growing recognition and acceptance of the fact that mutual love, respect, and responsibility between the generations do not depend on aging parents sharing the living units of their children, many older adults choose to live independently in a community of age mates where the dignity and worth of old age are recognized. Such a decision does necessitate some major personal adjustments. Influencing factors are the older person's emotional and physical health, whether the decision was his free choice or whether it was made to please other people, and his own ego resources for adapting to new situations. Adjustment to the new environment will be dependent on the older person's overall satisfaction with the attractiveness, comfort, and adequacy of his new home; with the policies and rules that have been established to regulate group living; with the quality of the services and program; and the warmth and friendliness of the other residents and the staff.

Group living fosters a sense of community and involvement and requires the individual to give up a degree of personal freedom in order to conform to rules and regulations that permit the comfort and welfare of all. The individual must be able to accept as a roommate or near neighbor another resident who may not be completely compatible, to eat his meals within set times, and to regulate the use of his radio and television in ways that will not be disturbing to his neighbor.

The older adult's need for privacy, self-determination, and independence persists and must be recognized. If he experiences too great a loss of privacy and too much pressure for conformity and socialization, the older person may feel frustrated and fearful that he has made a mistake in giving up his former living arrangements. An older adult will also face the necessity to adjust to his anxieties and changing perceptions of himself as he lives in the midst of physically ill and deteriorating individuals. He must understand and adjust to the petty personal jealousies, the competitive behavior, and the idle gossip that frequently are found in group living situations.

Many positive reactions result from congregate living with age mates

Residents experience many positive reactions as members of a community of age mates. For some individuals there is a great sense of relief from the necessity to shop and prepare meals, to clean the house, or to care for the garden. The new environment also provides a wide variety of social roles and ready companions with whom to enjoy activities and interests. In a study of individual adjustment to institutional living it was found that the best adjustment was made by those older adults (1) who were not excessively afraid of authority, (2) who maintained outside contacts, (3) who participated in activities in the home, and (4) who could face the frustrations inherent in the regulations necessary for group living.[1]

Not all residents of retirement housing are interested in social activities

The need for housing that is congenial to their life-styles at rents they can afford is the common need of older adults who move into retirement housing projects. They may or may not be interested in participating in a common social life. As with older adults who live independently in the community, some will welcome the opportunity for social activities with their peers, and others will not want to become involved. There will be some mature, integrated residents who will take initiative and responsibility as leaders and other rocking-chair personalities who will become progressively more dependent and passive in an environment where everything is provided for them. The managements of both proprietary and nonprofit residential projects recognize that, although shelter and physical care are their primary responsibilities, they must also make adequate provision for the social, educational, cultural, and religious needs and interests of their older residents. In many retirement

[1] Ruth Bennett, "The Meaning of Institutional Life," *The Gerontologist,* 3:121 (September 1963, Part I).

housing projects, recreational leaders and social workers are employed; social rooms, swimming pools, golf courses, and hobby shops are provided; and governmental licensing bodies set guidelines and standards for individual services and group programs. The American Association of Homes for the Aging, an affiliate of the National Council on Aging, has developed the following policy statement on the social components of care that its member nonprofit homes are expected to provide for their residents:

> We believe that older persons in our homes or in other types of congregate living facilities have the same rights and requirements as other citizens; namely, the right to self-determination, the right of privacy of person and thought, the right to personal dignity, the right to have social needs met and social roles fulfilled, and the right to good medical and personal care. These are inalienable rights and their infringement or our failure to provide the means for exercising them violate the older person's prerogatives as a human being. Accordingly our homes are not disease-treatment or patient-centered; they are person-centered.

Activities Program

All residents, regardless of their physical and mental condition, can and should be involved in a variety of recreational activities, depending on their capabilities and interests. To a large extent the interest of the individual should be the primary factor in determining the components of an activities program. An appropriately trained and qualified individual or individuals should be responsible for maintaining and sustaining an activities program. The activities program, moreover, is part of the basic service being offered by the facility and no additional charges should be made for general involvement in this program; this in no way should impinge, however, on the need for the resident to pay his own way for outside activities.

In developing group programs in a Home for the Aged, the following principles serve as guidelines:

1. That recreational services are of fundamental importance; that a program is offered not as the frills, the luxuries, the show aspects, but because of the basically essential value of these services to a good adjustment and a satisfying life for residents, not instead of or in place of a medical or any other program, but because of its own right it is valuable;

2. That programs in which the residents themselves take part are far more valuable to the participant and the observer than programs put on for the "dear little old people"; that the generic principles of doing *with* and not *for* people applies as well in a Home for the Aged as in any situation;

3. That nothing of interest to an adult human being is alien to the program in a Home for the Aged;

4. That activity is only a part and parcel of group work service. That program changes as needs change, and needs change as program changes. That program is not offered as a means of escape;

5. That the vital fluid of all services is *relationship*. That nothing will happen without it and that through it things will happen.

6. That the knowledge we have of what has happened to groups in other situations is transferable; the information we have on the problems of older people must be used for effective programming;

7. That basic social work principles apply; "recognizing the rights of individuals" and "accepting group members for what they are," and "beginning at the level of the group" cannot be bypassed or violated.[2]

The following regulations, set down in the Welfare and Institutional Code of the State of California, are typical of those established by many states to set standards in the old-age institutions that they license:

Social and Recreational Activities

PROGRAM OF ACTIVITIES. Every home shall make provision for social and recreational activities in accordance with the interests, abilities and needs of the persons under care.

SOCIAL ACTIVITIES. Social activities which ordinarily take place in family life shall be part of the program of the home, in addition to group social activities designed to promote group relationships and the feeling of belonging.

RECREATIONAL ACTIVITIES. Opportunities for participation in a variety of recreational activities shall be made available to the residents, according to their interests and abilities.

Every home shall provide for activities in the home of the type ordinarily found in family living, such as reading, listening to the radio, table games, etc.

Opportunity for participation in activities outside of the home shall be provided for residents who are interested and able.

Additional activities in the home shall be provided as needed to round out the total activity program.

RELIGIOUS PROGRAM. The home shall secure information from every resident as to his religious affiliation, if any.

No resident shall be deprived of the right to have visits from the minister, priest, or rabbi of his choice.

Homes which accept persons of varied religious faiths shall respect the right of each individual to worship in his own way, and consideration shall be given to the religious customs of daily living of the different faiths represented.

[2] American Association of Homes for the Aged, *Social Components of Care of the Aged*. (Washington, D.C.: 1966).

Every resident shall have freedom to attend the church of his own choice.

Attendance at religious services held in the home shall be on a completely voluntary basis.

FACILITIES FOR RECREATIONAL ACTIVITIES. Sufficient equipment and materials for the home's recreation program shall be provided.

Such things as radios, television, books, magazines, newspapers, indoor and outdoor games, piano, record player, which are ordinarily part of family life shall be available.

Additional equipment and materials for activities conducted in the home shall be provided as needed, or obtained through community agencies.[3]

The following proposed (1970-71) revisions of the California Code pertaining to Residential Care Homes (RCH) reflect current thinking, and are worth comparing with the present Code.

Program Requirements: Social and Recreational Activities

PROGRAM OF ACTIVITIES. Every home shall make provision for social and recreational activities in accordance with the interests, abilities, and needs of the persons under care. There shall be a staff member assigned responsibility for implementing an activity program.

RESIDENT PARTICIPATION. The RCH administrator or the staff member responsible shall occasionally discuss with residents the type of social and recreational activities they desire. The information obtained by interviews shall be used in planning future recreational and social activities and the purchasing of necessary equipment and materials.

SOCIAL ACTIVITIES. Social activities which ordinarily take place in family life shall be designed to promote individual and group relationships and a feeling of belonging. They include, but are not limited to, birthday parties, craft displays, open house and Christmas parties.

RECREATIONAL ACTIVITIES. Opportunities for participation in a variety of recreational activities shall be made available to the residents, according to their interests and abilities.

Every RCH shall provide for and encourage activities in the home such as, but not limited to, reading, listening to the radio, writing letters, songfests, television and table games.

Opportunity for participation in activities outside the home shall be provided for residents who are interested and able.

EQUIPMENT AND MATERIALS. Sufficient equipment and materials for the home's recreation program shall be provided. Such equipment and materials include but are not limited to, radios, television, books, magazines, newspapers, indoor and outdoor games and record players.

RELIGIOUS PROGRAM. Homes which accept persons of varied religious faiths shall respect the right of each individual to worship in his own

[3] California, *Welfare and Institutions Code* (1970, 1971).

way, and consideration shall be given to the religious customs of daily living of the different faiths represented.

1. Every resident shall have freedom to attend the church of his choice.

2. Attendance at religious services held in the home shall be on a completely voluntary basis.

Program Requirements: General Provisions

GENERAL. Every RCH shall make available to all residents sympathetic, understanding help in making use of group living, in adjusting to the routines of the facility and to whatever limitations may be imposed by the resident's individual circumstances. All RCH's shall assure that residents are treated with dignity, respect, kindness, and consideration. Problems and complaints shall be listened to and adjustments made in the program or room assignments whenever possible to alleviate conflict situations.

VISITORS. Residents shall be assisted to have private visits both within and outside the RCH. Visitors include, but are not limited to, friends, relatives, and professional persons such as social workers, attorneys, and ministers. Any exceptions to this section shall be documented and are subject to the approval of the licensing agency.

RESIDENTS' COUNCIL. An RCH may form a Residents Council. A Residents Council usually has committees for such purposes as considering complaints made by residents, recommending changes in the operation and services of the RCH, and assisting staff in planning social recreational events.

TRANSPORTATION. The licensee is responsible for providing or arranging for transportation for residents when the resident needs to visit a doctor's office, for occasional shopping, and for attending religious or social events in the local community.

VOLUNTEERS. An RCH may use volunteers in the social-recreational program to provide transportation for residents, and to perform unusual personal services such as shopping for gifts or letter writing.

There are no established standards that regulate services in proprietary, nonlicensed housing projects and communities. The importance of recreational facilities and social programs, however, is indicated by the great emphasis placed on them in promotional and sales literature.

Each type of retirement living arrangement makes its own unique contribution to housing needs of older adults

In 1960 approximately 61 percent of all residents of retirement housing projects were living in nonlicensed proprietary homes, constructed by private builders with private capital; 24 percent were residents in licensed nonprofit homes built by religious and fraternal organizations largely with government financing; 12 percent lived in county or municipally operated homes; and 3 percent in federal, state, and veterans homes and hospitals.[4] A clear picture of the unique contribution of the various types of retirement housing to the social and emotional well-being of their residents is important.

Nonlicensed, Fixed Dwelling, and Mobile Home Facilities

The new high-rise apartments and hotels located in the centers of large cities and the self-contained retirement communities and country club parks for mobile homes located in suburbs and on the periphery of big cities are built by private capital as investments for individuals and corporations. In these proprietary projects individuals purchase their units with a down payment and continuing monthly mortgage payments. An owner may sell his unit at any time and his equity becomes a part of his estate. With their fixed dwelling units, these complexes provide a totally new way of life for those who can afford them. Residents usually also pay a monthly membership or recreation fee for the use of golf courses, swimming pools, riding stables, and craft shops. These facilities are for the exclusive use of the residents and their guests, with security guards on duty at all times.

Mobile home parks are usually located outside of city limits in unincorporated areas. Mobile homes may be purchased at prices ranging from $4,500 to $10,000. It is a common practice to make a down payment of one-third of the total price, with the remainder paid off in monthly payments over a period of years. An additional sum for space rental and an annual license fee are also required. These charges run as low as $15 to as high as $250, depending on the size of the individual unit, the value of the land, and the recreational and social facilities provided. Not all nonlicensed fixed-dwellings and mobile homes provide programs and facilities for the social lives of their residents. Tables 2 and 3, taken from a study of various types of retirement housing made by a group of investigators from the School of Public Health of the University of California at Los Angeles, give the percentages of nonlicensed fixed-dwelling-unit facilities and mobile home parks providing programs and facilities for social activities for residents.

There are no provisions for life care or hospital and nursing services

---

[4] U.S., Department of Commerce, Bureau of the Census, 1960.

TABLE 2. Nonlicensed, Fixed-Dwelling Units: Recreational, Cultural, and Other Programs and Services [5]

Total sites	Sites completed or under construction (131)			Planned, new construction sites (28)
Kinds of programs or services:	Now on premises	Will be on premises	Total	Will be on premises
	PERCENT			
Recreation programs	47	16	63	100
Cultural programs	37	16	53	64
Educational programs	19	18	37	46
Resident self-government	34	17	51	64
Facilities for religious services	28	8	36	54
Swimming pool	35	7	42	54
Golf course	21	5	26	46
Special recreation building	43	6	49	50
Special recreation room(s)	32	5	37	50
Commercial enterprises	21	12	33	46
Off-premises transportation	17	—	17	—

TABLE 3. Mobile Home Parks: Recreational, Cultural, and Other Programs and Services, by Size of Sites [5]

	On the premises of mobile home parks			
Size of sites	Large (100 or more spaces)	Medium (50-60 spaces)	Small (49 or fewer)	All sites
Total sites	(36)	(56)	(79)	(171)
Kinds of programs or services:	PERCENT			
Recreation programs	81	63	9	42
Cultural programs	39	18	1	15
Educational programs	25	7	—	8
Resident self-government	53	14	3	17
Facilities for religious services	3	7	—	3
Swimming pool	81	45	6	35
Golf course	22	2	—	5
Special recreation building	92	77	13	50
Special recreation room(s)	3	2	6	4
Commercial enterprises	8	2	5	5

in mobile home parks or in proprietary retirement communities. Many have a nurse or a doctor from nearby communities on call. These projects are usually located near hospitals and pharmacies that residents use independently. In the case of serious illness, most management

[5] Rosabella Walkley, Daniel Wilner, and associates, *Retirement Housing in California* (Berkeley, Calif.: Diablo Press, 1966).

officials take responsibility for contacting the medical facility or a member of the resident's family.

In self-contained retirement communities, which are usually attractive and even luxurious in appearance, residents create their own society, standards, and expectations for individual social behavior. The residents are, as a group, of a higher socioeconomic class than the residents of nonprofit homes, and an atmosphere of activity and busyness characterizes most such retirement communities. Action and involvement are a part of the life-style. The residents are, as a group, younger and there are more couples than in other kinds of retirement settings. Many of the residents are still employed. Grandchildren are welcomed visitors in most retirement communities but long stays are not encouraged. As husbands and wives die, such settings provide the remaining spouse unique opportunities for continuing heterosexual companionships.

All studies of residents of these age-segregated communities show a high level of enthusiasm and individual satisfaction with the patterns of retirement life that these projects make possible. No studies indicate that they impose an unwelcome need to conform to patterns or pose a threat to the individuality of the residents. These projects are still too new to have provided any long-term research on the pattern of idealization, disillusionment, and stabilization of attitudes and the final level of individual satisfaction or dissatisfaction that takes place.

Retirement Homes for the Aged

Modern residential facilities that are sponsored by benevolent organizations, financed by federal and charitable foundation funds, and licensed by the department of welfare as well as the health department are replacing the "Old Folks' Home." They must provide nursing and hospital care and are designed to provide housing for individuals who do not wish, or are unable, to live alone. Many need the kind of help and supervision that in other days were provided by children or close relatives. In general, individuals who live in such settings are older, have fewer family ties, and are less likely to have a spouse than the residents of nonlicensed residential communities.

These facilities vary in size. Some have as few as six residents; others can accommodate as many as four hundred. Some such institutions have a fixed entrance fee with a life-lease agreement providing housing and life-care. Others, operating on the premise that an older person does not necessarily need to commit himself to live there for the remainder of his life, charge a minimum entrance fee and monthly rental fees. The managements of these modern institutions are committed to the need to provide a continuum of kinds and degrees of care to serve the changing needs of residents. When an individual first becomes a resident, his primary needs will be for safe and comfortable shelter, meals, companionship, and meaningful roles and activities. If he becomes physically frail or mentally confused, then he will need help and supervision in dressing, bathing, eating, and taking medication. Separate dining rooms and therapeutic recreation are usually provided for such residents. If the older person experiences a temporary or a long-term illness, convalescent or long-term care and rehabilitative therapies are then provided in the hospital and nursing section of the institution. This comprehensive-care institution with services adapted to changing individual needs is chosen by those older adults who can afford its higher fees.

Practice has not kept pace with knowledge about providing services

The modern concept of differentiated care for individual residents is implemented in few institutions. Many have not been able to finance the building of the additional physical facilities that will be needed. As the present generation of older residents grows into extreme old age as the result of the excellent care provided, these individual-care services will be needed by an increasingly larger number of residents.

Although guidelines have been established nationally, not all old age institutions have developed even minimum health care and social activity programs. Table 4, based on a study of old age institutions in California, gives, according to the size of the site, the percentages of those providing social programs and facilities for their residents.

Retirement homes should be resources for the total community

Excellent and highly diversified social programs to meet the wide interests of residents are found in most retirement homes today. House councils are organized by the residents, and they carry major responsibility for the planning and leadership of the activities within the home. In addition, boards of directors and administrators of many progressive retirement homes are accepting in imaginative and creative ways the responsibility and the opportunity to extend their physical facilities and staff to serve not only their residents but also the many other older people living independently within the neighborhood. Some homes are becoming integral parts of the total community organization structure

TABLE 4. Aged Institutions: Recreational, Cultural, and Other
Programs and Services by Size of Sites [6]

Size of sites Total sites	Large (75 or more units) (61)	Medium (20 to 74 units) (77)	Small (19 or fewer units) (146)	All sites (284)
Kinds of programs and services:		PERCENT		
Recreation programs	72	60	40	52
Cultural programs	87	52	18	42
Educational programs	51	10	4	16
Resident self-govern- ment	44	12	1	13
Facilities for religious services	85	58	43	56
Swimming pool	20		2	5
Golf course	7	3	1	2
Special recreation building	34	12	3	12
Special recreation room(s)	57	58	42	50
Commercial enterprises	30	10	1	10
Off-premises transportation	56	68	62	62

for serving older adults. Old-age institutions *can,* and many already *do,*
perform many of the functions of a highly developed multiservice senior
center. The attractive and comfortable lounges become the settings for
adult education classes and programs of all kinds, social events, and
holiday parties. The home arranges trips and excursions for its residents
as well as their neighbors. The physically able person residing in the
home becomes a friendly visitor, going out into the neighborhood to
visit homebound individuals and making daily reassurance telephone
calls to them. The kitchen facility of the home prepares refreshments for
special occasions, as well as extra hot meals for residents in the neighborhood who are unable to shop and cook for themselves. The home's
social worker and nurse make home visits to older people in the neighborhood at times of crisis, and make referrals to health and welfare
agencies who are able to help. The flow of well, older people from the
community into the home to share with the residents in their activities
and services and the opportunities for residents to go out into the community to participate in hobby shows, trips, excursions, conferences,
and community service projects can be extremely beneficial to all. The
residential care institution is facing a real challenge to take its place
along with centers in the growing network of resources to serve all the
older people of the community.

[6] Walkley and Wilner, *Retirement Housing in California,* p. 62.

Boarding Homes

The boarding home, sometimes called a residential care facility, is a small institution usually operated by an individual or by corporate owners. In California they are licensed for a maximum of fifteen and a minimum of six or fewer residents. Their monthly rates are lower than the large retirement homes and the residents are mostly public welfare recipients. The extent and the quality of the social program depend on the interest of the owner in the welfare of his residents and his willingness to expend funds from his limited income for services and programs. A television in a crowded parlor is often the only entertainment provided except at holidays, when church and youth groups visit and give a party for the residents.

Government Financed Housing Projects

Age-segregated housing projects for older adults have been greatly expanded during the past decade by various programs providing government financing. These include the Federal Housing Administration (FHA), which makes insured loans available to private builders of housing for the aged; the Public Housing Administration (PHA), which makes funds available to local communities for rental housing for families and older adults of very low income; and the Community Facilities Administration (CFA), which makes long-term direct loans at low interest to private, nonprofit, corporate sponsors for developing rental housing and related facilities for older persons (age sixty-two or older). The rent supplement program of PHA also makes it possible for older adults to rent individual housing on the open market with a supplement from the government through the welfare program to meet rents over and above 25 percent of the individual's income. Many projects built by PHA for low-income older adults have been located near public recreation areas. Their residents form the core of the membership of the senior centers located there along with other older people of the neighborhood. Other such public housing projects have included specially designed areas for multiservice senior centers. The operation of these centers is usually under the direction of the public recreation and parks department. In some communities the Housing Authority contracts with a nonprofit voluntary agency to direct the social services and recreational program for the residents and their neighbors in the community.

Funds are granted to nonprofit groups under Sections 202 and 236 of the Community Facilities Administration essentially for the purpose of providing housekeeping units. Some projects also include common rooms for congregate dining and social and recreational activities. Recent revisions in the regulations also make it possible to provide convalescent and rehabilitative care for residents of 202 and 236 housing projects. These projects are designed to serve lower-middle-income older persons and are subject to rigid operational control and review by the CFA.

The residents of these projects usually organize themselves into resident associations. The officers of the association and elected representatives meet regularly with the manager or administrator of the project to discuss and make recommendations on all matters that affect the safety, comfort, and physical well-being of the residents. In some nonprofit housing projects the sponsoring group makes special funds available to employ part or full-time staff to work with the residents in a program council. In other projects volunteers are recruited from the community to advise the residents and give leadership in developing social programs, classes, and interest group activities. In a housing setting, as in a community senior center, it is difficult for a resident or a group of residents to carry long-term consistent responsibility for an activity program for all other residents. A nonresident, acting as an enabler and nondirective adviser to the residents' council or tenants' association, is able to remain objective and impartial in his relationships with all residents and is therefore able to be effective in his leadership. Without this help, programs are usually limited to diversional activities such as bingo, movies, and card playing. Socially adequate and aggressive individuals carry all the responsibilities and receive all the satisfactions. Timid, retiring individuals become even more timid. The material in chapters 11 through 14 on leadership and program is as applicable to groups in residential settings as to those in multiservice centers in the community. Chart 7 shows the possible relationship in a sponsored housing project between the manager and the residents' association, the program director, and the residents' program council.

Nursing Homes and Extended Care Facilities

The institutions whose primary functions are physical care of ill, older adults are not usually classified as residential settings. In theory they are not residential settings but they are often so in practice because older people recover much more slowly from critical illnesses than do young patients and must remain in nursing homes for long periods of time. Older adults who live alone and have no one to care for them when they

Chart 7
Organizational Chart Showing the
Relationship of Programs and Services for Residents to the
Management of a Nonprofit Sponsored Housing Project

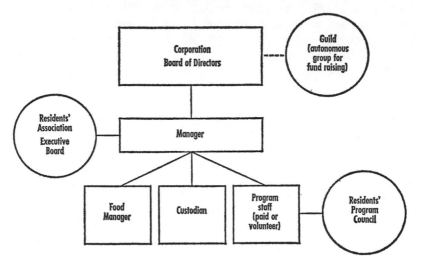

RESIDENTS' ASSOCIATION—EXECUTIVE BOARD
Officers of the Residents' Association
Two elected representatives from each house or floor
Chairman of the Food Committee

RESIDENTS' PROGRAM COUNCIL
Chairman of following committees
of the Residents' Association:
    Arts and Crafts
    Needlecraft
    Entertainments and Social Events
    Library
    Newspaper
    Music
    Recreation
    Trips and Excursions
    Hostess
    Others

AREAS OF CONCERN
Advisory to the Manager on all matters
that affect safety, comfort, physical
and social well-being of the residents.

AREAS OF RESPONSIBILITY
Planning and promoting services
and activities of interest to
the residents.

return to their homes may extend their stays so that they can get needed personal attention.

An older person may be a patient in a nursing home, but he is more importantly an individual with his own social and emotional needs. As staff members perform their nursing and rehabilitation tasks, their services can be therapeutic only if they relate to their patients as total persons. Convalescence is more rapid, patients are happier, and morale is higher when the environment is stimulating and there are opportunities to enjoy informal conversations and relationships and to participate in social activities with others.

Although meeting the social needs of patients has not been conceived of as a part of the function of nursing and boarding homes in the past, a change has come about with the passage of the Medicare legislation, which recognizes the social needs of individuals even though they are ill. Medicare provides for reimbursements to operators of such facilities for salaries of physical, occupational, recreational, and other therapists who work with patients on an individual basis as well as in group activities. These therapists serve as important adjuncts to the medical treatment program and encourage the convalescing patient to resume self-care and normal activities. Medicare regulations require the director of the nursing home to designate an individual to be in charge of patient activities. For the smaller homes that are unable to employ such persons, the regulation stipulates that consultation from a qualified recreational therapist or group activity leader may be used. Participation in group activities must, of course, be on a voluntary basis, and patients are to be encouraged—not forced—to participate. The legislation stipulates that suitable activities must be provided for those patients who are not ambulatory or who are unable to leave their rooms. It further states that at least one centrally located day room or lounge should be provided to accommodate the diversional and social activities of the patients. In addition, several smaller day rooms convenient to the patients' bedrooms should be provided.

Volunteers working under the direction of staff will be necessary to provide truly effective social programs in nursing homes. Volunteers must have great skill in relating in warm personal ways to each of the patients and in motivating them to become involved in such activities as their physical and mental conditions make possible.

A voluntary activity program within an institution, which attracted a large number of patients and resulted in significant physical, mental, and emotional benefits, has been described by Siegmund H. May, medical director of the Nassau County Home for the Aged and Infirm, New

York. This institution, serving chronically ill patients, offered residents an opportunity to assist in preparing a large mailing for the United States Committee for the United Nations International Children's Emergency Fund. The response was gratifying, and within a few weeks between 80 to 112 aged residents were participating in half-day work sessions five days each week. The work was adapted to each individual's ability and the jobs were rotated to avoid monotony. Efforts were made to provide a relaxed, cheerful, congenial atmosphere without any pressures. At the end of the project each participant received a badge identifying him as a UNICEF volunteer. Dr. May reports that the effect soon became visible in better hygiene, more attractive clothing, and friendlier attitudes. The patients were less emotionally disturbed and depressed than formerly, and a great improvement in their ability to socialize was evident. Good nursing and medical care, no matter how excellent, can no longer be accepted as the total function of a convalescent hospital or nursing home. With the implementation of the provisions of the Medicare legislation, programs geared to the socialization needs of the patient must become an integral part of the total services of all care-taking institutions.

Research studies show that heightened morale results from congregate living with age mates

There has been little research on the long-term impact of different kinds of housing on the social adjustment and life satisfactions of those older people who become residents. Survey studies made of residents in various kinds of housing projects after a year's residency all indicate high levels of satisfaction with their new homes. Ambulatory, well, older people living in public and sponsored congregate settings with age mates report that they had more friends and enjoyed increased activity and higher morale after living one year in the project, as compared with their experiences in the community before moving.[7] Enthusiastic reactions are also characteristic of financially comfortable upper-middle-class older people who move from independent living in age-integrated communities to age-segregated retirement communities.

A variety of housing patterns will be required to meet differing needs

As more projects similar to those described in this chapter are built, an increasing number of older adults will choose to become members of

7 Frances Carp, *A Future for the Aged: The Residents of Victoria Plaza* (Austin: University of Texas Press, 1966).

age-segregated communities. It will be important to have a variety of facilities to give individuals the freedom of choice; no present pattern of congregate retirement housing can be accepted as being the only and the best solution for all. Most older adults will continue to live independently in the community, either in their own homes or apartments with their children or close relatives. Unless they become so critically ill that they need intensive nursing care or so mentally ill that they become dangerous to themselves, it is clear that many older adults are better off remaining in their own homes. Nevertheless, they will need the development of many new community-based services that can, when necessary, be taken into their homes. These would include visiting nurses, housekeepers, home health aides, meals-on-wheels, friendly visitors and telephone reassurance services, multiservice senior centers, and programs extended from the centers by closed television. Such a development would permit the individual to remain in the circle of his neighborhood friends and contacts and would provide for him a normal environment as he reaches the years of extreme old age.

BIBLIOGRAPHY

American Association of Homes for the Aging. *The Social Components of Care.* Washington, D.C.: American Association of Homes for the Aging, 1966.

Bennett, Ruth. "The Meaning of Institutional Life." *The Gerontologist* 3 (1963): 117-25.

Beyer, Glenn H., and Woods, Margaret E. *Living and Activity Patterns of the Aged.* Research Report, no. 6, Ithaca, N.Y.: Cornell University, Center for Housing and Environmental Studies, 1963.

Carp, Frances. *A Future for the Aged: The Residents of Victoria Plaza.* Austin: University of Texas Press, 1966.

Crandall, Mae. *Recreation for Nursery Home Residents.* Raleigh: North Carolina Association of Nursing Homes, 1964.

Faunce, Frances Avery. *The Nursing Home Visitor; Handbook Written From Inside.* Nashville, Tenn.: Abingdon Press, 1969.

Fink, H. "The Relationship of Time Perspective to Age, Institutionalization and Activity." *Journal of Gerontology* 12 (1957): 414-17.

Friedman, Edward. "Spatial Proximity and Social Interaction in a Home for the Aged." *Journal of Gerontology* 21 (1966): 556-70.

Goldfarb, Alvin. "Mental Health in the Institution." *The Gerontologist* 1 (1960): 178-84.

Hoyt, G. C. "The Life of the Retired in a Trailer Park." *American Journal of Sociology* 59 (1968): 361-70.

Hunter, Woodrow W. "Recreation Needs." In *Nursing Care for the Aged,* pp. 43-56, Continued Education Series, no. 59. Ann Arbor: School of Public Health, University of Michigan, 1955.

Jacobs, Ruth Harriet. "One-Way Street: An Intimate View of Adjustment To a Home for the Aged." *The Gerontologist* 9 (1969): 268-75.

Kleemeier, R. "The Use and Meaning of Time in Special Settings." In *Aging and Leisure,* edited by R. Kleemeier, pp. 273-308. New York: Oxford University Press, 1961.

Kurasik, Steve. "The Need for Recreational Therapy in Hospitals, Nursing Homes, and Homes for the Aged." *Journal of American Geriatrics Society* 13 (1965): 556-60.

Lieberman, M. A.; Prock, V.; and Tobin, S. S. "Psychological Effects of Institutionalization." *Journal of Gerontology* 23 (1968): 343-53.

Lieberman, M. A., and Lakin, M. "On Becoming an Aged Institutionalized Individual." In *Social and Psychological Processes of Aging,* edited by W. Donahue, C. Tibbits, and R. Williams, pp. 475-503. New York: Atherton Press, 1963.

Mazer, June L. "The Volunteer in Relation to Activity Programs for the Institutionalized." *Journal of the American Geriatrics Society* 11 (1963): 607-11.

Mumford, Lewis. "For Older People—Not Segregation but Integration." *Architectural Record,* May 1956, pp. 191-94.

Natenshon, Louis J. "The Architectural Dilemma: Design, Individual Needs, and Social Living." *The Gerontologist* 9 (1969): 60-65.

Newmark, Louis. "The Development of a Residents' Council in a Home for the Aged." *The Gerontologist* 3 (1963): 22-25.

Poe, William D. *The Old Person in Your Home.* New York: Scribner, 1969.

Sherman, Susan R. et al. "Psychological Effects of Retirement Housing." *The Gerontologist* 8 (1968): 170-75.

Switzer, Mary E., and Rusk, Howard A. "Keeping Older People Fit for Participation." *The Annals of the American Academy of Political and Social Science.* 279 (January 1952).

Thompson, Morton. *Starting a Recreation Program in Institutions for the Ill and Handicapped Aged.* New York: National Recreation Association, 1960.

U.S. Department of Health, Education and Welfare. *Patterns of Living and Housing of Middle-Aged and Older People.* U.S. Department of Health, Education and Welfare. Public Health Services Publication, no. 1496. Washington, D.C., 1965.

Walkley, Rosabelle; Wilner, David; and associates. *Retirement Housing in California.* Berkeley: School of Public Health, University of California at Los Angeles, Diablo Press, 1966.

Wolf, Aaron S. "Participation of the Aged in the Group Process." *Mental Hygiene* 51 (1967): 381-86.

Wyman, Randolph A., M.D., and Alessandrini, Norma. "Recreation in a Hospital Center." *Hospital Management* 89 (1960): 37-38.

Zelditch, M. "The Home for the Aged—a Community." *Journal of Gerontology* 2 (1962): 37-41.

19 / Developing a Philosophy About Aging

IN THE FOREGOING CHAPTERS some of the advances in biological research and medical care that have extended the life span of man have been cited. Programs and services described are society's efforts to help add quality and meaning to the added years. Continuing research in the next decade will probably make much of our present knowledge obsolete. Overriding the possibility that man's life span may be still further extended is the reality that intrinsic factors within each living organism inevitably limit life. Some perspective on this fact and some philosophy that recognizes the decrements of age as well as its many increments are essential. Anne Morrow Lindbergh has stated her philosophy about the totality of life and the potential richness of the final years in *Gift from the Sea*. She calls the active years between forty and fifty the morning of life and reminds her readers:

> There is still the afternoon opening up, which one can spend not in the feverish pace of the morning but in having time at last for those intellectual, cultural, and spiritual activities that were pushed aside in the heat of the race. We, Americans, with our terrific emphasis on youth, action, and material success, certainly tend to belittle the afternoon of life and even to pretend it never comes. We push the clock back and try to prolong the morning, overreaching and overstraining ourselves in the unnatural effort . . . In our breathless attempts we often miss the flowering that waits for afternoon.[1]

How any one individual adapts to his inevitable physical decline and death will depend on the attitudes and reactions he established earlier in life. These attitudes and reactions are determined by his experiences,

[1] Anne Morrow Lindbergh, *Gift from the Sea* (New York: Pantheon Books, 1955).

313

his emotional security, and the meanings he has found at each stage of his life.

Every person lives his life not only through what he experiences in time and space but also through what he experiences in mind and spirit as he reacts inwardly to his own given set of environmental and personal facts. Out of the freedom to choose his inner reactions to his outer circumstances has come his personal integrity and meaning. If during life an individual has not grown in inner resources, his reactions in old age will flow not from an inner core but from the anxieties that his changing circumstances inevitably bring.

In old age an individual has two options—to give up and allow his life to diminish into meaningless oblivion or to move courageously into dimensions that will permit him to consummate his life with the attainment of new levels of consciousness. Which one is actualized will depend not on the specific conditions the individual faces but on his decision of how he will use his spiritual freedom to meet and handle new experiences. The measure of his meaning and inner security will lie in his ability to say, in the words of Dag Hammarskjöld:

> "—Night is drawing nigh—"
> For all that has been—thanks!
> For all that shall be—Yes! [2]

Loneliness is a universal experience. The need for communication with and relationships to one's fellow men persists throughout all of life. For many older people, feelings of isolation and loneliness become increasingly disturbing as opportunities for social and psychological interaction become progressively limited. Nevertheless, the aged person still has the option to choose his reactions to the circumstances causing his increasing loneliness. He may choose to react in ways that will increase his anxieties, insecurities, and egocentricity or in ways that help him remain an interesting human being with a mind that is flexible, humorous, and resourceful and a spirit that accepts himself gracefully. His choices will determine whether he will continue to have the company of the young as well as his own contemporaries, or whether he will be living in a narrow world of his own, filled with complaints, boredom, and self-pity. When he was seventy-five, the noted historian, Arnold Toynbee reminded his contemporaries in *Man's Concern with Death,* "Our minds, so long as they keep their cutting edge, are not bound by our physical limits. They can range over time and space into infinity."

During this decade of the 1970s a new society is in the making. The

[2] Dag Hammarskjöld, *Markings* (New York: Alfred A. Knopf, 1964), p. 87.

problems that are calling for solutions are not those only of youth—they are problems common to all, and all are caught up in the powerful currents that are carrying modern man away from his known ways. What society is to become is dependent on all its members, not just on those of a certain age group. Life requires all to help develop the best solutions for its problems. Those now in the older years cannot take to the sidelines in resignation and despair, believing that there is nothing more to expect from life. Life still expects something from them, now that they are free of the pressures for personal achievement, aggression, competition, and the need to control.

Mrs. Florida Scott-Maxwell, who at the age of fifty began training to become a psychotherapist, wrote in her book, *The Measure of My Days,* "My seventies were interesting, and fairly serene, but my eighties are passionate. . . . I am so disturbed by the outer world and by human quality in general, that I want to put things right as though I still owed a debt to life." [3]

Through all the dichotomies and the alienation so apparent in life today runs the persistent reality of the interdependence and interrelatedness of all of life—of man and his natural environment, of nation with nation, race with race, and the common humanity that encompasses the young and the old. The young are the crucial group for change in the societal attitudes toward the old. They will need to enlarge their concept of self to encompass the idea that they themselves will eventually become old. Only then will those who are now old no longer be "they." They will become "those of us."

BIBLIOGRAPHY

Frankl, Victor E. *Man's Search for Meaning: An Introduction to Logotherapy.* New York: Washington Square Press, 1968.

Hersey, Joan, and Hersey, Robert. *These Rich Years: A Journal of Retirement.* New York: Charles Scribner's Sons, 1970.

Hoffer, Eric. *The Ordeal of Change.* New York: Harper & Row, 1964.

Jung, Carl G. *Memories, Dreams, Reflections.* New York: Vintage Books, 1963.

Lindbergh, Anne Morrow. *Gift From the Sea.* New York: Random House, Pantheon Books, 1955.

Maslow, Abraham H. *Toward a Psychology of Being.* New York: D. Van Nostrand Co., 1968.

[3] Florida Scott-Maxwell, *The Measure of My Days* (New York: Alfred A. Knopf, 1968), pp. 13-14.

Moberg, David O. "Religiosity in Old Age." *The Gerontologist* 5 (1965): 78-87.

Scott-Maxwell, Florida. *The Measure of My Days*. New York: Alfred A. Knopf, 1968.

Webber, Howard. "Games." *The New Yorker*, 30 March 1963.

Index

Please remember that this is a library book,
and that it belongs only temporarily to each
person who uses it. Be considerate. Do
not write in this, or any, library book.